Mastering Music Fundamentals

A GUIDED STEP-BY-STEP APPROACH

Michael Kinney

SUNY Broome Community College

SCHIRMER
CENGAGE Learning™

Australia • Brazil • Japan • Korea • Mexico • Singapore • Spain • United Kingdom • United States

SCHIRMER
CENGAGE Learning™

Mastering Music Fundamentals
A Guided Step-By-Step Approach
Michael Kinney

Publisher: Clark Baxter

Senior Assistant Editor: Julie Yardley

Editorial Assistant: Anne Gittinger

Technology Project Manager:
Michelle Vardeman

Marketing Manager: Diane Wenckebach

Marketing Assistant: Rachel Bairstow

Advertising Project Manager: Brian Chaffee

Signing Representative: Tim Kenney

Project Manager, Editorial Production:
Emily Smith

Print/Media Buyer: Judy Inouye

Permissions Editor: Stephanie Lee

Production Service: Stratford Publishing
Services

Copy Editor: Carrie Crompton

Cover Designer: Krista Pierson

Cover Image: Corbis/Royalty Free

Compositor: Stratford Publishing Services

For product information and technology assistance, contact us at
Cengage Learning Customer & Sales Support, 1-800-354-9706
For permission to use material from this text or product, submit all requests online at **cengage.com/permissions**
Further permissions questions can be emailed to
permissionrequest@cengage.com

Library of Congress Control Number: 2003116481

ISBN-13: 978-0-534-61834-6
ISBN-10: 0-534-61834-0

Wadsworth
25 Thomson Place
Boston, MA 02210
USA

Cengage Learning is a leading provider of customized learning solutions with office locations around the globe, including Singapore, the United Kingdom, Australia, Mexico, Brazil and Japan. Locate your local office at:
international.cengage.com/region

Cengage Learning products are represented in Canada by Nelson Education, Ltd.

For your course and learning solutions, visit **academic.cengage.com**
Purchase any of our products at your local college store or at our preferred online store **www.ichapters.com**

Printed in the U.S.A.
4 5 6 7 8 11

This book is dedicated to

*all of the composers, both past and present, who have
created music for humankind to enjoy;*

*my teachers, who gave me the confidence
to pursue dreams;*

*my students, who have taught and continue to teach me
how to be a nurturing teacher; and*

*my wife, Patricia, and my daughters, Lisa and Jennifer,
who are the true embodiment of all
that is good in the world.*

Contents

CHAPTER SEVEN　*Triads*　305

CHAPTER EIGHT *Harmonic Functions of Triads* 347

To the Instructor

This book is designed with one main focus: to help reduce the time it takes you to teach your students the fundamentals of music theory.

The information is presented as if the reader were interacting with an instructor in a classroom and is predicated on pedagogical techniques that anticipate questions and difficulties students are likely to encounter. As new concepts are introduced, students are asked to complete written, and occasionally aural, exercises that will develop their understanding of the material. The correct answers to the written exercises, and additional worksheets, are provided at the end of every chapter.

The accompanying CD includes supplementary worksheets for each chapter and recorded examples of selected pieces of music. Answers to the chapter worksheets are available to instructors only on the Instructor's Resources portion of the book companion Web site: http://music.wadsworth.com/kinney1e. The student can access additional worksheets, called "Skill Development Drills," on both the CD-ROM and on the book companion Web site: http://music.wadsworth.com/kinney1e.

The musical examples employed to illustrate various concepts are tunes with which everyone should be familiar. Because many students have a limited acquaintance with "art music," the musical examples are not representative of the masterworks of the greater composers. Students' musical interests might encompass jazz, folk, commercial, religious, traditional and non-traditional rock and roll, some degree of classical instrumental and vocal music, and many other styles; but through no fault of their own, a shared musical heritage is very limited in scope and in many instances, virtually nonexistent. For this reason, the illustrated musical selections throughout the text are limited to familiar popular tunes.

There are numerous approaches to teaching the fundamentals of music. This text supports some of the more conventional models. If the method used to introduce a student to a particular topic is slightly different from your approach, this, in all likelihood, will be conducive to student learning since it provides an additional means to understanding the material.

Acknowledgments

Thanks to the reviewers who commented on this manuscript: Kevin Moore, Onondaga Community College; Ken Bales, University of Nebraska at Omaha; Heidi Pintner, Western Kentucky University; Janice Wyma, Irvine Valley College; Paul S. Carter, SUNY at Oneonta; and Zae Munn, St. Mary's College.

1

The Tools of Music

Music is a moral law. It gives soul to the universe, wings to the mind, flight to the imagination, a charm to sadness, and gaiety and life to everything. It is the essence of order and lends to all that is good, just, and beautiful.

—PLATO

THE MUSICAL ALPHABET

The musical alphabet represents the names of the basic pitches used in music and consists of the letters A, B, C, D, E, F, and G. The illustration below indicates how the fifty-two white keys of the piano keyboard are identified by repeating the musical alphabet beginning with the lowest note (A) on the far left side of the keyboard and ending with the highest note (C) on the far right side. The remaining thirty-six black keys, which also are identified using the musical alphabet, are labeled as altered white keys and will be addressed later on.

If you were to play every white and black key located on the piano keyboard from left to right, you would perceive the eighty-eight sounds progressively getting higher. Each key's sound has a unique lowness or highness associated with it that is commonly referred to as **pitch**. The eighty-eight keys of the piano keyboard, which encompass the majority of musical pitches we hear on a daily basis in Western music (music from Europe), are represented on the **Grand Staff** (or **Great Staff**).

THE GRAND STAFF

The Grand Staff consists of two staves of five lines each that are separated by the pitch identified as "**middle C**."

1.1a

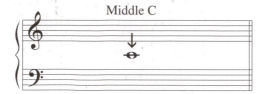

Middle C results from applying the musical alphabet to specific pitches located on each space and line of the Grand Staff, beginning with the bottom space, as follows:

1.1b   *The Grand Staff*

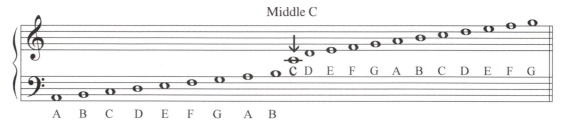

Altogether, there are eight Cs located on the piano keyboard. Middle C is identified as C4.

1.1c

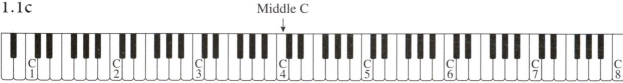

The remaining pitches may be identified in the same manner by associating a number with each pitch of the musical alphabet:

1.1d

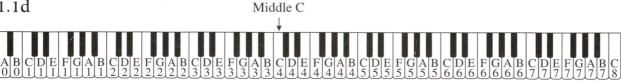

CLEFS

The upper staff of the Grand Staff is called the **treble clef** or **G clef** and is indicated with the treble clef sign. It is composed of five lines and four spaces:

1.2   Treble clef sign

The lower part of the Grand Staff is called the **bass clef** or **F clef** and is indicated with a bass clef sign. It too has five lines and four spaces:

1.3

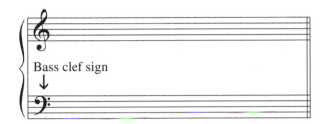

Bass clef sign

The two clefs are joined on the left side by a **brace** (**accolade**), which designates the Grand Staff:

1.4

Brace →

BAR LINES

The Grand Staff may be divided into **measures** separated by **bar lines**, as follows:

1.5a   Four measures separated by three bar lines

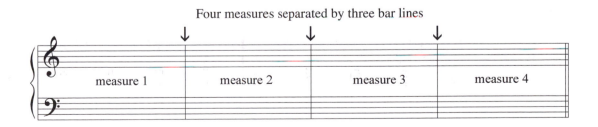

measure 1   measure 2   measure 3   measure 4

LEDGER LINES

Pitches may be located *above* or *below* each clef by using **ledger lines** and are identified by using the musical alphabet in the same manner as when identifying them on the Grand Staff.

1.5b   *Treble Clef*   1.5c   *Bass Clef*

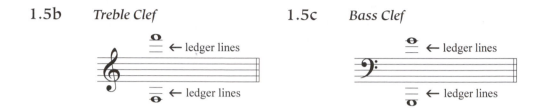

In the following example, a pitch has been written on the first ledger line above the treble clef. To correctly identify this pitch, you will need to alphabetically count the space and line above the top line F until you arrive on A. Since the pitch G is located on the first space above the staff, the pitch located on the first ledger line above the staff must be A. Please recall from example 1.1b that the musical alphabet is from A through G and continually repeats.

1.6a

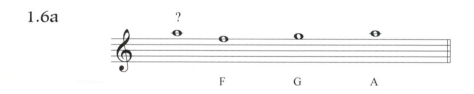

The process of counting lines and spaces to identify a pitch located on a ledger line *above or below* the staff also applies to the bass clef. Example 1.6b illustrates how to identify the name of a pitch located two ledger lines above the bass clef. Middle C, which always is located one ledger line above the staff, is a good reference point when determining pitches located above the bass clef. Beginning with middle C, alphabetically count each line and space until you arrive at the pitch located on the second ledger line above the staff. The pitch located on the second ledger line above the bass clef is E.

1.6b

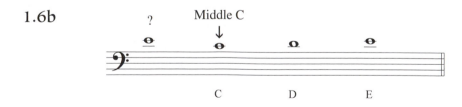

Pitches located below the staff are identified in a similar manner. Example 1.7a illustrates how it is necessary to say the alphabet backwards in order to identify the name of the pitch located three spaces below the staff.

1.7a

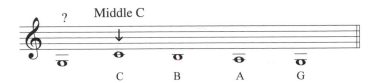

To identify the following pitch located on the third ledger line below the bass clef, you will have to count each space and ledger line until you arrive on the pitch.

1.7b

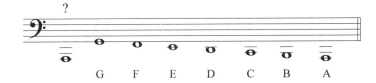

LEDGER LINES AND MIDDLE C

In identifying pitches more than two ledger lines *above the bass clef* or *below the treble clef,* middle C is a good reference point. When middle C is written in the bass clef, it is placed close to the top line (A). When it is written in the treble clef, it is placed close to the bottom line (E):

1.8

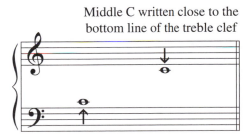

Remember that there only is one ledger line between the treble and the bass clef; the note located on it is called middle C. *If you are identifying a note written two ledger lines above the bass clef, you should be aware that it is the exact same note that is located on the first line of the treble clef!*

1.9

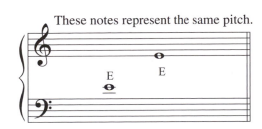

Example 1.10a further illustrates how the two pitches in example 1.9 are equal.

1.10a

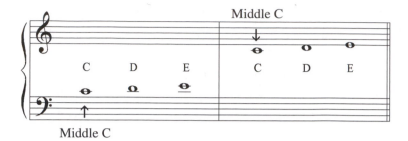

Principle *1*

There is only one line between the treble and bass clefs, and the pitch written on it is called "middle C." Any note written on a ledger line above or below middle C is identical to a pitch located on the staff.

1.10b

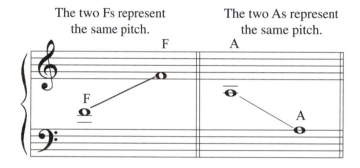

Exercise *1*

Identify the following pitches. (The answers are located at the end of this chapter.)

1.11

1.12

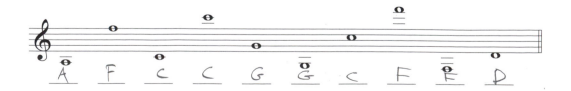

1.13

D A A C E F F B B G

1.14

G F E B D A D G B C

NOTES AND THEIR STEMS

The notes used to indicate various pitches in examples 1.11–1.14 are called **whole notes**.

1.15

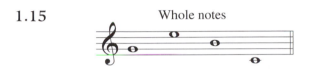

Whole notes

A whole note is but one musical symbol denoting a pitch's **rhythmic value**, or how long it is to be sustained over a period of time. There are numerous types of notes representing other rhythmic values that require a **stem** attached to the **note head**. Example 1.16 illustrates two half notes and their respective stems.

1.16

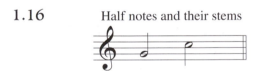

Half notes and their stems

Notice that in example 1.16 the stem on the first half note, G, is located on the right side and goes up. The stem on the second half note, C, is on the left side and goes down.

Principle 2

Stems associated with notes below the middle line of both the treble and bass clefs are written on the right side and will go up; stems associated with notes on or above the middle line in both clefs are written on the left side and go down.

Examples 1.17a and 1.17b illustrate the stem directions of various notes written in the treble and bass clefs:

1.17a

1.17b

NOTE BEAMS

There are instances when the stem direction of a pitch will not reflect **Principle 2** because of its context within a group of pitches. Example 1.18 illustrates one example of how the stem direction of another type of rhythmic value, the eighth note, reflects the stem direction of the majority of the pitches grouped with a **beam**.

1.18

Principle 3

When a pitch is part of a rhythmic grouping, its stem direction reflects the direction of the majority of the notes in the group.

WRITING INTERVALS ON THE STAFF

In Chapter 6 you will learn about **intervals**—the measured distance between two pitches. One interval you can easily practice writing on the staff is called the **octave**. An octave may be identified by moving up or down the musical alphabet until you arrive at the same alphabet letter of the pitch with which you started.

THE OCTAVE

Locate C toward the middle of the piano keyboard, and, counting this as step 1, ascend on the white keys to step 8. You will arrive on a C located one octave above your starting pitch.

1.19a

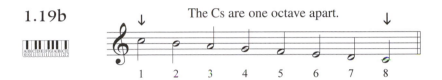

The Cs are one octave apart.

1 2 3 4 5 6 7 8

If you descend in the same manner, you will arrive on a pitch located one octave below your starting pitch.

1.19b

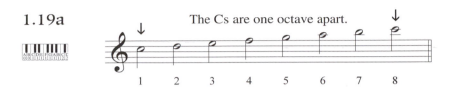

The Cs are one octave apart.

1 2 3 4 5 6 7 8

Exercise 2

In the following exercise, practice writing pitches one octave *higher* in the space provided. (The stem for each note head should be about one octave in length.) Be sure to place the stems of the note heads on the appropriate side (refer to **Principle 2** if you have questions regarding stem placement). After checking your solutions with the answer key located at the end of this chapter, try playing these pitches on a piano in order to familiarize yourself with the sounds of these intervals. This is a very important part of the process of understanding intervals.

1.20a

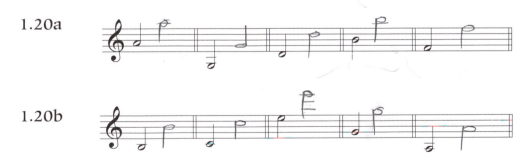

1.20b

Write the following notes one octave lower in the bass clef.

1.20c

1.20d

ACCIDENTALS AND SEMITONES (HALF STEPS)

Accidentals are used to indicate the raising or lowering of a pitch by one half step or more. (The term **accidental** is a misnomer because when a pitch is raised or lowered it is usually by intention and not by accident.) Five basic accidentals will be presented in this section:

♯   sharp   ♭♭   double flat

♭   flat   ♮   natural sign

×   double sharp

On the piano keyboard below, observe that there are adjacent black keys immediately to the right and left of the white key labeled "A." These black keys represent pitches that are said to be one **half step,** or one **semitone**, away from A. *On the piano keyboard, a movement to the key to the immediate right or left of a key is one half step.*

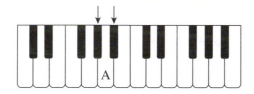

The half step generally is considered to be the smallest distance between pitches in music from the Western world (Europe), but there are musical styles in which the distance between adjacent pitches is a quarter step (**quarter tone** or **microtone**—one half of a half step) or less. Historically, **microtonal music** has been an important part of the music of various cultures—in China, India, Persia, South America, and in Native American music, to name a few. Although microtonal music will not be addressed in this book, it is worth noting that it is an important element of music in cultures around the world.

Principle 4

The nearest key to the right or left of any key on the piano keyboard is said to be one half step away.

SHARPS AND FLATS

Locate the key identified as "D," and observe that there is an adjacent black key to its immediate left and right. The black key to the left of D is called D flat and the black key to the right of D is called D sharp. Both black keys are said to be one half step away from D.

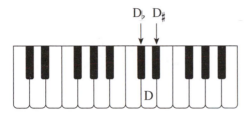

D flat sounds one half step lower than D. D sharp sounds one half step higher than D.

Principle 5

On the piano keyboard, a sharped pitch will always be the next nearest adjacent key to the right of a key, while a flatted pitch will always be the next nearest adjacent key to the left of a key.

D flat and D sharp are written on the staff as follows, with the appropriate flat and sharp placed on the left side of each pitch:

1.21

Principle 6

A flat placed before a note lowers it one half step.

Principle 7

A sharp placed before a note raises it one half step.

Observe on the piano keyboard that the pitch G has black keys immediately to its left and right.

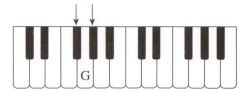

In the following example, the pitches to the immediate left and right of G are identified as G flat and G sharp, respectively, and reflect **Principles 6** and **7**:

1.22

Principle 8

Every white key on the piano keyboard has an associated flat and sharp.

The following example illustrates the sharped and flatted notes within the span of one octave on the piano keyboard, that are associated with each letter of the musical alphabet (A–G):

1.23

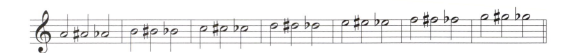

Notice that there is no black key separating the pitches B and C. The distance between them is one half step (one semitone).

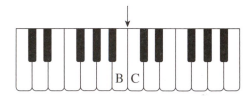

This same relationship holds for the pitches E and F. The distance between them also is one half step.

Principle **9**

The distance between the pitch pairs on the piano keyboard representing B and C, and E and F is one half step.

ENHARMONICS

Observe on the piano keyboard that G sharp (the black key to the immediate right of G) may also be identified as A flat.

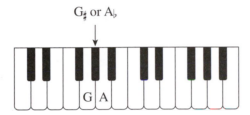

The notes G sharp and A flat are said to be **enharmonically equivalent** because, although they are written differently, they sound the same.

Principle **10**

Two pitches that are written differently but sound the same are said to be enharmonically equivalent.

1.24   G sharp and A flat are enharmonically equivalent.

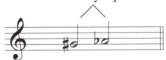

You may be wondering why it is necessary to identify a black key on the piano by two different names. The answer will become clear to you as you study scales in Chapter 3, but for now, please be aware that *every pitch of the musical alphabet has an enharmonically equivalent pitch*.

The following example illustrates a few pairs of enharmonically equivalent pitches:

1.25

On the piano keyboard, locate the pitches illustrated in each measure of example 1.25 and observe that, although they are written differently, each pair of pitches is represented by one black key.

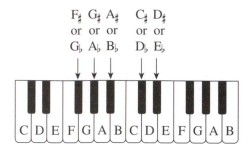

Principle 9 stated that the distance between the pitch pairs on the piano keyboard representing B and C, and E and F is one half step because there is no black key separating them.

Once again, observe on the piano keyboard that there is no black key between the pitch pairs B and C, and E and F.

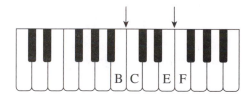

The enharmonically equivalent pitches that are *not* represented by a black key on the piano keyboard appear on the staff as follows:

1.26   Enharmonically equivalent pitches that are not represented by a black key on the piano keyboard

The *lack of a black key between these pitch pairs* means that C flat is **enharmonic** to B (two pitches that sound the same but are written differently), B sharp is enharmonic to C, F flat is enharmonic to E, and E sharp is enharmonic to F. Observe these enharmonically equivalent relationships on the piano keyboard:

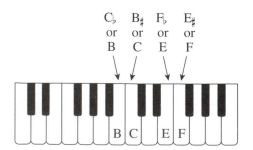

Exercise 3

In the following exercises, write the enharmonically equivalent pitch immediately to the right of each note.

1.27a

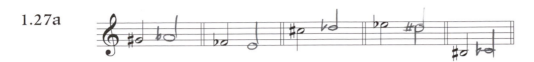

1.27b

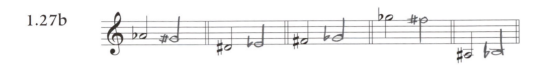

DOUBLE SHARPS AND FLATS

Occasionally it becomes necessary to raise or lower a pitch that is *already* either sharped or flatted. To accomplish this, a **double sharp** or **double flat** is used. The effect of one of these accidentals placed before a natural pitch (any white key on the piano keyboard) is that it raises or lowers it one whole step (two half steps). The symbols used for these accidentals are written as follows:

     ✗   double sharp

     ♭♭   double flat

1.28   These pitches illustrate double sharps and double flats.

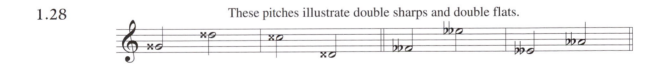

Principle 11

A double sharp raises a pitch one whole step, and a double flat lowers a pitch one whole step.

Observe that the pitch G, when double flatted, is enharmonically equivalent to F, and when double sharped, it is enharmonically equivalent to A.

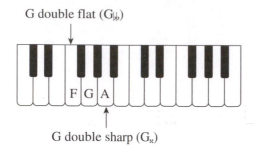

G double flat (G♭♭)

G double sharp (G✕)

The following example illustrates this concept:

1.29a

 G double flat = F   G double sharp = A

Every pitch expressed as a double sharp or double flat has an associated enharmonically equivalent pitch. The following example illustrates this relationship using F double flat and A double sharp:

1.29b   F double flat and E flat are   A double sharp and B are
enharmonically equivalent.   enharmonically equivalent.

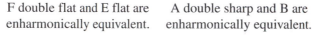

Observe the enharmonic relationships illustrated in example 1.29b on the piano keyboard:

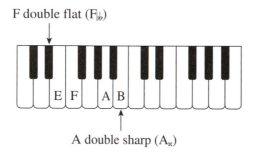

F double flat (F♭♭)

A double sharp (A✕)

Exercise 4

Refer to the piano keyboard below, and, in the space provided next to each note, write the enharmonically equivalent pitch.

1.30a

1.30b

THE NATURAL SIGN

Any type of accidental placed before a pitch is canceled by the **natural sign**:

♮   natural sign

Observe how the pitches G sharp and G flat are restored to G by placing the natural sign before each pitch:

1.31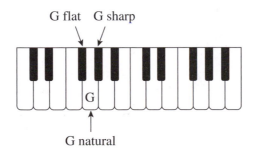

Observe these relationships on the piano keyboard:

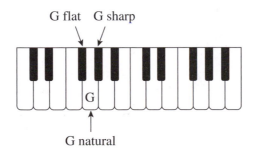

Principle **12**

An accidental placed before a pitch is canceled by the natural sign.

In the majority of instances, the natural sign will restore a sharped or flatted pitch to a white key on the piano. For example, if the pitch G sharp, which is a black key on the piano keyboard, is written as G natural, it will have been lowered one half step to the white key, G.

G sharp

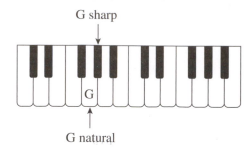

G natural

If G flat, which is a black key on the piano keyboard, is written as G natural, it will have been raised one half step to the white key, G.

G flat

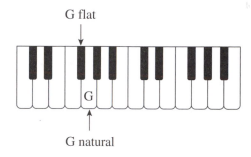

G natural

Principle 13

When the natural sign cancels a sharp, a pitch is lowered one half step; when it cancels a flat, a pitch is raised one half step.

You may consider all of the white keys on the piano keyboard as "natural pitches" and the black keys as "sharps" and "flats." The only exception to this is that, since there are no black keys between B and C, and E and F, these white keys sometimes function as sharps and flats. For example, although on the piano keyboard there is a black key for G sharp, there is no black key for B sharp because this pitch is located on its enharmonically equivalent white key, C. This means that the white key, C, will serve as B sharp. This same situation occurs between the pitches E and F.

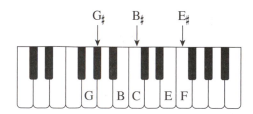

Observe on the piano keyboard that (1) C flat is the enharmonic equivalent of B, (2) B sharp is the enharmonic equivalent of C, (3) F flat is the enharmonic equivalent of E, and (4) E sharp is the enharmonic equivalent of F.

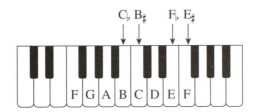

On the piano keyboard below, please observe the enharmonic equivalent possibilities associated with sharping and flatting the pitches of the musical alphabet (double sharps and flats are not included):

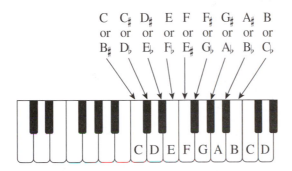

The natural sign may also be used to adjust pitches that are double sharped or double flatted. Although this situation occurs very infrequently, when it does, the pitches must be carefully written.

A natural sign placed before the pitches F double sharp and F double flat cancels both accidentals and restores the pitches to F natural.

1.32   The natural sign cancels the
         double sharp and double flat.

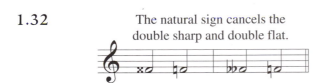

If you wanted *to cancel only one of the sharps or flats* of F double sharp or F double flat, you would write this in one of two ways, as illustrated in the following example:

1.33   Two ways of canceling only one   Two ways of canceling only one
         of the sharps of F double sharp: of the flats of F double flat:

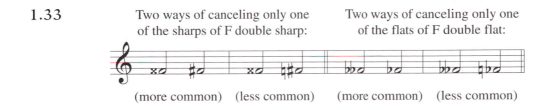

(more common)   (less common)   (more common)   (less common)

CHROMATIC AND DIATONIC HALF STEPS

The following example illustrates two ways of writing the enharmonically equivalent pitches located one half step above F.

1.34

In the first measure of the following example, F has been raised one **chromatic half step** by placing a sharp before the second pitch. In the second measure, F is not raised, but has moved up one **diatonic half step** to G flat.

1.35

Principle *14*

A half step movement from a pitch, in any direction, to a pitch of the same letter name is called a chromatic half step.

1.36a

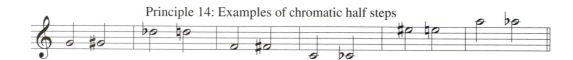

Principle 14: Examples of chromatic half steps

Principle *15*

A half step movement from a pitch, in any direction, to a pitch of a different letter name is called a diatonic half step.

1.36b

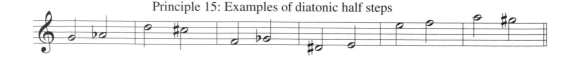

Principle 15: Examples of diatonic half steps

Exercise *5*

In the following exercise, write, in the space provided next to the given pitch, the pitch that is **one *diatonic* half step *above*** it:

1.37

In the following exercise, write, in the space provided next to the given pitch, the pitch that is **one *diatonic* half step *below*** it:

1.38

In the following exercise, write the pitch that is **one *chromatic* half step *above*** the given pitch.

1.39

In the following exercise, write the pitch that is located **one *chromatic* half step *below*** the given pitch.

1.40

THE MOVABLE C CLEF

Up to this point, pitches have been written in the treble and bass clefs. Other clefs are used to write pitches for instruments whose normal playing ranges encompass *both the treble and bass clefs*. The following example shows the normal playing range for the viola.

1.41   The normal playing range for the viola

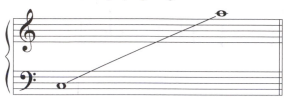

It is impractical to write the upper pitches for the viola in the bass clef because it would require an inordinate number of ledger lines, resulting in music that is extremely difficult to read.

1.42

It is equally impractical to write the lower pitches for the viola in the treble clef because it, too, would require an inordinate number of ledger lines.

1.43a

The solution to this problem is to *relocate middle C* to a line on the staff so that the writing of the higher and lower pitches requires fewer ledger lines. This may be accomplished by employing the **movable C clef**. Example 1.43b illustrates how the pitches in example 1.43a would appear if written in a movable C clef.

1.43b

The following example identifies the names of the most commonly used movable C clefs and illustrates their respective positions on the staff.

1.44

Principle 16

Middle C is located on the line at which the center of the movable C clef is placed.

In the following example, middle C is the note written on the line at which the center of the movable clef is placed:

1.45

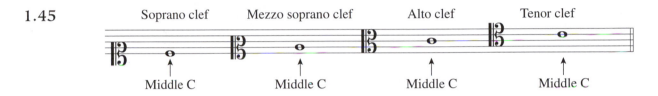

The middle C illustrated in each of the four C clefs in example 1.45 is the same middle C located on the *first ledger line below the treble clef* and on the *first ledger line located above the bass clef*.

1.46a 1.46b

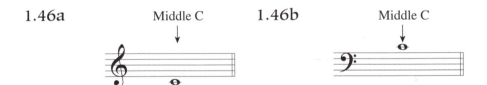

In the following example, the pitches written in the treble clef would appear in the alto clef, as follows:

1.47

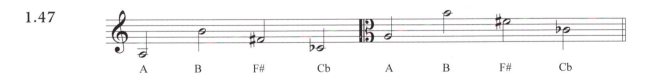

Pitches written in the tenor clef would appear in the treble clef, as follows:

1.48

In order to avoid using excessive ledger lines, the music for the viola is written in the alto clef. The example below illustrates how much more difficult it would be for a musician to read the music for the viola if it were written in the treble clef:

1.49

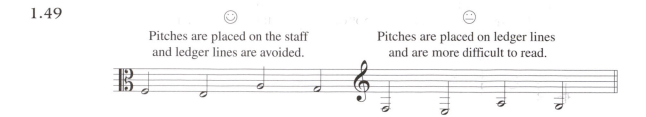

The tenor clef is used occasionally for the trombone, bassoon, and cello when a musical passage is written in their extreme high registers. The example below illustrates a musical passage written for the tenor trombone in which the pitches in the third and fourth measures are placed in the tenor clef in order to avoid writing excessive ledger lines:

1.50   Trombone

If the music in example 1.50 did not employ the tenor clef in measures three and four, it would appear as follows:

1.51   Trombone

The soprano and mezzo soprano clefs were important historically for the notation of vocal music. They are not commonly used today.

Skill Development

Identify the following pitch in the mezzo soprano clef:

1.52a

Process

Step 1. Identify where middle C is located. Since the pitch above is written in the mezzo soprano clef, middle C is located on the second line from the bottom.

1.52b

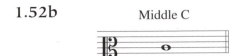

Middle C

Step 2. Next, count up the spaces and lines from middle C until you arrive at the pitch on the fourth line up from the bottom of the staff. This pitch is identified as G.

1.52c

C D E F G

Exercise 6

Identify the following pitches in the various clefs. Remember to locate middle C first.

1.53

E A C A B F B C E D F G D G D C

Skill Development

Where in the treble clef would the following pitch be written?

1.54a

Process

Step 1. Identify the pitch. Since the pitch is written in the alto clef, middle C is located on the third line up from the bottom. Identify each space and line until you arrive at A.

1.54b

C B A

Step 2. To write this pitch in the treble clef, you must not forget that it is located below middle C. Be sure to place it below middle C in the treble clef.

1.55

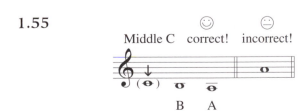

Middle C   ☺ correct!   ☹ incorrect!

B A

Exercise 7

Write the following pitches in the treble clef:

1.56

DYNAMICS

Dynamics refers to the various degrees of loud and soft volume levels at which a musical composition is to be performed. "Loud" refers to music that is to be played strongly, and "soft" refers to music that is to be played quietly. The following dynamics, which generally are written in Italian, are abbreviations representing various degrees of soft (quiet) and loud (strong):

pp (pianissimo)—very soft   *mf (mezzo forte)*—moderately loud
p (piano)—soft   *f (forte)*—loud
mp (mezzo piano)—moderately soft   *ff (fortissimo)*—very loud

Conductors and performers rely on numerous dynamic levels indicated in a musical score to assist them in expressing a composer's intentions and as a means to achieving a meaningful musical experience for listeners. It is a musician's responsibility to appropriately apply and interpret these various dynamic levels, and their respective nuances, in order to fulfill the expectations of the composer and bring "musical life" to a composition.

Crescendos (gradually increasing the musical volume) and **decrescendos** (gradually decreasing the musical volume) may be placed throughout a composition to help make the music more expressive. The specific dynamic ranges associated with a crescendo or a decrescendo depend on a composer's preference, but they always are indicated at the beginning, middle, and end of a musical phrase, as illustrated in the following example:

1.57

The range of the crescendo and decrescendo in example 1.57 begins with piano (p), increases to fortissimo (ff), and ends with piano (p). There are numerous variations of this dynamic device. Composers determine the suitable ranges of both soft and loud necessary to accomplish their musical goals.

REPEAT SIGNS

There are various ways of indicating to a performer that particular sections within a piece of music must be replayed. Sometimes it is necessary to repeat only one or two measures of music, while at other times it may be necessary to repeat large sections of a composition. The practice of using **repeat signs** is an efficient way to reduce the number of measures required to write a piece of music because it obviates the necessity of rewriting the music that needs to be replayed.

One of the most common signs indicating that a small or large section of music is to be repeated is notated as follows:

1.58

The repeat sign in the following example indicates that the performer must return to the beginning of the piece and replay all of the music:

1.59   The repeat goes back to the beginning.

In example 1.60, the music written within the repeat signs must be replayed:

1.60

When composers wish only to have *one measure* repeated, they may indicate this by using the following symbol:

1.61

In other instances, composers will indicate that they want only the *two previous measures* repeated. In order to save time writing music manuscript, the following symbol is used:

1.62

FIRST AND SECOND ENDINGS

In the following musical example, a repeat sign is required in the first ending because a performer must return to the beginning of the song in order to begin the second verse. The performer will then sing the second verse up to the first ending and then proceed directly to the second ending to conclude the song. The popular American folk song "She'll Be Comin' Round the Mountain" illustrates first and second endings:

1.63   *She'll Be Comin' Round the Mountain*

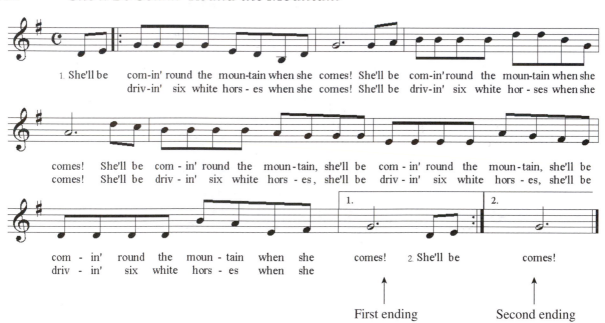

Repeating a large section (or sections) of music within a longer and more complicated musical composition may be achieved by using one or more of the following types of repeats:

D.C. al Fine (*da capo al fine*): From the beginning, play up to the D.C. al Fine; then return to the beginning and stop at the Fine.

1.64

D.C. al Coda (*da capo al coda*): From the beginning, play up to the D.C. al Coda; then go back to the beginning and play up to the coda sign (⊕). Skip directly to the coda section to bring the piece to a conclusion.

1.65

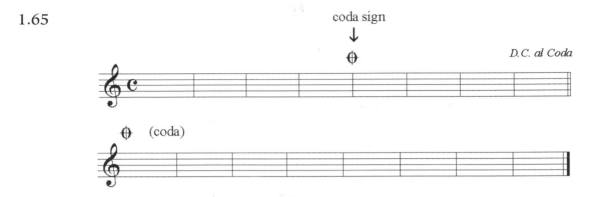

D.S. al Fine (*dal segno al fine*): From the beginning, play up to the D.S. al Fine, then repeat to the sign (𝄋), and then stop at the Fine.

1.66

D.S. al Coda (*dal segno al coda*): From the beginning, play up to the D.S. al Coda. Go back to the sign (𝄋), then play up to the coda sign (⊕). Skip directly to the coda section, which will conclude the piece.

1.67

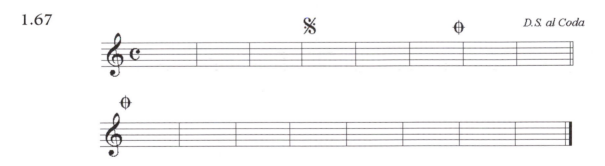

Now that you have been introduced to the basic tools of music notation, the following chapters will explain and illustrate how these elements combine to provide a means of organizing and representing musical sounds that are an important part of our daily lives.

REVIEW OF PRINCIPLES

Principle 1
There is only one line between the treble and bass clefs, and the pitch written on it is called "middle C." Any note written on a ledger line above or below middle C is identical to a pitch located on the staff.

Principle 2
Stems associated with notes below the middle line of both the treble and bass clefs are written on the right side and will go up; stems associated with notes on or above the middle line in both clefs are written on the left side and go down.

Principle 3
When a pitch is part of a rhythmic grouping, its stem direction reflects the direction of the majority of the notes in the group.

Principle 4
The nearest key to the right or left of any key on the piano keyboard is said to be one half step away.

Principle 5
On the piano keyboard, a sharped pitch will always be the next nearest adjacent key to the right of a key, while a flatted pitch will always be the next nearest adjacent key to the left of a key.

Principle 6
A flat placed before a note lowers it one half step.

Principle 7
A sharp placed before a note raises it one half step.

Principle 8
Every white key on the piano keyboard has an associated flat and sharp.

Principle 9
The distance between the pitch pairs on the piano keyboard representing B and C, and E and F is one half step.

Principle 10
Two pitches that are written differently but sound the same are said to be enharmonically equivalent.

Principle 11
A double sharp raises a pitch one whole step, and a double flat lowers a pitch one whole step.

Principle 12
An accidental placed before a pitch is canceled by the natural sign.

Principle 13
When the natural sign cancels a sharp, a pitch is lowered one half step; when it cancels a flat, a pitch is raised one half step.

Principle 14
A half step movement from a pitch, in any direction, to a pitch of the same letter name is called a chromatic half step.

Principle 15
A half step movement from a pitch, in any direction, to a pitch of a different letter name is called a diatonic half step.

Principle 16
Middle C is located on the line at which the center of the movable C clef is placed.

ANSWER SHEETS FOR CHAPTER 1

Exercise 1

1.11

G F D B C E E A D G

1.12

A F C C G G C F F D

1.13

D A A C E F F B B G

1.14

G F E B D A D G B C

Exercise 2

1.20a

1.20b

1.20c

1.20d

Exercise 3

1.27a

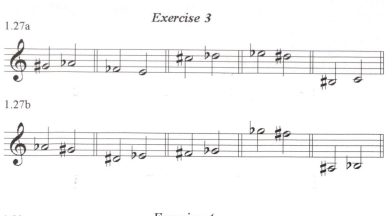

1.27b

1.30a

Exercise 4

1.30b

Exercise 5

1.37

1.38

1.39

1.40

Exercise 6

1.53

E A C F   B F B C   E D F G   D G D C

Exercise 7

1.56

2

Rhythm and Meter

Rhythm and motion, not the element of feeling, are the foundations of musical art.

—Igor Stravinsky

Rhythm is the aurally perceived relationship of the sequential durations of sound and silence patterns occurring over time. If you were to sing "Jingle Bells," you would be performing the melody with its text and rhythms. Try singing the melody, and notice how the words and their associated musical tones have long and short patterns of duration. If you feel as though you are unable to sing, ask a musically inclined friend or teacher to perform the melody for you or listen to it on the accompanying CD.

2.1a   *Jingle Bells*

If the same tune were performed in a monotone (without the high and low pitches of the melody), you would be singing the rhythms:

2.1b   *The rhythm to "Jingle Bells"*

Another song with which you probably are familiar is "America the Beautiful." Sing the first part of the tune as you know it, and observe how the words and their associated musical tones have long and short patterns of duration. These patterns are called rhythms:

2.2a   *America the Beautiful*

If the same tune were performed without the actual high and low pitches of the melody, you would be singing the rhythms:

2.2b   *The rhythm to "America the Beautiful"*

The writing and reading of rhythms is a rather complicated task. Although this chapter will present a method of understanding the logic of counting rhythms, it is not meant to replace the valuable experience of learning to perform them through the process of taking vocal or instrumental music lessons.

Notes and Rests

Rhythm is written by using specific types of notes and rests to indicate various durations of sounds and silences. Example 2.3 illustrates a few of the most commonly used notes and rests as they appear on the staff:

2.3

THE BEAT (PULSE)

Rhythm is an integral part of all music that is associated with a **beat** (or **pulse**). The beat is aurally perceived as a steady unvarying pulse that underlies music. Its rate determines the **tempo** of a musical composition. If you have ever danced to a piece of music, you know that a good beat is important. You probably have observed people tapping their feet as they listen to a piece of music with a clearly defined beat.

The grouping of beats into regularly recurring patterns of strong and weak accents produces a sense of **meter**.

METER

The majority of music we listen to reflects the grouping of beats into easily countable patterns of two, three, and four. The differences among these beat patterns are easily distinguishable because the first beat of a group is usually stronger than the rest. In addition to the grouping of beats, there is another layer of activity in which *the beat* of a musical composition is aurally perceived to be evenly divided into either two or three parts.

Music is said to be in a **simple meter** when the beat fundamentally may be divided into two parts (halves), and is said to be in a **compound meter** when the beat fundamentally may be divided into three parts.

Say the following phrases out loud and observe this comparison (the arrows indicate the beats):

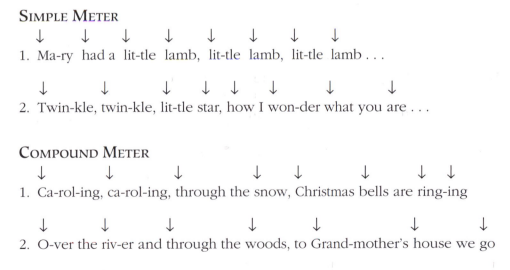

SIMPLE METER

↓　　↓　　↓　　↓　　↓　　↓　　↓　　↓
1. Ma-ry had a lit-tle lamb, lit-tle lamb, lit-tle lamb . . .

↓　　　↓　　　↓　↓　↓　↓　　↓　　　↓
2. Twin-kle, twin-kle, lit-tle star, how I won-der what you are . . .

COMPOUND METER

↓　　　↓　　　↓　　　↓　↓　　↓　　↓　↓
1. Ca-rol-ing, ca-rol-ing, through the snow, Christmas bells are ring-ing

↓　　↓　　↓　　↓　　↓　　↓　　↓
2. O-ver the riv-er and through the woods, to Grand-mother's house we go

The next section will present a discussion of simple meter and how rhythms are derived, counted, and performed when the beat first is evenly divided into two parts and then subdivided into smaller rhythmic units.

PART I ∾ *Simple Meter*

It is relatively easy to "feel" beats that are grouped into regularly recurring patterns of two, three, and four. Although the majority of music you hear generally will be performed using one of these grouping patterns, in more complex modern music, and in certain ethnic music traditions, a clearly defined symmetrical beat pattern is not always intended.

In order to "feel" a specific grouping of four beats, tap your foot four times and place a heavy accent on beat one and a lighter accent on beat three as you count: ONE, two, *three*, four. The counting of the numbers, along with the tapping of the foot, will help you establish a four-beat pattern called **quadruple meter**.

In the following example, establish a clearly defined pattern of four beats, then, using any pitch that is in your comfortable singing range, sing whole notes using the syllable "la." Sustain each whole note as you mentally count to four, then rest for four counts. If you are convinced you cannot sing, try to produce a pitch that sounds like a musical note, and perform the following example to the best of your ability. With practice, you will become better at this!

2.4
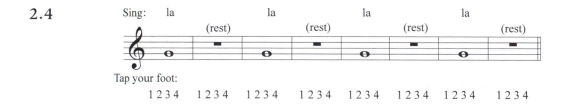

NOTES AND THEIR RESPECTIVE RESTS

Now try to perform the half notes in example 2.5 in the same manner in which you sang whole notes in example 2.4. Half notes and their respective rests often receive two beats each in quadruple meter, so sing "la" for two beats and rest for two beats. Please notice that you will need to tap your foot evenly and mentally count one, two while singing a half note, then continue counting the remainder of the four beats (three and four) during the half rest.

2.5

Quarter notes and quarter rests in quadruple meter usually receive one beat each. In example 2.6, mentally count from one to four while tapping your foot. Give each quarter note and quarter rest one beat while singing "la" on every quarter note:

2.6   Sing "la" on every quarter note
      while mentally counting 1 2 3 4.

1 2 3 4   1 2 3 4   1 2 3 4   1 2 3 4   1 2 3 4   1 2 3 4   1 2 3 4   1 2 3 4

THE METER SIGNATURE

While you were singing examples 2.4 through 2.6, mentally you were counting the beats in quadruple meter as one, two, three, and four. The method of counting in this pattern may be indicated on the staff at the beginning of a piece of music with a **meter signature** (or **time signature**).

In a **simple meter**, the top number indicates the number of beats per measure, and the lower number indicates the beat unit that will receive one beat. The two numbers placed one on top of the other indicate the meter signature.

In the following example, the meter signature indicates that there are four beats per measure (upper number) and the quarter note will receive the beat (lower number):

2.7   The arrow indicates where the
      meter is placed on the staff.

The meter signature in example 2.7 may more quickly be written by using the "C" symbol, which refers to "**common time**," as illustrated below:

2.8a   or   2.8b

The "C" in example 2.8a and the meter signature in example 2.8b both indicate four beats per measure with the quarter note receiving one beat.

Principle 1

The top number of a meter signature in simple meter indicates the number of beats per measure, while the lower number indicates the beat unit that receives one beat.

There are different types of simple meters. Some of the more common ones are illustrated in the following example:

2.9

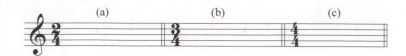

The first meter signature in example 2.9 indicates that there are two beats per measure, with the quarter note receiving the beat. It is identified as simple duple. The second meter signature (b) indicates three beats per measure, with the quarter note receiving the beat. It is identified as simple triple. The last meter signature (c) indicates four beats per measure, with the quarter note receiving the beat. It is identified as simple quadruple.

The four most commonly used simple meters are displayed as follows:

Some Common Simple Meters

$\frac{2}{2}$ Simple Duple	Two beats per measure with the half note receiving one beat
$\frac{2}{4}$ Simple Duple	Two beats per measure with the quarter note receiving one beat
$\frac{3}{4}$ Simple Triple	Three beats per measure with the quarter note receiving one beat
$\frac{4}{4}$ Simple Quadruple	Four beats per measure with the quarter note receiving one beat

In the following example of simple quadruple meter (common time), various patterns of whole, half, and quarter notes have been written with their correct beat numbers. Each measure has been separated by a bar line.

2.10

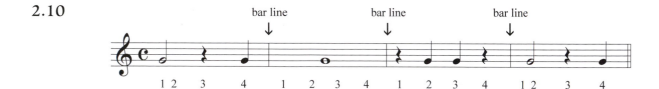

Exercise 1

In the following exercises, place the correct beat number(s) under each note and rest, and sing the rhythms using "la." Remember to tap your foot and keep an even and steady beat. The correct answers to these exercises are provided at the end of this chapter.

DIVIDING THE BEAT INTO HALVES

The beat in simple meter may continually be split into halves (or **sub-divided**), resulting in smaller parts of the beat unit (the note value receiving one count). This is analogous to dividing a one dollar ($1) bill: the first division would produce two fifty-cent pieces, and a further subdivision would produce four quarters.

The Subdivision Chart on page 46 represents (through the sixty-fourth note) how in simple meters, rhythmic units beginning with the whole note, may be continually divided into equal halves.

If a quarter note receives the beat in a simple meter, it may be divided into two eighth notes and then evenly subdivided into smaller rhythmic units. The division of the quarter note into two eighth notes and the division of the quarter rest into two eighth rests are illustrated in the following example. Observe in example 2.12 that a quarter note is changed to two eighth notes by the addition of **flags** to the note **stems.**

2.12

Principle 2

A simple meter results from dividing the beat into halves.

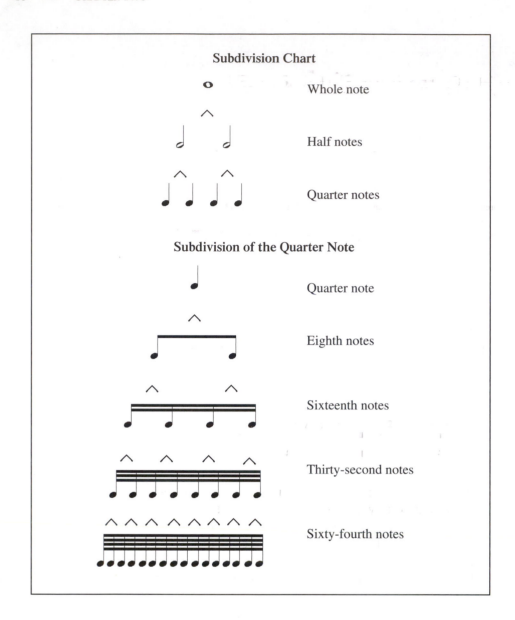

EIGHTH NOTES AND EIGHTH RESTS

Eighth notes and eighth rests are written on the staff as follows:

2.13　

When eighth notes are written in pairs or groups, they are usually connected with a **beam** that makes them easier to read.

2.14

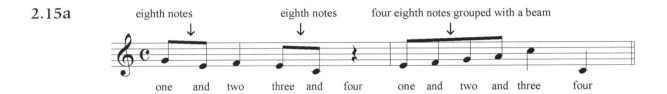

eighth notes   eighth notes   four eighth notes grouped with a beam

In simple quadruple meter, two eighth notes equal one beat and are counted as follows:

2.15a

eighth notes   eighth notes   four eighth notes grouped with a beam

one   and   two   three   and   four   one   and   two   and   three   four

Since eighth notes represent both halves of the quarter note, the first half is counted with a number, while the second half, "and," is replaced by a plus sign (+), as follows:

2.15b

1   +   2   3   +   4   1   +   2   +   3   4

Tap your foot with an even beat, and sing the following familiar melody in example 2.16, which was popularized by Wolfgang Mozart. The eighth notes will fall into place if you sing two of them evenly spaced within the beat every time you tap your foot down and up. The arrows indicate the position of the foot as you sing each note.

Notice that four eighth notes in each measure have been grouped with a beam to facilitate the reading and counting of the rhythm. It is recommended that, before beginning this exercise, you consult a music teacher to confirm your understanding of this concept.

2.16

Tap your foot evenly down and up as the arrows indicate.

Twin - kle, twin - kle, lit - tle star,   how   I   won - der what you   are.

"Twinkle, Twinkle, Little Star" is counted as follows:

2.17

1   +   2   +   3   +   4   1   +   2   +   3   +   4

When eighth notes are alternated with their respective eighth rests, they are counted as follows:

2.18

The arrows indicate the foot position.

The following examples (2.19–2.23) illustrate the mental process required to successfully place the correct beat number and its division under each note and rest value as necessary, and also how to place bar lines where they are required. When you have completed studying these examples, try singing the rhythms using "la."

Skill Development

Under each note and rest, please write the correct beat number and its division as necessary and draw bar lines where appropriate.

2.19

Process

Step 1. Determine the meter by identifying the meter signature located directly to the right of the treble clef.

2.20

The C under the arrow indicates common time, which means there must be four beats per measure.

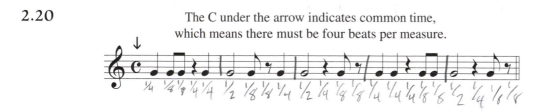

Step 2. Under each note and rest identify the correct beat number and its division, where necessary. Draw a bar line after you have identified beats one through four. If you need to review this process, please refer to examples 2.12–2.18.

2.21

Step 3. The next two measures would be completed as follows:

2.22

1 2 + 3 4   1 2 3 + 4   1 2 3 4 +

Step 4. The final two measures would appear as follows:

2.23

1 2 + 3 4   1 2 3 + 4   1 2 3 4 +   1 2 3 4 +   1 2 3 4 +

Exercise 2

Under each note and rest in the following melodies, please indicate the correct beat number (and division of the beat as necessary) and draw the bar lines where appropriate. *Be sure to check the meter signature so you know how many beats are required per measure.* Sing these rhythms using "la," and be sure to keep a steady beat by evenly tapping your foot:

2.24a

2.24b

2.24c

2.24d

2.24e

SUBDIVIDING THE QUARTER NOTE

In the previous section you learned that when the bottom number of a simple meter signature is a four, the quarter note receives one beat. Also, you observed that when the quarter note is divided in half, the result is two eighth notes. If you think in terms of money and imagine that the beat (which is the quarter note in this instance) is equal to one dollar, then eighth notes would each be equal to fifty cents (50¢).

2.25

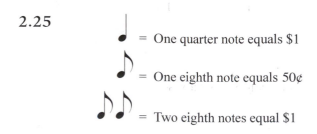

= One quarter note equals $1

= One eighth note equals 50¢

= Two eighth notes equal $1

SIXTEENTH NOTES

The quarter note also may be subdivided into four equal parts called sixteenth notes, each of which is one fourth of the beat.

2.26

A sixteenth note is written with two flags on the note stem. In terms of money, each sixteenth note would be worth twenty-five cents:

2.27

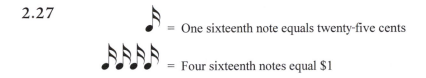

= One sixteenth note equals twenty-five cents

= Four sixteenth notes equal $1

Sixteenth notes are counted in the following manner:

2.28a

1 e + a 2 e + a 3 e + a 4 e + a

DOWNBEATS AND UPBEATS

Tap your foot and sing the following example. Your goal is to place four notes evenly within a beat (or pulse). Begin by raising your foot and then tapping it down and up while saying "Mississippi" evenly within the beat. Place "Mis-sis" on the **downbeat** (when your foot goes down) and "sip-pi" on the **upbeat** (when your foot goes up). If you do this evenly, you will be singing *sixteenth notes*. In the following example, the arrows indicate the position of the foot:

2.28b

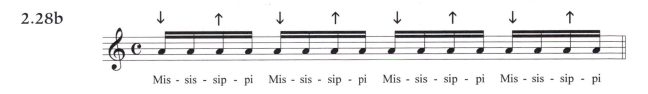

Mis - sis - sip - pi Mis - sis - sip - pi Mis - sis - sip - pi Mis - sis - sip - pi

SIXTEENTH REST

A sixteenth note also has a corresponding rest, which is written as follows:

2.29

♪ = sixteenth note   ⅞ = sixteenth rest

The sixteenth rest is counted in exactly the same manner as the sixteenth note and may occur on any quarterly segment of the beat:

2.30a

1   e   +   a   2   e   +   a   3   e   +   a   4   e   +   a

Example 2.30b illustrates that the notes or rests of a subdivided beat may be connected with a beam (refer to example 2.14 to clarify the definition of a beam). The visual result is a rhythmic unit the eye quickly identifies as the total beat. Also notice that when a *sixteenth rest* is part of a group of beamed pitches within a subdivided beat unit, the *sixteenth note* immediately following or preceding it is written slightly differently from other sixteenth notes:

2.30b

Sixteenth notes written within a subdivided and beamed beat
unit that are preceded and followed by a sixteenth rest

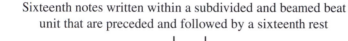

When the subdivision of the quarter note into four parts is combined with quarter notes and eighth notes, and their respective rests, the music is counted as follows:

2.31

1 2 e + a 3 4   1 + 2 3 e + a 4   1 + 2 e + a 3 4 +   1   2 3 4 e + a

Exercise 3

Under each note and rest in the following melodies, indicate the correct beat number (and portion of the beat as necessary) and bar lines where appropriate. Sing these rhythms using "la," and be sure to keep a steady beat by evenly tapping your foot.

2.32a

2.32j

Up to this point, the quarter note has received one beat and has been divided evenly into two eighth notes, then subdivided into four sixteenth notes. The next two subdivisions produce eight thirty-second notes and sixteen sixty-fourth notes. Although the subdivision of the quarter note generally does not exceed eight notes per beat (the thirty-second note), the sixty-fourth note does appear in musical literature:

2.33a 1 quarter note = 2 eighth notes = 4 sixteenth notes = 8 thirty-second notes = 16 sixty-fourth notes

Another way to understand the even subdivision of the beat from the quarter through the sixty-fourth note is to visualize it as mathematical fractions:

2.33b

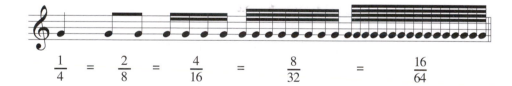

$$\frac{1}{4} \quad = \quad \frac{2}{8} \quad = \quad \frac{4}{16} \quad = \quad \frac{8}{32} \quad = \quad \frac{16}{64}$$

DOTTED AND TIED NOTES

It is possible to *increase the rhythmic value* of any note or rest by fifty percent with the addition of a dot.

*Principle **3***

A dot placed after a note or rest lengthens its rhythmic duration by one half of its original value.

In the following example, a half note, which receives two beats in simple quadruple meter when the quarter note receives the beat, now is worth three beats because the dot after it has increased its rhythmic value by fifty percent.

2.34

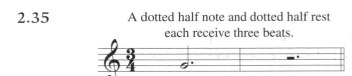

= 2 beats   = 3 beats

In a simple meter in which the quarter note receives the beat, the dotted half note and dotted half rest are counted as follows:

2.35

A dotted half note and dotted half rest each receive three beats.

1 2 3   1 2 3

Sing the following rhythm using "la," and remember to keep a steady beat with your foot as you mentally count from one to four in each measure.

2.36

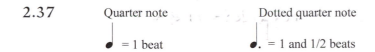

la   la   la   la   la   la   la

1   2   3 4   1 2 3   4   1   2   3   4   1   2 3 4

When the *quarter note* receives the beat in a simple meter, the addition of a dot, placed directly after the note, increases its rhythmic value by fifty percent. Its rhythmic value now is worth one and one half beats:

2.37

Quarter note   Dotted quarter note

= 1 beat   = 1 and 1/2 beats

The following example illustrates how a dot placed after a note or rest increases its duration by half.

2.38

o· = o + ↑   ‖   ▬· = ▬ + ▬

A dotted whole note equals a   A dotted whole rest equals a
whole note plus a half note.   whole rest plus a half rest.

↑· = ↑ + ↑   ‖   ▬· = ▬ + ↑

A dotted half note equals a   A dotted half rest equals a
half note plus a quarter note.   half rest plus a quarter rest.

↑· = ↑ + ♪   ‖   ↑· = ↑ + ↑

A dotted quarter note equals a   A dotted quarter rest equals a
quarter note plus an eighth note.   quarter rest plus an eighth rest.

♪· = ♪ + ♫   ‖   ↑· = ↑ + ↑

A dotted eighth note equals an   A dotted eighth rest equals an
eighth note plus a sixteenth note.   eighth rest plus a sixteenth rest.

When, in a simple meter, a note's rhythmic value is increased by fifty percent by the addition of a dot, it generally means that the added value is a portion of the remaining beats within a measure. Example 2.39 illustrates how beat three, in simple quadruple meter, may be added to a half note by using a dot or a **tie**.

2.39

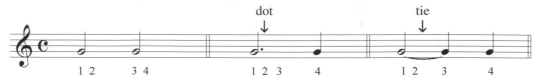

It is important for composers and **arrangers** to provide performers reading their music with a clear visual image of how a beat unit has been subdivided or lengthened. When writing rhythms in which the value of a note has been lengthened by half, dots are generally used more than ties. (Rests that are lengthened in this way are *never* written with a tie.) The relative complexity of a rhythm within a particular musical context will determine whether the tie or the dot is used to lengthen the rhythmic value of a note.

Now, let's study how to count a *dotted quarter* note's rhythmic value as it relates to the beat that directly follows it in a measure.

In the following simple quadruple meter the top number indicates that there are four beats to the measure, and the bottom number indicates that the quarter note receives one beat:

2.40   Simple quadruple meter

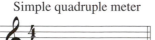

The dot placed after a quarter note is, in effect, the first part of the next beat. This also may be expressed by using a tie:

2.41a   Dotted quarter note   Tied quarter note

    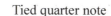 = 1 and 1/2 beats

It is important to realize that the dotted quarter note and the quarter note tied to one eighth note have the exact same rhythmic value:

2.41b   Dotted quarter note   Tied quarter note

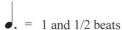. = 1 and 1/2 beats   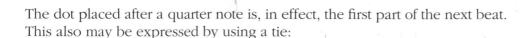 = 1 and 1/2 beats

The eighth note that is tied to the quarter note is the *first half* of the next beat, so there must be one half of the next beat remaining. The remaining half of the next beat is identified by using the "and" (+) sign:

2.42

The quarter note tied to the eighth note in example 2.42 also may be expressed as a dotted quarter note:

2.43

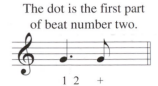

In order to experience the musical effect of the dot on a quarter note, please sing "la" in the following example. When you arrive at the tied or dotted quarter note, sustain it until you sing "la" on the "and" (+) of the beat. Remember to tap your foot down on the number and up on the "and" of each beat (see examples 2.16 and 2.18 for review).

2.44

Another way to experience the dotted quarter and eighth note combination is to sing the beginning of the popular folk song "I've Been Workin' On the Railroad."

2.45

The dotted quarter and eighth note combination is expressed in the following sections of two patriotic songs:

2.46a   *America the Beautiful*

2.46b   *America*

Exercise 4

Under each note and rest in the following melodies, indicate the correct beat number (and portion of the beat as necessary), and draw the bar lines where appropriate. *Be sure to check the meter signatures so you know how many beats are required per measure.* Sing these rhythms using "la," and be sure to keep a steady beat by evenly tapping your foot. It is not necessary to sing the actual pitches of the melody.

2.47a

2.47b

2.47c

2.47d

Now let's explore an important rhythmic pattern that involves the division of the eighth note.

THE DOTTED EIGHTH NOTE

In a simple quadruple meter such as 4/4, two eighth notes equal one quarter note.

2.48a   ♪♪ = ♩

One eighth note divided into two equal parts (cut in half) produces two sixteenth notes.

2.48b ♪ = 𝅘𝅥𝅯𝅘𝅥𝅯

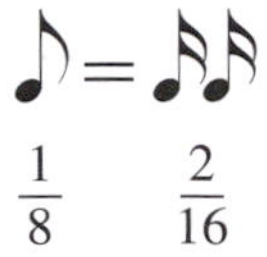

$\frac{1}{8}$ $\frac{2}{16}$

Two divided eighth notes, therefore, would produce four sixteenth notes, which equal one quarter note in simple quadruple meter (see Subdivision Chart on page 46).

The diagram below illustrates two eighth notes being divided into four sixteenth notes, which equal one quarter note:

2.49

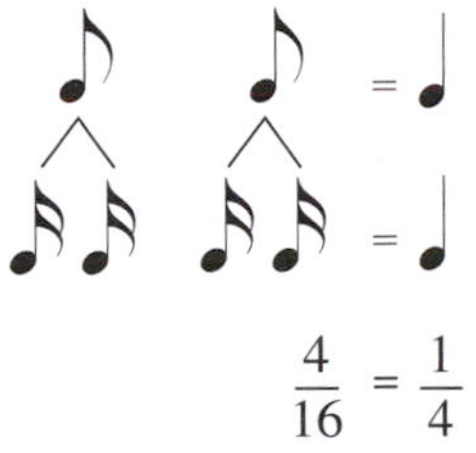

$\frac{4}{16} = \frac{1}{4}$

Now let's review **Principle 3**, which states that a dot placed after a note or rest lengthens its rhythmic duration by one half of its original value.

Example 2.50 illustrates how the placing of a dot after an eighth note increases its rhythmic value by one half:

2.50 ♪ = 𝅘𝅥𝅯𝅘𝅥𝅯   ♪. = 𝅘𝅥𝅯𝅘𝅥𝅯𝅘𝅥𝅯

The following example illustrates how a tie (the curved line under each pair of sixteenth notes) is used to connect the *first three* of the four sixteenth notes of the subdivided quarter note. When the quarter note receives the beat, the tie indicates that the three sixteenth notes are to be performed as one sound with a duration of 3/4 of one entire beat! In other words, the rhythmic length of one quarter note has been shortened by 1/4 of the beat (one sixteenth note). The three sixteenth notes, which are counted as 1, e, +, comprise the dotted eighth note. The remaining sixteenth note is counted as "a."

2.51

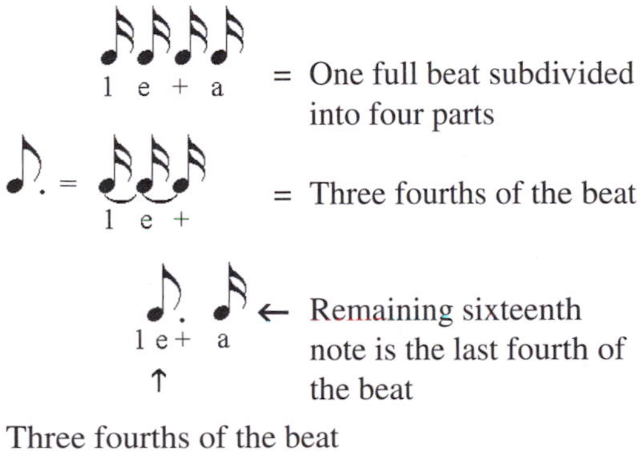

𝅘𝅥𝅯𝅘𝅥𝅯𝅘𝅥𝅯𝅘𝅥𝅯
1 e + a   = One full beat subdivided
                   into four parts

♪. = 𝅘𝅥𝅯𝅘𝅥𝅯𝅘𝅥𝅯
1 e +   = Three fourths of the beat

♪. 𝅘𝅥𝅯 ← Remaining sixteenth
1 e+ a   note is the last fourth of
   ↑   the beat

Three fourths of the beat

The dotted eighth note followed by a remaining sixteenth note is a common rhythmic pattern that normally is written with a beam, in the following manner:

2.52

1 e + a

Another way to think about this rhythm is to realize that of the four sixteenth notes comprising one beat, the "dot" is the first half of the second part of the beat, "and" (+), which is added to the length of the rhythmic value of the first eighth note:

2.53

To understand the dotted eighth-sixteenth rhythmic unit in another way, let's compare it to money. If one-quarter note equals $1.00 . . .

2.54

. . . each eighth note would be worth 50¢ . . .

2.55

. . . and each sixteenth note would be worth 25¢.

2.56a

Example 2.56b illustrates how, in terms of a one dollar bill, the dotted eighth note is equal to 75¢ (or 3/4 of the one dollar bill), with 25¢ remaining:

2.56b

25¢ 25¢ 25¢ 25¢   75¢ 25¢

1 e + a   may be written as   1 e + a

In the next example, let's look at the mental process required to correctly perform dotted rhythms. In measure one, the dotted eighth-sixteenth note pattern occurs on beat two:

2.57

In order to perform the rhythm on the second beat in measure one, you must *mentally subdivide* the beat unit (the quarter note) into four sixteenth notes and place "2 e + a" evenly within the beat. This rhythmic unit is counted as follows:

2.58

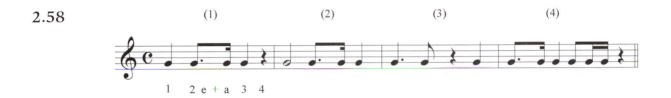

Remember, it is the dot that is counted as the "and (+)" because it is the first half of the second part of the beat. The remaining note is the last sixteenth note of beat, which will be called "a" (see example 2.56b).

In the second measure of example 2.59, the dotted eighth-sixteenth pattern occurs on beat three and is counted as follows:

2.59

In measure three of the following example, the dot that follows the quarter note is counted as the first half of beat number two. If you need to review this, please refer to examples 2.37–2.44.

2.60

In the last measure of example 2.61 the dotted eighth-sixteenth pattern occurs on the first beat and is counted as follows:

2.61

The rhythms presented in example 2.61 are difficult to perform accurately if you are not an experienced musician. It is very important to have a music teacher or an accomplished musician assist you with understanding how these rhythms are to be correctly interpreted.

The following excerpts of three popular melodies illustrate how the dotted eighth-sixteenth note pattern sounds within the context of a song:

2.62   *The Star-Spangled Banner*

2.63   *The Farmer in the Dell*

2.64   *O Christmas Tree*

Exercise 5

Under each note and rest in the following melodies, indicate the correct beat number (and portion of the beat as necessary) and draw the bar lines where appropriate. *Be sure to check the meter signature so you know how many beats are required per measure!* Sing these rhythms using "la," and be sure to keep a steady beat by evenly tapping your foot. It is not necessary to sing the actual pitches of the melody.

CUT TIME (ALLA BREVE)

"**Cut time**" is the colloquial term for "***alla breve***," which represents a simple duple meter in which there are two beats per measure, with the half note receiving the beat. (Up to this point, the quarter note has received the beat.) Example 2.66 illustrates how the "C" that represented 4/4 meter now is "cut in half" to represent 2/2.

2.66

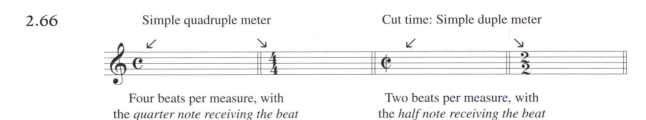

Simple quadruple meter   Cut time: Simple duple meter

Four beats per measure, with   Two beats per measure, with
the *quarter note receiving the beat*   the *half note receiving the beat*

Since the *half note* in "cut time" receives the beat, the *quarter note* is now one half of the beat. The following example would be counted:

2.67

The half rest receives one beat.

The subdivided beat is counted:

2.68a

Each rhythmic value has a corresponding rest that is counted in exactly the same manner.

2.68b

Although any rhythm written in cut time may also be written in simple quadruple meter, cut time is helpful to a performer because it simplifies the reading of rhythms played at fast tempos.

The following example, written in simple quadruple meter, normally would be counted as follows:

2.69

If example 2.69 were to be played at a fast tempo, a performer would need to visually focus on each of the four beats per measure, which would, over time, be more difficult to read than if the four beats were grouped into two larger beat units.

The following example illustrates how the rhythms written in simple quadruple meter may be regrouped into two larger beat units (two half notes) and counted in cut time.

2.70

Simple quadruple

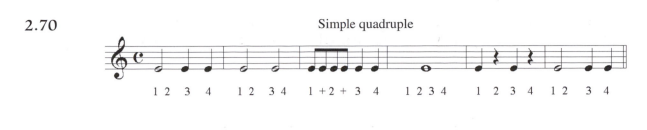

1 2 3 4   1 2 3 4   1 +2 + 3 4   1 2 3 4   1 2 3 4   1 2 3 4

Cut time (simple duple)

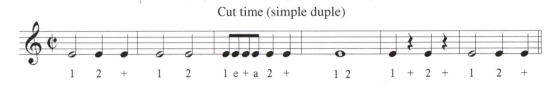

1   2   +   1   2   1 e + a 2 +   1 2   1 + 2 +   1   2   +

Exercise 6

In the following examples written in cut time, place the correct beat number under each note and rest.

2.71a

1 2   12   1 2 +   12   1 + 2   1 2

2.71b

12   1 + 2   1 2   1 + 2   1 2 +   1 2 +

2.71c

1 2 +   12   1 e + a 2   1 e + a 2   1 + 2   1 2

2.71d

1 + 2   1 e + a 2 +   1 2 +   12   1 e + a 2   1 + 2 e a

2.71e

1 + 2 +   1 2 +   1 + 2 e a   12   1 + 2 e a   1 2

When a beat is *divided into halves,* the resulting meter is identified as "simple." A beat also may be *divided into thirds,* which produces a unique rhythmic effect identified as "compound meter."

PART II ∞ *Compound Meter*

Music written in a **compound meter** has a different "rhythmic feel" than music written in a simple meter because the beat is divided into three parts rather than two. Please say the following phrases out loud and notice how the rhythms of the words illustrate the differences between the two meters. The arrows indicate where the beats occur.

SIMPLE METER

1. Ma-ry had a lit-tle lamb, lit-tle lamb, lit-tle lamb . . .

↓   ↓   ↓   ↓↓   ↓   ↓   ↓

2. Twin-kle, twin-kle, lit-tle star, how I won-der what you are . . .

COMPOUND METER

1. Ca-rol-ing, ca-rol-ing, through the snow, Christmas bells are ring-ing . . .

↓   ↓   ↓   ↓   ↓   ↓   ↓

2. O-ver the riv-er and through the woods, to Grand-mother's house we go . . .

The following musical examples illustrate the basic differences between how music sounds when a melody written in simple quadruple meter is rewritten in compound quadruple meter. Although both meters are counted as one, two, three, four, the simple quadruple meter divides the beat into two and four parts, while the compound quadruple meter divides the beat into three parts:

2.72a   *A Melody Written in* Simple Quadruple Meter

2.72b   *The Same Melody Rewritten in* Compound Quadruple Meter

The division of the beat into three parts produces a unique "rhythmic feel" quite different from the division of the beat into two parts (simple meter). Tunes written in compound meter include "In the Still of the Night," "Unchained Melody," "Blueberry Hill," "For He's A Jolly Good Fellow," and the Christmas songs "Oh Holy Night" and "What Child Is This?"

Principle 4

A compound meter results from dividing the beat into thirds.

Perhaps the simplest *visual* method of ascertaining whether or not a piece of music is written in a compound meter is first to determine if the upper number of the meter signature is evenly divisible by three. If the upper number is 6, 9, 12, or 15 (these numbers are the most common), the meter is compound. The number 3 is not included in this grouping. Three-four time is considered a simple meter.

Some examples of compound meters are illustrated below.

$$\frac{6}{4} \quad \frac{9}{4} \quad \frac{12}{4} \quad \frac{15}{4} \quad \text{and} \quad \frac{6}{8} \quad \frac{9}{8} \quad \frac{12}{8} \quad \frac{15}{8} \quad \text{and} \quad \frac{6}{16} \quad \frac{9}{16} \quad \frac{12}{16} \quad \frac{15}{16}$$

In a compound meter, the *number of beats per measure* is determined by dividing the upper number of the meter signature by three. If the upper number of the meter signature is 6, there will be two beats per measure (compound duple meter). If the upper number is 9, there will be three beats per measure (compound triple meter), and so on.

Compound Duple Meter
(Two beats per measure)

$$\frac{6}{4} \qquad \frac{6}{8} \qquad \frac{6}{16}$$

Compound Triple Meter
(Three beats per measure)

$$\frac{9}{4} \qquad \frac{9}{8} \qquad \frac{9}{16}$$

Compound Quadruple Meter
(Four beats per measure)

$$\frac{12}{4} \qquad \frac{12}{8} \qquad \frac{12}{16}$$

Compound Quintuple Meter
(Five beats per measure)

$$\frac{15}{4} \qquad \frac{15}{8} \qquad \frac{15}{16}$$

Principle 5

In a compound meter, the number of beats per measure is determined by dividing the upper number of the meter signature by three.

The lower number of a compound meter signature *does not* designate the note that will receive one beat. This number indicates the rhythmic value of one third of the beat unit. Recall **Principle 4**, which states that a compound meter results from dividing the beat into thirds. To determine the rhythmic value of the note that will receive one beat (the beat unit), it will be necessary to combine three notes of the value represented by the bottom number of the meter signature.

If the meter signature is 6/8, the lower number indicates that *one third of the beat unit* is the eighth note:

     6 ←— (dividing the upper number by three indicates that there will be two beats per measure)

     8 ←— (*indicates that the eighth note is one third of the beat unit*)

Because in a 6/8 meter signature, the lower number (8) indicates that the eighth note is *one third of the beat unit,* the *beat unit* must be the result of the combination of *three* eighth notes. Three eighth notes combine to produce the dotted quarter note, which always will represent the beat unit in a compound meter when the lower number is 8:

2.73   The lower number indicates that the eighth note is 1/3 of the beat unit.

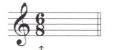 

     The dotted quarter note is the combination of three eighth notes and is the beat unit, which will receive one beat when the lower number of a compound meter is the number 8.

Principle 6

To determine the beat unit in a compound meter (the note receiving one beat), combine three notes of the value that is represented by the bottom number of the meter signature; the resulting beat unit always will be some type of a dotted note.

Let's suppose that the meter signature of a piece of music is 9/4. Since the upper number 9 is evenly divisible by three, this meter must be **compound triple**:

     9 ←— (dividing the upper number by three indicates that there will be
     4   three beats per measure)

Now, let's determine the rhythmic unit that will receive one beat in a 9/4 meter signature. The lower number indicates that *one third of the beat unit* is the quarter note:

     9
     4 ←— (*indicates that the quarter note is one third of the beat unit*)

Three quarter notes now must be combined into one note that will represent the beat unit. Three quarter notes equal the dotted half note, and it is this rhythmic unit that will receive one beat in a compound meter when the lower number is 4.

2.74   The lower number indicates that the quarter note is 1/3 of the beat unit.

The dotted half note is the combination of three quarter notes and is the rhythmic unit that will receive one beat when the lower number of a compound meter is the number 4.

The Compound Meter Table indicates some common compound meters and their associated beats per measure and the note value that will receive one beat.

Compound Meter Table

	Compound Duple Meter (Two beats per measure)			Compound Triple Meter (Three beats per measure)		
	6/4	6/8	6/16	9/4	9/8	9/16
notes receiving one beat	𝅗𝅥.	♩.	♪.	𝅗𝅥.	♩.	♪.

	Compound Quadruple Meter (Four beats per measure)			Compound Quintuple Meter (Five beats per measure)		
	12/4	12/8	12/16	15/4	15/8	15/16
notes receiving one beat	𝅗𝅥.	♩.	♪.	𝅗𝅥.	♩.	♪.

Perhaps a more efficient and less confusing way to express a compound meter signature, occasionally used by composers and arrangers, is to indicate the exact number of beats per measure (upper number), and the note unit receiving the beat (placed beneath the upper number), as indicated in the following example.

2.75   *A more efficient way of expressing compound meter?*

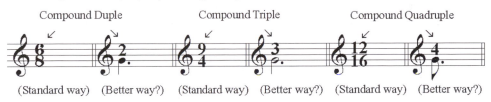

Exercise 7

In the following examples, identify the meter, the number of beats per measure and the beat unit (the note that will receive one beat):

	Meter	Beats per Measure	Beat Unit
4 / 8			
3 / 4			
12 / 2			
9 / 16			
5 / 4			
6 / 8			
3 / 2			
9 / 4			
4 / 4			
12 / 8			

COMPOUND METER
BEAT UNIT DIVISIONS

Although it is always a dotted note that is the rhythmic unit that will receive one beat in a compound meter (see **Principle 6**), *in order to perform and write rhythms correctly, it helps a great deal to identify and count the smaller divisions and subdivisions of the beat unit.* For example, in 6/8 time there are two beats per measure, but it is possible to count each division of the beat unit, the eighth note.

2.76

Example 2.77a illustrates how some of the more common compound duple meter rhythms appear on the staff as the beat unit is subdivided. The numbers above the staff indicate the counting of the beat units, while the numbers below the staff indicate how to count the divided and subdivided beat unit:

2.77a

Count the beat subdivisions as follows: 1 2 3 + 4 5 6   1 2 3 4 5 6   1 2 3 4 5 + 6   1 + 2 3 4 5 6

In the *first measure* of example 2.77a, the *second note*'s rhythmic value has been increased by half with the addition of the dot (this reflects **Principle 3** on page 54). Half of the value of an eighth note is a sixteenth note, which must come from the first half of the next eighth note. The remaining sixteenth note in this grouping is the second half of the eighth note and is counted as "and" (+) as follows:

2.77b

Count the beat subdivisions as follows: 1 2 3 + 4 5 6

Example 2.78 indicates how to count the beats (indicated above the staff) and its various divisions and subdivisions (indicated below the staff) in the remaining measures of example 2.77b:

2.78

Beat subdivisions: 1 2 3 + 4 5 6   1 2 3 4 5 6   1 2 3 4 5 + 6   1 + 2 3 4 5 6

Skill Development

In the following example, indicate *below* the staff the correct counting of each individual note (the beat unit divisions and subdivisions) and *above* the staff where the beats occur in this meter:

2.79

Process

Step 1. Observe that the compound duple meter signature indicates there will be two beats per measure (upper number), with the dotted quarter note receiving one beat (the lower number indicates one third of the beat unit). (See **Principles 5** and **6** to review.) Before you place the beat numbers above the staff, first indicate the *beat divisions and subdivisions* under the staff. Remember, you will be counting the eighth note and eighth rest as the fundamental rhythmic division of the beat.

2.80

Step 2. In the second measure, the dotted quarter note is worth three counts because it contains all three parts of the divided beat (the eighth note). Also, observe that the two sixteenth notes in the remaining part of the second measure reflect that one third of the beat unit (the second eighth note) has been divided into two sixteenth notes. The second half of this rhythmic unit (the sixteenth note) is counted as "and" (+):

2.81

Step 3. In the *third measure*, the first eighth note's rhythmic value has been increased by half because of the addition of the dot (see **Principle 3**). Half of the value of an eighth note is a sixteenth note, which must come from the first half of the next beat unit division (the eighth note). The remaining sixteenth note in this grouping is the second half of the eighth note and is counted as "and" (+), as follows:

2.82

Step 4. Now indicate above the staff where the beats occur in 6/8 meter. Recall that, in compound duple meter, when the lower number of the meter signature is 8, the dotted quarter note will be the rhythmic unit receiving one beat. Therefore, every combination of various rhythmic values in 6/8 meter equalling the rhythmic value of a dotted quarter note will combine to make one beat.

2.83

Exercise 8

In the following melodies, indicate the correct beat number above the staff. Below the staff, number each note and rest and its division as necessary and draw in the bar lines where appropriate. *Be sure to check the meter signature so you know how many beats are required per measure!* Sing these rhythms using "la," and be sure to keep a steady beat by evenly tapping your foot. It is not necessary to sing the actual pitches of the melody.

With practice, you will become familiar enough with compound meter rhythmic patterns so that you will be able to read and play them by visualizing and "feeling" the underlying subdivision of the beat.

PART III ∽ *Rhythmic Mode Mixture*

The placing of a rhythmic figure from a compound meter into a simple meter, and vice versa, is identified as **rhythmic mode mixture.** This brief borrowing or sharing of a particular rhythmic figure is extremely effective because the rhythmic diversity of a composition is greatly enhanced.

Principles 2 and **4** state that (1) a simple meter results from dividing the beat into halves and (2) a compound meter results from dividing the beat into thirds. When the grouping of *three note values* to *one beat*, which is common to a compound meter, is placed within a piece of music written in a simple meter, it is identified as a **triplet**. (Remember, in simple meter, the basic subdivision of the beat is in halves, not thirds!)

EIGHT-NOTE TRIPLETS

In the following example, the three-note rhythmic unit from compound duple meter (6/8) has been moved to simple quadruple meter (4/4) and is called an eighth-note triplet.

2.85

(triplet)

Example 2.86 illustrates how in the second measure the eighth-note triplet is placed within one beat and counted in simple quadruple meter:

2.86

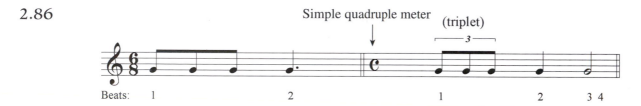

Beats: 1   2   1   2   3 4

Principle 7

Triplets result from placing a compound meter's rhythmic pattern into a simple meter in which three notes of an equal rhythmic value are played in the amount of time it takes to play two of those notes.

Please observe how the correct beat numbers are placed under each note in the first two measures written in "common time":

2.87

1 2   3   4   1 + 2 + 3 4

In the third and fourth measures of example 2.87, the triplet pattern occurs on beat two. Since it takes one beat to play two eighth notes in a simple meter, the eighth note triplet also must be played within one beat (a ratio of

3:1), with each note receiving one third of the beat. Example 2.88 illustrates how each of the rhythmic figures is counted:

2.88

1 2 3 4   1 + 2 + 3 4   1 2   3 4 1 + 2   3 4

One method of learning how to perform a triplet is to practice saying "tri-po-let" evenly on one beat:

2.89

Beats: 1   2   3   4

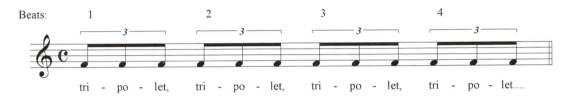

tri - po - let,   tri - po - let,   tri - po - let,   tri - po - let....

Also, previously in this chapter you were introduced to the triplet as a three-note rhythmic unit occurring within word patterns in compound meters, as follows:

Compound meter words:

             (triplet)   (triplet)

[Ca-rol-ing,] [ca-rol-ing,] through the snow, Chrismas bells are ring-ing. . . .

             (triplet)   (triplet)

[O-ver the] [riv-er and] through the woods, to **[Grand-mother's]** house we go . . .

Exercise 9

In the following examples, place the correct beat numbers *under* the notes and then, using "la," sing the various rhythmic patterns. Be sure first to check the meter signature and then provide yourself a steady beat by evenly tapping your foot down and up. While singing the eighth-note triplets, mentally think "tri-po-let."

2.90a

2.90b

QUARTER-NOTE TRIPLETS

Another common type of rhythmic mode mixture occurs when *three quarter notes from a compound meter* are performed within *two beats in a simple meter*. This three-note pattern in simple meter is called a quarter-note triplet and is very similar to the eighth-note triplet discussed in the previous section. Both triplets illustrate **Principle 7**: Triplets result from placing a compound meter's rhythmic pattern into a simple meter in which three notes of an equal rhythmic value are played in the amount of time it takes to play two of those notes.

The quarter-note triplet is grouped as a three-note rhythmic unit within a horizontal bracket and is written in simple meter as follows:

The quarter-note triplet is a difficult rhythm to perform accurately because the second and third notes within this rhythmic unit do not occur on a normally divided part of the beat. Please notice where beat three is placed in example 2.91; it occurs between the second and third note of the quarter-note triplet.

Since the quarter-note triplet is "borrowed" from a compound meter, the precise rhythmic value of each note easily may be understood by observing how it occurs in any of the compound meters, such as 6/8, 9/8, or 12/8.

In compound duple meter, six eighth notes are grouped into two beats:

To develop an understanding of how three quarter notes are rhythmically placed within two beats, you first must create quarter notes by "tying" every two eighth notes as follows:

2.93

Since two eighth notes are equal to one quarter note, the rhythm in example 2.93 could be expressed as follows:

2.94

The arrows in example 2.95 indicate how, in compound duple meter, the accent that normally would occur on the second beat of the measure has been shifted to a different portion of the divided beat unit. An additional accent will be applied to the last two tied eighth notes of the second measure (and also to the last quarter note in the last measure). It is the displacement of the normally accented beats in a simple or a compound meter that makes the rhythmic figure in measures two and three unique:

2.95

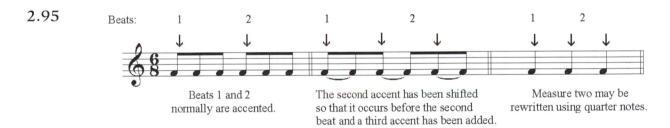

When the rhythm in the third measure of example 2.95 is placed in a simple meter in which the quarter note receives the beat, it must be written as a quarter-note triplet so that the musician knows that it must be performed within two beats. Remember, **Principle 7** states: Triplets result from placing a compound meter's rhythmic pattern into a simple meter in which three notes of an equal rhythmic value are played in the amount of time it takes to play two of those notes.

In the following example, the three quarter notes from the last measure of example 2.95 (which is in compound duple meter) have been placed in a simple quadruple meter and written with the number 3 placed above the notes within a horizontal bracket.

This rhythmic figure is called a quarter-note triplet because these three quarter notes are to be performed within two beats in simple meter.

2.96

In order to perform the quarter-note triplet correctly, you need to think in terms of how six eighth notes would occur within two beats in compound meter:

2.97

In example 2.98 the rhythmic value of a quarter note in the triplet figure has been established by connecting every two adjacent eighth notes with a tie. Please review examples 2.92–2.94 if you need clarification of this process.

2.98

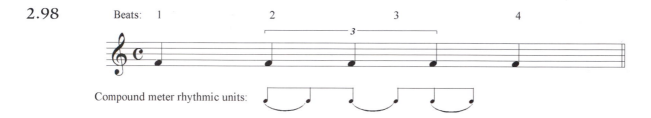

In order to perform the rhythm in example 2.98 correctly, you must mentally count beats two and three as eighth-note triplets and play the connected eighth notes as quarter notes:

2.99

Performing the quarter-note triplet actually is much easier than it seems. Although it may be somewhat cumbersome to determine how it is to be counted, it is relatively easy to remember how it is to be played. It is recommended that you consult a musician who is thoroughly familiar with this rhythm to play or sing it for you so that you may establish a linkage between how the quarter-note triplet is written and how it actually sounds.

DUPLETS

Up to this point you have studied how the eighth- and quarter-note triplet rhythms have been borrowed from compound meters and placed into simple meters. Now let's learn how to place a two-note rhythmic unit from simple meter, the **duplet**, into a compound meter.

Please recall that one of the distinguishing features of a compound meter is that the beat is divided into thirds. Example 2.100 illustrates how two beats in *simple duple meter* are divided in half by writing eighth notes, and how in *compound duple meter* they are divided into thirds by writing three eighth notes. The underlying rhythmic feel of a divided beat in simple meter is 2:1, while in compound meter it is 3:1.

2.100

In a compound meter, the underlying feeling of the subdivision of the beat into thirds may be temporarily disrupted by inserting a borrowed rhythm from a simple meter. Example 2.101 illustrates how the duplet (two notes played in the time of three in a compound meter) is counted within one beat in a compound meter and temporarily suspends the feeling of the beat unit being divided into thirds:

2.101

Performing the duplet correctly may be achieved first by evenly tapping your foot down and up and then practicing singing two notes and three notes evenly within one beat. After you feel comfortable with this, try singing the duplet within one beat of 12/8 time, as illustrated in the following example.

2.102

The meters and rhythms presented in this chapter are among the most commonly used in the writing and performing of music. Although there are numerous and interesting complex rhythmic variations among many diverse musical styles, the basic principles and methods of counting, performing, and writing rhythms remain consistent, regardless of the intricacies one might confront.

PART IV ∞ *Anacrusis, Metronome, and Tempo*

THE ANACRUSIS

Anacrusis is an elegant word that identifies the notes (or note) that precede the first stressed beat of a musical phrase. Musicians also refer to these notes as "pickup notes." Each of the following tunes begins with an anacrusis:

2.103a *America the Beautiful*

2.103b *The Star-Spangled Banner*

2.103c *Happy Birthday!*

Practice singing these tunes and accentuate the second word of the text (not the anacrusis). By stressing the second word and not the first, you will "feel" the musical effect of the anacrusis functioning as a pickup into the tune.

Although the anacrusis may occur at the beginning of a musical composition, it also may appear within a piece of music. The following example illustrates the anacrusis introducing four distinct musical phrases:

2.103d *America the Beautiful*

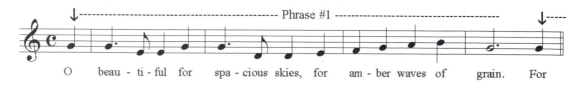

Each anacrusis in "America, the Beautiful" occurs on beat four *because in each case it precedes beat one of the musical phrase:*

2.103e   *America the Beautiful*

Notice in example 2.103e that the anacrusis *at the beginning* of "America the Beautiful" is labeled as count number four. Observe that in the last measure there are only three beats. These three beats plus the anacrusis at the beginning add up to the meter signature's required four beats per measure.

THE METRONOME MARKING AND TEMPO

The **metronome** was invented in 1812 by Dietrich Nikolaus Winkler of Amsterdam (ca. 1780–1826), but it is the name of Johann Nepomuk Maelzel (1772–1838) that is associated with the device. The early mechanical versions of the metronome indicated the speed of the beat by providing a ticking sound produced by a double pendulum housed within a wooden pyramid-like structure. The modern metronome is a portable electronic device accomplishing the same task by using optional blinking lights, audible bleep sounds, and a digitally enhanced visual display of the beat.

Musicians often rely on the metronome marking placed at the beginning of a piece of music to indicate the **tempo** (speed) of a musical composition. The metronome marking is indicated by the abbreviation M.M. (Maelzel's Metronome), followed by the note that will receive one beat and then a number indicating how many beats there will be in one minute. In the following example, the metronome marking indicates that the quarter note receives one beat and that there will be sixty beats in one minute (or one beat per second):

Quarter note
↓
M.M. ♩ = 60

If you have a watch or clock with a second hand, notice that it moves sixty times per minute (or once per second). It is this basic rate of speed that is used as a reference point to compute a metronome marking. The second hand of your watch is moving at a Maelzel's Metronome marking of

M.M. ♩ = 60

A metronome marking of

M.M. ♩ = 120

indicates that the quarter note will receive one beat and that there will be 120 beats per measure (or two beats per second). This is the tempo of a traditional Sousa march.

Try singing the following familiar melody at the speed of sixty beats per minute, or one beat per second. (Refer to the second hand on your watch for the speed of the beat.) This may seem a bit slow, but singing at this tempo will allow you to experience what it is like to maintain a strict beat of one per second.

2.104 *America the Beautiful*

O   beau - ti - ful for   spa - cious skies, for   am - ber waves of   grain. For . . .

If you wanted to indicate that "America the Beautiful" should be performed at a slightly faster tempo, you could set the metronome marking at:

$$\text{M.M. } \quad = 90$$

which indicates that there are ninety beats per minute (or one and one half beats per second) and that the quarter note receives one beat. If you have a metronome available, set it at this marking, and try singing the following example at this tempo. If you do not have a metronome available, you should consult a music teacher for assistance.

2.105 *America the Beautiful*

O   beau - ti - ful for   spa - cious skies, for   am - ber waves of   grain. For . . .

Prior to the invention of the metronome, composers indicated the tempo of a musical composition by writing one or two adjectives above the first measure of a score and on the performer's part. Although these adjectives served as a guide to convey the general speed and feeling of the music, they left a great deal of room for interpretation among performers and conductors.

By the 18th century, various Italian **tempi** (plural of tempo) indicators became conventional throughout Europe. Because of their popularity, Maelzel placed them on his metronome along with their associated ranges of speed. For example, the Italian tempo indicator of "Allegro" (merry, lively) does not imply any one strict metronome marking, but rather a speed within a range of a "not too fast Allegro" to a "fast Allegro."

Although the term "Allegro" partly reflects the characteristic "feeling" of a piece of music and suggests a tempo, the exact speed at which a composition is to be performed is largely dependent upon the musical era in which it was composed and the range of tempi variations acceptable at that time. For example, the speed of the "Allegro" tempo during most of the Baroque era (1600–1750) generally was slower than in the Classical era (1750–1825).

The Italian Tempi Chart illustrates, from slow to fast, some of the more common Italian tempi associated with metronome markings.

Italian Tempi

Grave	solemn, very slow
Largo	broad, large, very slow
Adagio	slow, slower than andante but not as slow as largo
Andante	moderately slow, walking speed
Moderato	moderate (not as fast as Allegro but not as slow as Andante)
Allegretto	a little slower than Allegro (played lightly)
Allegro	merry, lively
Vivace	lively, brisk
Presto	quite fast
Prestissimo	very fast (as fast as possible)

To clarify the precise or general tempo of a piece of music, many composers (since the development of the metronome in 1812) have combined an adjective (or appropriate phrase), often in their native language, with or without a metronome marking, such as:

Allegro vivace (♩ = 158)—Italian

Animé et très rude (♩ = 138)—French

Im Anfang sehr gemächlich (German—metronome marking omitted)

Brisk, with a good beat (♩ = 140)—American

At times, composers may wish only to *suggest a general feeling* of the tempo of a composition, and therefore they indicate this by writing the word "about" or the abbreviation "ca." (circa), as follows:

Molto moderato—with simple expression (♩ = ca. 52)—Italian and American

They also may wish to suggest that the tempo of a composition is satisfactorily playable within a *given range* of beats per minute:

Allegro (♩ = 108–112)

Metronome markings are always helpful to the conductor and performer in fulfilling the composer's musical intentions.

REVIEW OF PRINCIPLES

Principle 1
The top number of a meter signature in simple meter indicates the number of beats per measure, while the lower number indicates the beat unit that receives one beat.

Principle 2
A simple meter results from dividing the beat into halves.

Principle 3
A dot placed after a note or rest lengthens its rhythmic duration by one half of its original value.

Principle 4
A compound meter results from dividing the beat into thirds.

Principle 5
In a compound meter, the number of beats per measure is determined by dividing the upper number of the meter signature by three.

Principle 6
To determine the beat unit in a compound meter (the note receiving one beat), combine three notes of the value that is represented by the bottom number of the meter signature; the resulting beat unit always will be some type of a dotted note.

Principle 7
Triplets result from placing a compound meter's rhythmic pattern into a simple meter in which three notes of an equal rhythmic value are played in the amount of time it takes to play two of those notes.

ANSWER SHEETS FOR CHAPTER 2

2.32e

1 2 3   + 4 e + a 1 e + a 2 + 3 4 1 e + a 2 + 3 + a 4

2.32f

1 2 + 3 e + a 4 1 + 2 3 4 e + a 1 2 +   3   4 1 e + a 2 3 + 4

2.32g

1 e + 2 3 + 1 + a 2 3 1 2 3 e + a 1 + a 2 + a 3 1 2 e + a 3

2.32h

1 + a 2 + 1 + a 2 1 e + a 2 1 e + a 2 1 + a 2 +

2.32i

1 + 2 3 + a 4 + 5 e + a 1 2 + 3 + 4+ 5 1 e + a 2 e + a 3 4 5

2.32j

1 + 2 3 e + a 4 + a 1 + a 2 e + a 3 4 1 e + 2 3 4 + a

Exercise 4

2.47a

1 2 + 3 4 1 2 + 3 4 + 1 2 + 3 4 + 1 2 + 3 4

2.47b

1 2 3 + 1 2 + 3 1 e + a 2 3 + 1 + 2 3 + 1 2 3

2.47c

1 + a 2 + 1 2 + 1 2 + a 1 e + a 2 + a 1 e + a 2 + 1 2

2.71c

1 2 +   1 2   1 e + a 2   1 + a 2   1 + 2   1   2

2.71d

1 + 2   1 e + 2+   1   2 +   1 2   1 e + a 2   1 + 2 + a

2.71e

1 + 2 +   1 2 +   1 2 + a   1 2   1 + 2 + a   1 2

Exercise 7

Meter		Beats per Measure	Beat Unit
4/8	Simple Quadruple	Four	Eighth Note
3/4	Simple Triple	Three	Quarter Note
12/2	Compound Quadruple	Four	Dotted Whole Note
9/16	Compound Triple	Three	Dotted Eighth Note
5/4	Simple Quintuple	Five	Quarter Note
6/8	Compound Duple	Two	Dotted Quarter Note
3/2	Simple Triple	Three	Half Note
9/4	Compound Triple	Three	Dotted Half Note
4/4	Simple Quadruple	Four	Quarter Note
12/8	Compound Quadruple	Four	Dotted Quarter Note

2.90d

1 2 + 3   4 1 e + a 2 3 + 4 1   2   3 + 4 1 + 2   3 4

2.90e

1   2 3 1   2 3 1 2   3 + 1 2   3

WORKSHEETS FOR CHAPTER 2

Name

1. In the following exercises, place the correct beat number under each note and rest and sing the rhythms using "la." In a compound meter, identify all notes and rests as parts of the divided beat. Remember to tap your foot and keep an even and steady beat!

2.

3.

4.

5.

6.

7.

8.

Name

9.

10.

11.

12.

13.

14.

15.

16.

17.

Name

Name

27.

28.

29.

30.

31.

32.

33.

34.

35.

Name

Find additional Skill Development Drills on the
accompanying CD-ROM and on the book companion
Web site: http://music.wadsworth.com/kinney1e.

3
∾

Scales

*Music is a higher revelation than all wisdom and philosophy; it is the wine
of a new procreation, and I am Bacchus who presses out this glorious
wine for men and makes them drunk with spirit.*

—Ludwig van Beethoven

Most of the music we hear is based on an organized pattern of ascending
and descending pitches known as a **scale**. The tones of a scale are vital to
constructing melodies and harmonies for nearly every type of musical composition and are pivotal to establishing an aural focal point in music, which
we call a **key center**. Scale tones are combined in various ways to produce
a variety of supporting harmonies called **chords**, which are used to: (1) support melodies, (2) enhance the overall aesthetic effect of a musical composition, and (3) provide listeners with a sense of forward movement as music
unfolds over time.

   In this chapter you will learn how to construct five types of scales: major,
minor, whole-tone, pentatonic, and chromatic. Although there are other
scales used by various cultures throughout the world, the major and minor
scales, in particular, are among the most important and fundamental elements contributing to the ways we perceive **tonal music**.

Aural Characteristics of Major and Minor Scales

The festive song "Happy Birthday," which has an overall "bright" melody, is
constructed from a **major scale**. Some other familiar tunes constructed from
a major scale that exhibit the same characteristic brightness include "The Star
Spangled Banner," "America the Beautiful," "God Bless America," "Jingle
Bells," and "Feliz Navidad" (a Christmas tune by Jose Feliciano).

   The songs "Summertime," "Autumn Leaves," and "My Funny Valentine,"
and the Christmas carols "What Child Is This?" "Carol of the Bells," and the

beginning of "We Three Kings of Orient Are" illustrate the characteristic sounds of music constructed from a **minor scale**. The "dark" tone quality, or tone color, is readily apparent and easily distinguished from those tunes constructed from a major scale.

In addition to these songs, there are numerous musical masterworks written in minor keys by master composers of the eighteenth and nineteenth centuries, such as **concertos**, **sonatas**, **symphonies**, **art songs**, and solo piano compositions, that constitute a significant part of the musical repertoire of many major symphony orchestras and concert soloists worldwide.

Musical masterworks such as Wolfgang Amadeus Mozart's Symphony no. 41 in C Major or Ludwig van Beethoven's Symphony no. 5 in C minor were composed using major and minor scales. For hundreds of years, composers and songwriters have used these scales to help craft beautiful and memorable musical compositions.

To develop a fundamental sense of the conceptual differences between music written in a major or minor tonality, try playing the following **triads** on the piano keyboard. If this is not possible, then ask a teacher or friend to play them on a guitar, piano, or electronic keyboard, and carefully listen to the differences between these two sonorities.

3.1   *Triads*

The C major triad in example 3.1 has a "bright" sound that distinguishes it from the "darker" sounding C minor triad in the same way in which the melody of "Jingle Bells," written in major, differs from the melodies of "What Child Is This?" and "Autumn Leaves," which are written in minor.

Now that you have a basic awareness of the conceptual differences between major and minor, let's take a moment to review some of the important concepts presented in Chapter 1, and then apply this information to more fully understand the important roles scales contribute to the structure of music.

BRIEF REVIEW OF IMPORTANT CONCEPTS

Whole and Half Steps

You will recall that on the piano keyboard the nearest pitch to the right or left of any black or white key indicates the distance of one semitone, or one half step. Any pitch may be raised or lowered one half step by adding a sharp or a flat, respectively.

If, on the piano keyboard, the white key G were to be raised one half step (by the addition of a sharp), it would move directly to the black key to its immediate right, G♯, which also may be identified by its enharmonic equivalent (two pitches sounding the same but written differently), A♭. If G were lowered one half step (by adding a flat), it would move to the black key to its immediate left, G♭, which also may be identified by its enharmonic equivalent, F♯. In both instances, the nearest pitch above or below G is said to be one half step away. Observe these relationships in the following example.

3.2

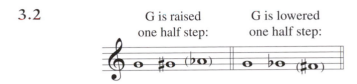

These relationships are easily visible on the piano keyboard by identifying the black key to the right of G as G♯ or A♭, and the black key to the left of G as either G♭ or F♯.

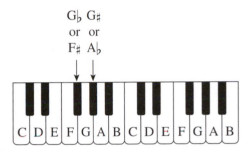

At this point you may be wondering, How will I know when to identify the black key immediately to the right of G as G♯ or A♭? or How will I know when to identify the black key immediately to the left of G as G♭ or F♯? The answer is, *context!*

The correct identification of an enharmonic pitch is determined by the way it is used in scales and also how it functions with respect to both melody and harmony within a musical composition. This issue will become clearer as you progress with your study of music theory, but at this point it is important to realize that enharmonic pitches do exist for all of the pitches in the musical alphabet (A–G).

Let's review another issue involving enharmonic pitches: double sharps and double flats.

Double Sharps and Double Flats

Your first two questions regarding double sharps and double flats might be: Why are they necessary? and In what situations will they be used? The answer to the first question is that they are logical outcomes resulting from an adherence to the rules that govern music theory. The system we use to write and discuss music reflects a coherent and consistent process of musical thought that will become clear to you as you progress through this textbook. The answer to the second question is largely the same reasoning as for enharmonic equivalents of pitches: It depends on the musical context! Double sharps and double flats result from a reasoned theoretical process that you will learn as you explore scales.

To illustrate the process of double sharping a pitch, locate F on the piano keyboard and raise it two half steps by sharping it twice. The first sharp will place you on F♯. When you sharp F♯ you will arrive on F double sharp (F𝄪), which is enharmonic with G. How will you know when to call it F double sharp or G? Context! Remember, this issue will become clearer as you learn about scales.

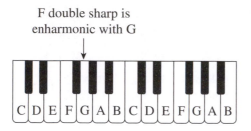

3.3   F has been raised two half steps (two semitones) to F double sharp, which is the enharmonic equivalent of G.

Now let's lower the pitch G one whole step (two half steps), first by flatting it and changing it to G♭, and then by flatting it again and changing it to G♭♭. The pitch now is enharmonic with F.

3.4   G has been lowered one whole step (two half steps) to G double flat, which is the enharmonic equivalent of F.

You may be wondering if it ever will be necessary to triple sharp or triple flat a pitch. The answer is no! The reason for this will become clear to you as you progress in this chapter.

The Musical Alphabet

A major scale is a specific pattern of eight successive musical alphabet pitches separated by whole and half steps occurring within the span of an

octave. Recall that in Chapter 1, the lines and spaces in the bass and treble clefs included the letters of the musical alphabet: A, B, C, D, E, F, and G. In the Western Hemisphere, these are the only alphabet letters used to name musical pitches. It is interesting to note that in Germany, the letter *B* refers to the key or pitch of B♭, and *H* refers to the key or pitch of B. For our purposes, if a scale begins on D, it will end on D and include, in ascending order, the remaining letter names of the musical alphabet: E, F, G, A, B, and C. If a scale begins on E♭, it will end on E♭ and include, in ascending order, the remaining letter names of the musical alphabet: F, G, A, B, C, and D.

THE SOUNDS OF SCALES

Perhaps the most important observation you may make regarding scales is that they have distinctively unique sounds. If possible, ask your teacher, or a musically inclined friend, to play the C major and C minor scales and carefully listen to the differences in their overall tonal characteristics. Does one scale sound brighter than the other? Is the pitch "C" approached from the note below by the same distance in both scales? Is it possible to associate a color (red, blue, yellow, and so forth) with each scale? If so, what color would it be? Although the differences among these scales might be somewhat difficult to articulate, their aural characteristics are distinct and relatively easy to distinguish.

The specific pitches that comprise a major and minor scale reflect an established pattern of whole and half steps occurring between adjacent **scale degrees** (or scale steps). The particular sound of a scale contributes to the creation of the characteristic-sounding melodies and supporting **harmonies** that collectively become the foundation for musical expression.

PART I ∞ *Major Scales*

MAJOR SCALES AND PITCH RELATIONSHIPS

Let's begin our study of major scales by observing the relationships between and among the pitches occurring in the C major scale. It is important to understand that these pitch relationships may be applied to all major scales.

The C major scale may be heard (and seen) on the piano keyboard by individually playing all of the white keys within one octave, beginning and ending on C. The black keys will be used in other scales when it becomes necessary to access pitches requiring sharps or flats. If possible, play this scale on a keyboard and pay close attention to its overall sound. The diagram on the next page identifies the white keys of the piano keyboard that must be played to produce the C major scale.

To play the C major scale on the piano, play the white keys from C to C in ascending order (left to right), as indicated by the arrows. Observe that C is the white key located immediately to the left of the two black keys.

C Major Scale

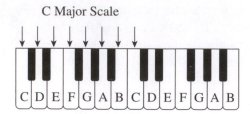

Notice that the C major scale is comprised of eight pitches placed on the staff in alphabetical order, beginning and ending on C.

3.5   ## C Major Scale

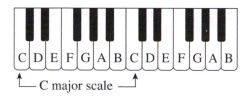

A major scale consists of a pattern of whole and half steps occurring between various adjacent scale degrees. Because the entire piano keyboard is constructed in half steps, it provides a visual display of the whole and half step relationships among and between pitches, and will serve as an important tool when constructing scales.

Principle *1*

A half step is the smallest distance between pitches and may be viewed on the piano keyboard as any two adjacent piano keys.

The following keyboard illustrates that the first two pitches of the C major scale, C and D, are separated by a black key that may be identified as either C♯ or its enharmonic equivalent, D♭.

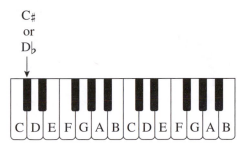

Now, using the piano keyboard, count the number of half steps occurring between C and D. Beginning on C, the next nearest key located above it is C♯, which is said to be one half step away.

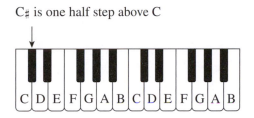

C♯ is one half step above C

The next key above C♯ is D, which also is said to be one half step away from C♯.

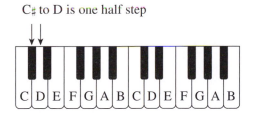

C♯ to D is one half step

Even though there is only one black key between C and D, these pitches are separated by two half steps: C to C♯ and C♯ to D. The distance from C to D therefore is called one **whole step**.

3.6

C to C♯ is one half step. C♯ to D is one half step. C to D is one whole step.

Principle *2*

Two half steps are equal to one whole step.

The pitches C and D are located on scale degrees 1 and 2 of the C major scale and are said to be one whole step apart. The next two pitches, D and E (located on scale degrees 2 and 3), are separated by one black key on the piano keyboard and also are one whole step apart.

D and E are separated by one black key

In the following example, please observe that among the first three pitches of the C major scale, the distance between any two adjacent pitches is one whole step.

3.7

The arrows indicate that there is one whole step between scale degrees 1 and 2, and 2 and 3.

Now let's examine the distance between scale degrees 3 and 4 of the C major scale. Please observe on the piano keyboard below that the next white key to the right of E is F, and that there is no black key separating these pitches.

There is no black key separating E and F

The pitch F is the next nearest note above E, and is said to be one half step above it. Please review **Principle 1,** which states that a half step is the smallest distance between pitches and may be viewed on the piano keyboard as any two adjacent piano keys.

3.8a

The distance between
E and F is one half step

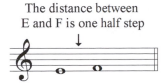

Observe that E and F are scale degrees 3 and 4 of the C major scale:

3.8b

E and F are located on scale degrees
3 and 4 of the C major scale.

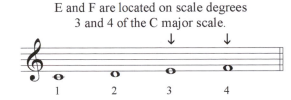

In the C major scale, the distance between the next three pitch pairs—F to G, G to A, and A to B—is one whole step because each pair is separated by a black key.

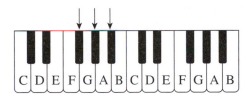

The half step will occur once again between the pitches B and C, because there is no black key separating these pitches.

There is no black key separating B and C

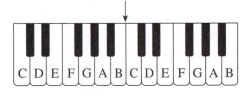

This may be illustrated on the staff as shown in example 3.9a.

3.9a

B and C are one half step apart

In example 3.9b, please observe that half steps in the C major scale occur only between scale degrees 3 and 4, and 7 and 8, as indicated by the caret sign (∧). All other distances between adjacent pitches are whole steps.

3.9b

Half steps in the C major scale occur only between E and F, and B and C because there is no black key separating these pitch pairs.

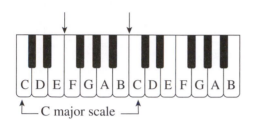

Principle 3

The distance between E and F, and B and C is one half step.

Because major and minor scales are constructed using whole and half steps, let's review the differences between diatonic and chromatic half steps.

REVIEW OF DIATONIC AND CHROMATIC HALF STEPS

In Chapter 1 **diatonic** and **chromatic** half steps were introduced, and soon you will have the opportunity to apply them to the construction of major and minor scales. As you will recall, the term *diatonic* generally means "step-wise," as in the ascending (or descending) pattern of the scale degrees in the C major scale.

In example (A) below, the distance from C to C♯ is said to be a **chromatic half step** because C♯ is an alteration of the pitch C, which shares the same basic letter name. In example (B), the pitch C has moved up one half step to D♭, which is a pitch with a different letter name and is enharmonic to C♯. This particular half step movement is called a **diatonic half step**.

3.10

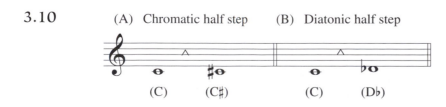

Please observe on the piano keyboard that the note C♯, or its enharmonic equivalent pitch D♭, is the only black key between the two white keys of C and D. Regardless of what this black key is called, it remains one half step above C.

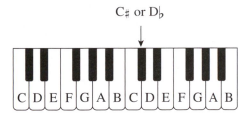

Let's practice writing diatonic and chromatic half steps. Refer to the piano keyboard below when computing your pitches.

Exercise 1

Write *diatonic* half steps *above* each of the following pitches. (Answers are provided at the end of this chapter.)

3.11a

3.11b

Write *diatonic* half steps *below* the following pitches:

3.12a

3.12b

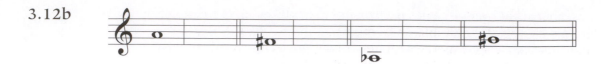

Write *chromatic* half steps *above* the following pitches:

3.13a

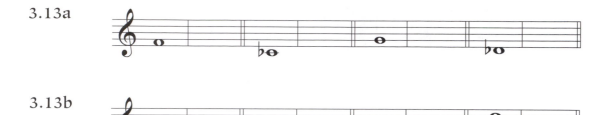

3.13b

Write *chromatic* half steps *below* the following pitches:

3.14a

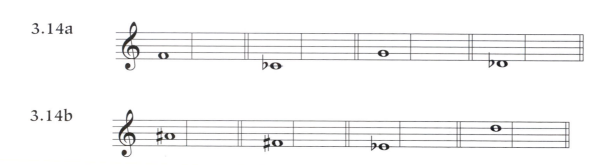

3.14b

THE ASYMMETRICAL AND SYMMETRICAL NATURE OF SCALES

As already discussed, the C major scale is constructed using a combination of whole and half steps, with half steps occurring between scale degrees 3 and 4, and 7 and 8. The distance between any two adjacent pitches of the remaining pitches of the scale will be one whole step.

3.15

Because the distance between adjacent scale degrees is one whole step, *except* for steps 3 and 4, and 7 and 8, the scale is asymmetrical. Scales that are asymmetrical by design exhibit unique characteristics that differentiate them from other types, and serve as the basis of providing a rich palette of musical colors for a **composer** and an **arranger**.

Scales are said to be **symmetrical** when the distances between all consecutive pitches are the same. The **chromatic scale** is such a scale; it is comprised entirely of half steps. Observe in the following example that the distance between any two adjacent pitches in the ascending and descending form of the C chromatic scale is no larger than one half step.

3.16a

Chromatic scale beginning on C (every note is one half step apart):

A chromatic scale may be played on the piano keyboard by beginning on any key and depressing all of the white and black keys within one octave above the starting note. The C chromatic scale, as illustrated in example 3.16a, would be played by depressing the keys from left to right (ascending) and from right to left (descending), as indicated by the arrows on the keyboard:

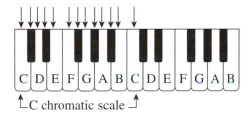

Although, for theoretical reasons, the D chromatic scale looks slightly different from the C chromatic scale, it uses the exact same pitches and is constructed entirely in half steps beginning and ending on D.

3.16b

Chromatic scale beginning on D (every note is one half step apart):

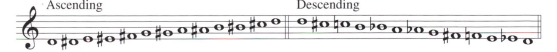

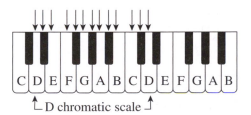

The construction of chromatic scales will be addressed more fully toward the end of this chapter.

The **whole-tone scale,** which will also be presented in greater detail later on in this chapter, is another type of symmetrical scale that is constructed entirely in whole steps.

3.17   Whole-tone scale beginning on C (all notes are one whole step apart):

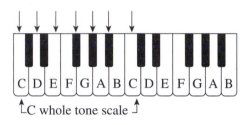

Although the major scale does not have the equidistant spacing between scale degrees that occurs in the chromatic and whole-tone scales, it does possess another kind of symmetry. The symmetrical nature of a major scale may be observed when it is divided into two sections that contain an identical distribution of the placement of whole and half steps.

THE TETRACHORD

Scale degrees 1 through 4 of a major scale are identified as the lower **tetrachord** (from the Greek *tetra,* the prefix meaning "four"), because they comprise the first four diatonic pitches of a scale. Scale degrees 5 through 8 comprise the upper four pitches of a scale and are referred to as the upper tetrachord.

The lower and upper tetrachords of the C major scale encompass the pitches C to F, and G to C, respectively, as illustrated in example 3.18.

3.18   C Major Scale: Lower and Upper Tetrachords

The lower and upper tetrachords in a major scale are symmetrical in that each group of four pitches is constructed in the same ordering of whole and half steps. The lower tetrachord in the C major scale consists of the following

pattern of whole and half steps: whole step (C to D), whole step (D to E), and half step (E to F). The upper tetrachord is constructed in an identical fashion: whole step (G to A), whole step (A to B), and half step (B to C).

3.19

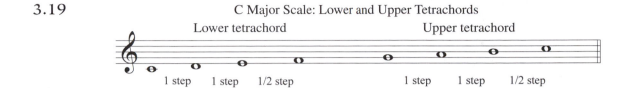

C Major Scale: Lower and Upper Tetrachords

The identical distribution of the whole and half steps in the two tetrachords provides a unique and important symmetry to the major scale that significantly distinguishes it from other types of scales. This important configuration contributes to establishing an aurally perceived sense of a major tonality and a key center within a musical composition.

CONSTRUCTING MAJOR SCALES

There are a total of fifteen different major scales: seven that require from one to seven sharps; seven that require from one to seven flats; and the C major scale, which has neither sharps nor flats. Sharps and flats are important to major scales because they are used to ensure that the required distances between the various scale degree pitches produce the correct upper and lower tetrachords.

Before we go further in studying major scale construction, it is important to restate that on the piano keyboard, it is between the adjacent white keys of E and F, and B and C that there are *no black keys*. These distances therefore are identified as "half steps" (semitones). The distance between any of the remaining adjacent white keys on the piano is "one whole step."

The distance between E and F, and B and C is one half step

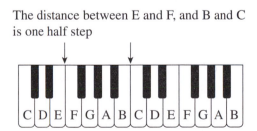

Principle **4**

When constructing a major scale, diatonic half steps must occur between the pitches located on scale degrees 3 and 4, and 7 and 8; all other distances between pitches located on adjacent scale degrees must be one diatonic whole step.

On the keyboard below, and in example 3.20, observe how the C major scale reflects **Principles 3** and **4**:

C D E F G A B C D E F G A B

1 2 3 4 5 6 7 8

3.20   C major scale   one half step   one half step

1   2   3   4   5   6   7   8

Principle 5

What is true for the key of C major is true for all other major keys.

Principle 5 is simple but important: It will allow you to apply the pitch relationships that exist in the key of C to the remaining fourteen major keys. For our purposes, this principle means that the whole and half step arrangements observed in the C major scale will apply to the construction of all other major scales.

Now let's begin to construct major scales by applying **Principle 4**, which states that when constructing a major scale, diatonic half steps must occur between the pitches located on scale degrees 3 and 4, and 7 and 8; all other distances between pitches located on adjacent scale degrees must be one diatonic whole step.

Skill Development

Please construct the F major scale.

Process

Step 1. In ascending order, write on the staff the pitches representing the musical alphabet beginning and ending on F.

3.21

Step 2. Under each pitch, place the correct scale degree number.

3.22

Step 3. Place the caret sign (^) above the appropriate pitches to indicate where diatonic half steps must occur in a major scale (between scale degrees 3 and 4, and 7 and 8).

3.23

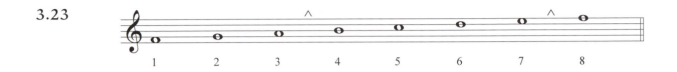

Step 4. Refer to the piano keyboard and, beginning with scale degree 1 (F), count up two half steps.

F to G is one whole step

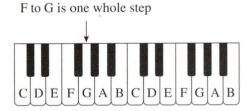

3.24 The note G is one whole step above F.

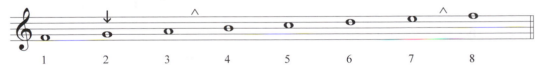

Step 5. Now that you know G is the second scale degree of the F major scale, refer to the piano keyboard and move one diatonic whole step above G (two half steps). You will arrive on A, which is scale degree 3 of the F major scale.

G to A is one whole step

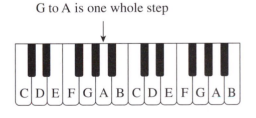

3.25 The note A is one whole step above G.

Step 6. At this point you know that the F major scale consists of the pitches F, G, and A. You now must determine what the correct pitch will be for scale degree 4. The caret sign (∧) placed between the pitches at scale degrees 3 and 4 (illustrated in example 3.25) is there to remind you that the distance between these pitches must be one *diatonic* half step! Refer to the piano keyboard and move up one diatonic half step from A to the next nearest pitch. This pitch is B♭.

You must *not* call this pitch by its enharmonic equivalent, A♯, because *scale degree 4 must be some kind of a B* (B, B♭, or B♯). Refer to example 3.25 and please notice that scale degree 4 of the F major scale involves the next letter of the musical alphabet (B). Therefore, one diatonic half step above A is B♭.

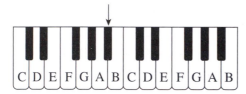

A to B♭ is one diatonic half step

3.26   The note B♭ is one half step above A

Step 7. Now you must determine the correct pitch at scale degree 5. The distance between steps 4 and 5 must be one whole step (see **Principle 4**: When constructing a major scale, diatonic half steps must occur between pitches located on scale degrees 3 and 4, and 7 and 8; all other distances between pitches located on adjacent scale degrees must be one diatonic whole step).

Refer to the piano keyboard and locate the pitch which is one whole step above scale degree 4 (B♭). You will arrive on C because one half step above B♭ is B, and one half step above B is C. Place C on the staff.

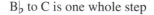

B♭ to C is one whole step

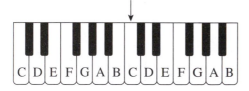

3.27   The note C is one whole step above B♭, and is scale degree 5 of the F major scale

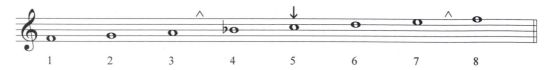

Step 8. To determine the correct pitch located on scale degree 6, you will need to count up one whole step (two half steps) from C. Look at the piano keyboard and locate the pitch that is one whole step above C. The note D is scale degree 6 of the F major scale.

D is one whole step above C

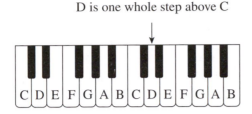

3.28 The note D is one whole step above C and is scale degree 6 of the F major scale

Step 9. To determine the correct pitch for scale degree 7 of the F major scale, you will need to go up one whole step from D. This pitch is E and it is scale degree 7 of the F major scale. Place E on the staff.

E is one whole step above D

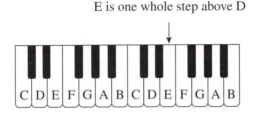

3.29

Step 10. As stated in **Principle 4**, the distance between the pitches located on scale degrees 7 and 8 must be one half step. The caret sign (∧) in example 3.29 is there to remind you of this. You have determined that E is scale degree 7 of the F major scale, so now you must move up one half step to establish the pitch located on scale degree 8. Recall that the next nearest adjacent key on the piano keyboard (white or black) immediately above or below any key is one half step away. Refer to the piano keyboard and notice that the next nearest key above E (to the right) is F. F is the pitch located on scale degree 8 of the F major scale.

F is one half step above E

3.30

1   2   3   4   5   6   7   8

Skill Development

Let's try constructing a major scale beginning on A.

Process

Step 1. In ascending order, write on the staff the pitches representing the musical alphabet beginning and ending on A.

3.31

Step 2. Under each pitch, place the correct scale degree number.

3.32

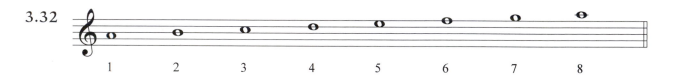

1   2   3   4   5   6   7   8

Step 3. Place the caret sign (∧) above the appropriate pitches to indicate where the half steps must occur in a major scale (between scale degrees 3 and 4, and 7 and 8).

3.33

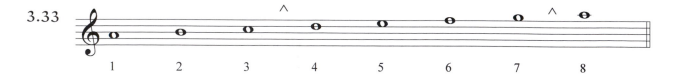

1   2   3   4   5   6   7   8

Step 4. Refer to the piano keyboard and, beginning with scale degree 1 (A), count up (movement to right of the A) two half steps. One half step above A is A♯, and one more half step above A♯ is B. B is the pitch that is located on the second scale degree of the A major scale.

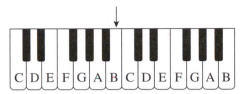

B is one whole step above A

3.34

Step 5. Now that you know that B is the second scale degree of the A major scale, refer to the piano keyboard and move one diatonic whole step above B. You will arrive on C♯. Please remember that you must not identify C♯ by its enharmonic equivalent name of D♭! Refer to the scale degree numbers under each pitch and you will see that scale degree 3 *must be* identified as some kind of C (C, C♯, or C♭).

C♯ is one whole step above B

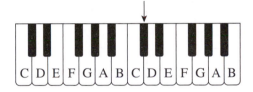

3.35   C♯ is one whole step above B and is scale degree 3 of the A major scale

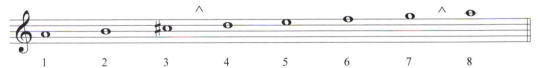

Step 6. At this point you know that the A major scale consists of the pitches A, B, and C♯. Now you must determine what the correct pitch will be for scale degree 4. The caret sign (∧) between the pitches at scale degrees 3 and 4 in example 3.35 is there to remind you that the distance between the pitches on these scale degrees must be one diatonic half step. Refer to the piano keyboard and move up one diatonic half step from C♯. You will arrive at D, which is scale degree 4 of the A major scale.

D is one diatonic step above C♯

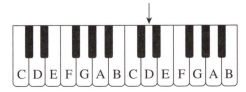

3.36   D is one half step above C♯ and is scale degree 4 of the A major scale.

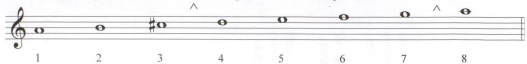

Step 7. You now must determine the correct pitch at scale degree 5. The distance between scale degrees 4 and 5 must be one *whole step,* because **Principle 4** states that when constructing a major scale, diatonic half steps must occur between pitches located on scale degrees 3 and 4, and 7 and 8; all other distances between pitches located on adjacent scale degrees must be one diatonic whole step.

     Refer to the piano keyboard and locate the pitch that is one whole step (two half steps) above step 4, D. You will arrive on E.

E is one whole step above D

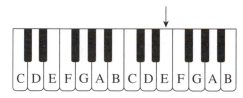

3.37

Step 8. To determine the correct pitch for scale degree 6, you will need to count up one *diatonic* whole step from E. Look at the piano keyboard and locate the pitch that is two half steps above E. One half step above E will place you on F, and one half step above F will place you on F♯. You must not identify F♯ by its enharmonic equivalent of G♭, because the pitch located on scale degree 6 must be some type of F (F, F♯, or F♭). The pitch located on scale degree 6 of the A major scale is F♯.

F♯ is one whole step above E

3.38

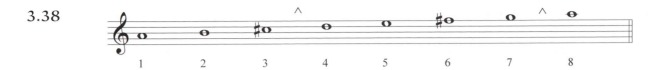

Step 9. To determine the correct pitch for scale degree 7 of the A major scale, you will need to move up one *diatonic* whole step from the pitch F♯. Look at the piano keyboard and locate the pitch that is two half steps to the right of F♯. The correct pitch is G♯.

G♯ is one whole step above F♯

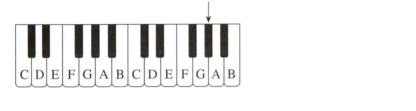

3.39

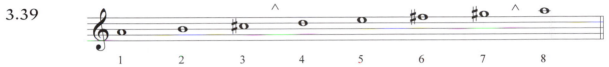

Step 10. As stated in **Principle 4**, the distance between the pitches located on scale degrees 7 and 8 must be one *diatonic* half step. The caret (∧) between these scale degrees is there to remind you of this. You have determined that the pitch G♯ is scale degree 7 of the A major scale, so now you must move up one half step to determine scale degree 8. The correct pitch located on scale degree 8 of the A major scale is A.

A is one diatonic half step above G♯

3.40

Exercise 2

Construct the following major scales and be sure to number the scale degrees 1 through 8, and place a caret (∧) between steps 3 and 4, and 7 and 8. For your convenience, pitches for each scale degree have been placed on the staff.

3.41a   Construct the B♭ major scale.

3.41b   Construct the D major scale.

3.41c   Construct the E♭ major scale.

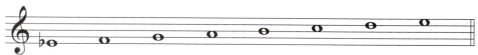

3.41d   Construct the F# major scale.

PART II   ∞   *Minor Scales*

CONSTRUCTING MINOR SCALES

Music written in the minor mode has, at its core, an associated **pure minor** scale. There are a total of fifteen different pure minor scales, seven of which require from one to seven sharps; seven of which require from one to seven flats; and the A pure minor scale, which has neither sharps nor flats.

Although the process of constructing minor scales is similar to the process of constructing major scales, there are some additional considerations that must be carefully addressed.

Minor scales are constructed in three forms: **pure minor** (which may be called the **natural minor**), **harmonic minor**, and **melodic minor**. The musical reasoning that explains the need for these three forms of the minor scale will be addressed toward the end of this chapter.

It is very important for you to try to sing and play each of the three forms of the minor scale. Developing your "mind's ear" to become sensitive to the subtleties unique to each form will assist you in understanding why there is a musical need for them. If you are unable to play these scales on an instrument, please ask your music teacher or a musically inclined friend to sing or play them for you.

THE PURE MINOR SCALE

Principle **6**

When constructing a pure minor scale, diatonic half steps must occur between the pitches located on scale degrees 2 and 3, and 5 and 6; all other distances between pitches located on adjacent scale degrees must be one diatonic whole step.

Skill Development

Let's construct the E pure minor scale and employ the same process used to construct major scales. The only difference is that half steps will occur between scale degrees 2 and 3, and 5 and 6.

Process

Step 1. In ascending order, write on the staff the pitches representing the musical alphabet beginning and ending on E.

3.42

Step 2. Under each pitch place the correct scale degree number.

3.43

Step 3. Place a caret sign (∧) above the appropriate pitches to indicate where diatonic half steps must occur in a pure minor scale (between scale degrees 2 and 3, and 5 and 6).

3.44

Step 4. Refer to the piano keyboard and, beginning with scale degree 1, count up one whole step. One half step above E is F, and one more half step above F is F♯. F♯ is the second scale degree of the E pure minor scale.

F♯ is one whole step above E

3.45

Step 5. Now that you know F♯ is the second scale degree of the E pure minor scale, refer to the keyboard and move one diatonic half step above it. (The caret (∧) between scale degrees 2 and 3 is there to remind you that the distance between the pitches at this point must be one diatonic half step!) The pitch one diatonic half step above F♯ is G. Please remember that half steps in the pure minor scale must occur at scale degrees 2 and 3, and 5 and 6.

G is one diatonic half step above F♯

3.46

Step 6. At this point you know that the E pure minor scale consists of the pitches E, F♯, and G. Now you must determine what the correct pitch will be for scale degree 4. Refer to the piano keyboard and move up one diatonic whole step from G to A. Remember, one diatonic whole step equals two half steps. You first must move up one half step from G to G♯ and then another half step above G♯ to A. The pitch located on scale degree 4 of the E pure minor scale is A.

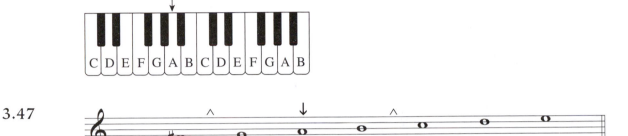

A is one whole step above G

3.47

Step 7. Now you must determine the correct pitch for scale degree 5. Because the distance between scale degrees 4 and 5 must be one diatonic whole step, scale degree 5 of the E pure minor scale is B.

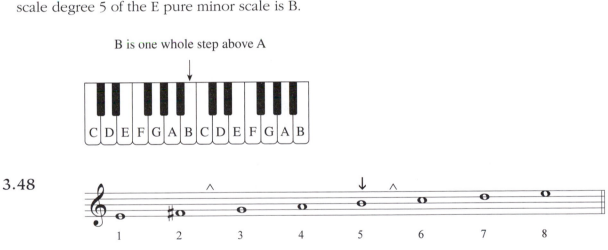

B is one whole step above A

3.48

Step 8. To determine scale degree 6, you will need to count up one diatonic half step from B. Please recall that the caret (∧) indicates that the distance between scale degrees 5 and 6 must be one diatonic half step. The nearest adjacent pitch above B is C, which is the sixth scale degree of the E pure minor scale.

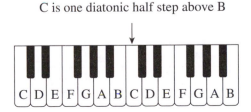

C is one diatonic half step above B

3.49

Step 9. To determine the correct pitch located on scale degree 7, you will need to go up one diatonic whole step from the note C. On the keyboard, locate the pitch that is two half steps to the right of C. One half step above C is C♯, and one half step above C♯ is D. The pitch D is located on the seventh scale degree of the E pure minor scale.

D is one whole step above C

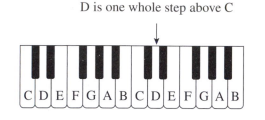

3.50a

Step 10. Now you must move up one diatonic whole step to determine the pitch located on scale degree 8. Refer to the keyboard, and notice that the note one whole step up from D is E.

E is one whole step above D

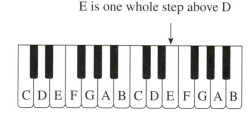

The E pure minor scale appears on the staff as follows.

E pure minor scale

3.50b

Exercise 3

Construct the following "pure minor" scales. Be sure to number the scale degrees 1 through 8, and place the caret (^) at 2 and 3, and 5 and 6. For your convenience, pitches for each scale degree have been placed on the staff.

3.51a   Construct the G pure minor scale.

3.51b   Construct the B♭ pure minor scale.

3.51c   Construct the F♯ pure minor scale.

3.51d   Construct the E♭ pure minor scale.

THE HARMONIC MINOR SCALE

The harmonic minor scale is a variation of the pure minor scale. In this scale, scale degree 7 of the pure minor is raised one half step. The reason for this will be explained later on in this chapter. For now, the focus will be on learning how to construct this form of the minor.

Principle 7

When constructing the harmonic minor scale, first establish the pure minor and then raise the pitch located on scale degree 7 one chromatic half step.

Skill Development

Let's construct the B harmonic minor scale. You must first construct the pure minor form of this scale.

Process

Step 1. Write on the staff, in ascending order, the pitches representing the musical alphabet beginning and ending on B.

3.52

Step 2. Under each pitch, place the correct scale degree number.

3.53

Step 3. Place the carets (^) between the appropriate pitches to indicate where diatonic half steps must occur in the pure minor scale (between scale degrees 2 and 3, and 5 and 6).

3.54

Step 4. Now place in the correct accidentals (sharps or flats) to complete the B pure minor scale. If you have trouble with this process, or wish to review it, see examples 3.42 through 3.50b. The completed B pure minor scale is illustrated in example 3.55.

3.55

B pure minor scale

Step 5. Now that you have constructed the B minor scale in its "pure" form, in order to make it "harmonic minor" you will need to apply **Principle 7** and raise the pitch located on scale degree 7 one *chromatic* half step. The pitch currently located on scale degree 7 is A. Refer to the piano keyboard and raise the pitch A one chromatic half step to A♯. The B harmonic minor scale is illustrated in example 3.56.

A to A♯ is one chromatic half step

3.56   B harmonic minor scale

Skill Development

Let's try constructing the F harmonic minor scale.

Process

Step 1. In ascending order, write on the staff the pitches representing the musical alphabet beginning and ending on F.

3.57

Step 2. Under each pitch place the correct scale degree number.

3.58

Step 3. Place carets (∧) between the appropriate pitches to indicate where diatonic half steps must occur in the pure minor scale (between scale degrees 2 and 3, and 5 and 6).

3.59

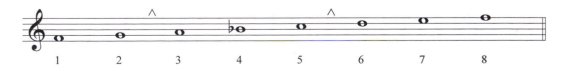

Step 4. Now add the correct accidentals (sharps or flats) to complete the F pure minor scale.

3.60

F pure minor scale

Step 5. Now that you have constructed the F minor scale in its "pure" form, in order to create the "harmonic minor" form, you will need to apply **Principle 7** and raise the pitch located on scale degree 7 one chromatic half step. The pitch located on scale degree 7 currently is E♭. Refer to the piano keyboard and raise E♭ one chromatic half step to E natural. The F harmonic minor scale is illustrated in example 3.61.

E natural is one chromatic half step above E♭

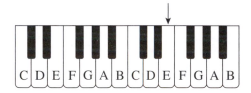

3.61

F harmonic minor scale

Exercise 4

Construct the following "harmonic minor" scales. Be sure to number the scale degrees 1 through 8, and place carets (∧) between 2 and 3, and 5 and 6. For your convenience, the notes for each scale have been placed on the staff.

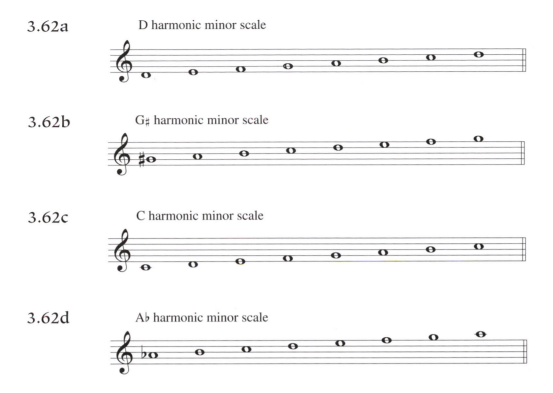

3.62a   D harmonic minor scale

3.62b   G♯ harmonic minor scale

3.62c   C harmonic minor scale

3.62d   A♭ harmonic minor scale

THE MELODIC MINOR SCALE

The melodic minor scale results from raising the pitches located on scale degrees 6 and 7 of the pure minor scale one chromatic half step while ascending, and then restoring these altered pitches to their original pitches while descending. As a result, this scale always must be constructed in an ascending and descending fashion. This may sound very confusing at first, but this scale, as well as the harmonic form of the minor, reflects a number of important aesthetic and theoretical musical considerations that will become clearer as you continue your study of music. A brief explanation of the necessity of both the melodic and harmonic scales will be addressed later on in this chapter.

Principle 8

The melodic minor scale is a variation of the pure minor scale in which pitches located on scale degrees 6 and 7 of the pure minor form are raised one chromatic half step while ascending, then lowered to their original pitches when descending (thereby restoring the pure minor).

One simple way to think about the melodic minor scale is to realize that it is the pure minor form written *ascending and descending,* with the pitches located on scale degrees 6 and 7 raised one half step on the ascending side only. Let's observe this pattern of raised pitches in the C melodic minor scale. Example 3.63 illustrates the C pure minor scale written in an ascending and descending pattern.

3.63

Notice in example 3.63 that the descending side of the C pure minor scale is a mirror image of the ascending side. The only adjustment needed to make this scale C melodic minor is for the pitches located on scale degrees 6 and 7 *on the ascending side* to be raised one chromatic half step. This may be accomplished by applying the natural sign to them. Please observe that the descending side remains the unaltered pure minor form of this scale. Example 3.64 reflects **Principle 8** and illustrates the C melodic minor scale written in its complete form.

3.64   C melodic minor scale

Let's now observe how **Principle 8** is reflected in the F♯ melodic minor scale. In example 3.65, the F♯ pure minor scale is written in an ascending and descending pattern.

3.65   F# pure minor scale written ascending and descending

To make this scale F♯ melodic minor, scale degrees 6 and 7 on the ascending side must be raised one chromatic half step. Please notice that the descending side must remain the pure minor form of this scale.

3.66

Natural signs have been applied to the pitches located at scale degrees 6 and 7 on the descending side in order to cancel the sharps originally used to raise them on the ascending side. This step is necessary because the

descending side of the scale must reflect the pure minor as written in example 3.65.

Skill Development

Now let's take a step-by-step approach and construct the G♯ melodic minor scale.

Process

Step 1. On the staff, write in ascending and descending order the pitches representing the musical alphabet beginning and ending on G♯. Include the appropriate scale degree number under each pitch.

3.67

Step 2. Place carets (∧) to indicate where the half steps occur (in a pure minor scale, half steps must occur at scale degrees 2 and 3, and 5 and 6).

3.68

Step 3. Now carefully construct the pure form of the G♯ minor scale on the ascending side, and then copy it to the descending side. Refer to the keyboard as necessary and place in the correct accidentals (sharps or flats). If you have trouble with this process, or need to review, see examples 3.42 through 3.50b.

The completed G♯ pure minor scale is illustrated in the following example.

3.69

Step 4. Example 3.69 illustrates the G♯ pure minor scale written both in an ascending and descending pattern. Now you must raise scale degrees 6

and 7 *one chromatic half step* on the ascending side only by sharping both E and F♯. Do not forget to restore them to their original forms on the right side by using a natural sign. Remember, the descending side of the melodic minor scale must reflect the pure form of the minor. Please refer to the piano keyboard below to assist with this process. In example 3.70, the G♯ melodic minor scale is written in its complete form.

3.70

The G# melodic minor scale written ascending and descending.

Let's look carefully at the G♯ melodic minor scale in example 3.70. Notice that scale degrees 6 and 7 in the pure form were E♮ and F♯, respectively (see example 3.69). They have been raised one chromatic half step to E♯ and F𝄪. On the descending side of the scale, a natural sign was placed before the F♯ in order to cancel the sharp that was added on the ascending side. The result is a pitch with a natural and a sharp. The pitch on scale degree 6, E, on the ascending side, was raised one chromatic half step to E♯, and needs a natural on the descending side to restore it to its original form in the pure minor, as illustrated in example 3.69.

Skill Development

Please construct the E♭ melodic minor scale.

Process

Step 1. On the staff, write in ascending and descending order the pitches representing the musical alphabet beginning and ending on E♭, and include the appropriate scale degree number under each pitch.

3.71

Step 2. Place carets (∧) to indicate where the half steps occur (in a pure minor scale half steps must occur at scale degrees 2 and 3, and 5 and 6).

3.72

Step 3. Now construct, in ascending and descending order, the pure form of the E♭ minor scale and be careful to add the correct accidentals. Example 3.73 illustrates the E♭ pure minor scale.

3.73

Step 4. Now raise the pitches on scale degrees 6 and 7 on the ascending side one chromatic half step using the natural sign. Please refer to the piano keyboard below to assist with this process. In example 3.74 the E♭ melodic minor scale is written in its complete form.

3.74

E♭ melodic minor scale

At this point, it would be beneficial to practice aural discrimination of the three types of minor scales. If at all possible, try playing these scales on an instrument and then practice singing them. If you are unable to do this, and if you are unfamiliar with the tunes mentioned at the beginning of this chapter that illustrate the differences between major and minor tonalities, try locating a recording of these popular songs so that you are able to compare their different tonal qualities.

As you progress through this book, you will be able to understand the various topics more clearly if you make an effort to *hear* the musical examples that are presented in each chapter. One important method of developing a discerning musical ear is to play, on the piano or on another instrument, each musical example you encounter. With minimal effort, and with sustained practice, over a period of time your "mind's ear" will begin to develop a sensitivity and awareness to the three forms of the minor scale and the theoretical principles that govern their construction.

Exercise 5

Construct the following "melodic minor" scales. Be sure to number the scale degrees 1 through 8, and place carets (∧) between 2 and 3, and 5 and 6. For your convenience, pitches for each scale degree have been placed on the staff.

3.75a   D melodic minor scale

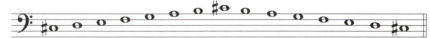

3.75b   C♯ melodic minor scale

3.75c   G melodic minor scale

3.75d   A melodic minor scale

THE NECESSITY OF THE HARMONIC AND MELODIC MINOR SCALES

Sing the Christmas tunes "What Child Is This?" and "Jingle Bells," which were addressed at the beginning of this chapter, and compare the differences in their overall musical character. "What Child Is This?" is written in the "dark" sounding "Aeolian" mode (minor) and "Jingle Bells" in the "bright" sounding "Ionian" mode (major).

A distinguishing feature of music in the major mode is that its key center, called the **tonic** (the pitch located on scale degrees 1 and 8 of a major scale), may be approached by a pitch located either *one whole step above* or *one half step below* it. Observe in example 3.76 how the tonic, C, is approached in the C major scale.

3.76

The C major scale in two octaves, indicating C being approached from above by one whole step and from below by one half step.

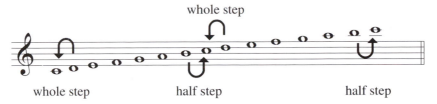

Approaching the tonic by one whole step from above is possible in both the major and minor modes. However, as example 3.77 illustrates, the tonic in the C *pure minor form* is *approached from below* by *one full step* and not by one half step, as was scale degree 8 in the C major scale illustrated in the previous example.

3.77

The C pure minor scale in two octaves, indicating the tonic C being approached from above and below by one whole step.

In a major scale, the pitch located on scale degree 7, which approaches the tonic from one half step below, is called the **leading tone**. In example 3.76, the tonic, C, is approached by its leading tone, B. The leading tone is one of the most significant of all pitches within a tonal musical composition because it assists in directing the "mind's ear" toward a clearly defined tonic (or key center). Please recall that in major scales, half steps occur between scale degrees 3 and 4, and 7 and 8. The required half step between scale degrees 7 and 8 ensures a leading tone.

Example 3.78 illustrates the leading tone as a diatonic pitch occurring on scale degree 7 in the key of C major. Remember that **Principle 5** states that what is true for the key of C major is true for all other major keys. All major keys, of which there are fifteen, have leading tones located one half step below the tonic.

3.78

C major scale

B is the leading tone to C.

Recall that half steps occur in a minor scale between pitches located on scale degrees 2 and 3, and 5 and 6. Because there is no diatonic half step occurring between scale degrees 7 and 8 in the pure minor form, this form of the scale *has no leading tone.* The tonic in the pure minor scale is approached instead by the **subtonic**, which is located one full step below it.

3.79

In music that is harmonically complex, it is not always an easy task for listeners to clearly identify the "tonic." The clear establishment of the tonic provides a key center and a sense of a melody's harmonic direction that continues to be preferred by the majority of listeners, regardless of the style of music being performed.

When key changes, or shifts from the tonic, occur in a piece of music, our "musical ears" generally require a leading tone to direct our attention to the new tonal center being established. These tonal shifts, or **modulations**, provide music with harmonic variety, and also help composers and arrangers more fully express their musical intentions.

When the *tonic* of the pure minor scale is approached from the subtonic, and not the leading tone, a strong sense of a key center is more difficult to establish, particularly if the music has frequent modulations or brief shifts toward new tonal centers. It is because of this lack of a clearly defined sense of a tonal center during these tonal shifts that a leading tone is frequently required in the minor mode, to help direct the "mind's ear" toward a new tonic.

At times, the pitch located on the seventh scale degree of the pure minor scale (the subtonic) must be altered by raising it one half step in order to create the leading tone necessary to assist in defining the tonic. The result is that the tonic of the pure minor scale now will be approached by one half step in the same way that it is approached in a major key. This alteration of the pure minor is referred to as the *harmonic minor form.* Example 3.80 illustrates this concept.

3.80

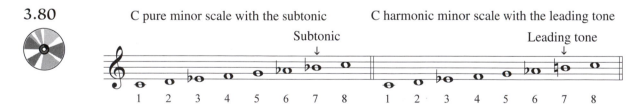

Principle 9

The leading tone is scale degree 7 of a major scale and the harmonic form of the minor scale, and is one half step below the tonic.

Now that the fundamental reasons for the creation of the harmonic minor scale have been reviewed, let's look at why there is the need for the melodic minor form of this scale.

Example 3.81 illustrates two scales: C major and C pure minor. Recall that in a major scale, half steps occur between scale degrees 3 and 4, and 7 and 8, and that in the pure minor scale, they occur between scale degrees 2 and 3, and 5 and 6. The distance between the remaining adjacent scale degrees is one whole step.

3.81

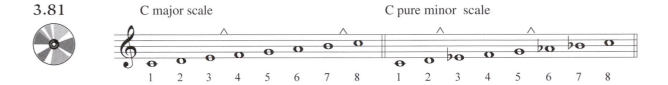

Example 3.82 illustrates the C harmonic minor scale. Please notice that, although the *smallest distance* between any two adjacent pitches is one half step, the *largest distance* between any two adjacent pitches is one and one half steps, which occurs between scale degrees 6 and 7 only in the harmonic form of the minor scale. This distance is the result of altering the pure minor by raising the pitch located on scale degree 7 one half step and creating a leading tone. The harmonic minor scale contains half steps between scale degrees 2 and 3, 5 and 6, and 7 and 8.

3.82

Play and sing each of the three scales below, or have your teacher play them for you. Notice their differences and the "exotic" nature of the harmonic minor.

3.83

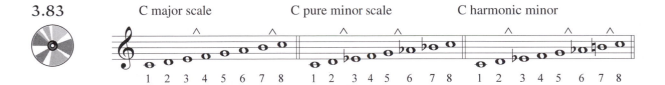

If you repeatedly play the pitches located on scale degrees 5 through 8 of the harmonic minor scale in an ascending and descending pattern, you will hear that this section of the scale has the characteristics of an exotic melody. The normal symmetry and linear smoothness occurring between the pitches located on scale degrees 6 and 7 of the pure minor form have been disrupted by the insertion of the one and one half step distance between these two scale degrees. The creation of the leading tone in the harmonic minor form has resulted in an awkward-sounding scale pattern that composers, historically, have sought to avoid, and have "corrected" by using the melodic minor form of the minor scale.

There are musical instances where the exploitation of this awkward distance (one and one half steps between scale degrees 6 and 7) is effectively used; but, in general, composers have sought to avoid this **interval** (the distance between pitches) when writing music for both singers and instrumentalists.

Play and sing the following musical example, both ascending and descending, using "la" and focus particularly on the pitches located on scale degrees 5 through 8. See if you agree with this assessment of the nature of the harmonic form of the minor scale.

3.84

To correct for the awkwardness of the one and one half step distance between scale degrees 6 and 7 of the harmonic minor, the melodic minor scale serves to "adjust" the scale by raising the pitch located on scale degree 6 one half step when ascending. This adjustment closes the "gap" of the one and one half step interval between scale degrees 6 and 7, and results in a linear scale that sounds much smoother and is easier to sing. Try singing or playing the scales in example 3.85a, and listen to the smooth, conjunct nature of the ascending melodic minor form.

3.85a

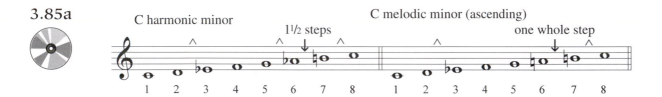

Recall that **Principle 8** states that the melodic scale must be written in an ascending and descending order. Let's discover the reason for this. Carefully observe in example 3.85b that the ascending form of the C melodic minor scale has altered pitches on scale degrees 6 and 7 of the pure minor scale.

3.85b

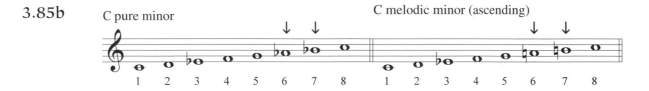

The melodic form of the C minor scale, which served to make the scale more conjunct and smoother to perform, must not be sustained for a long period of time in a minor key, because the character of the mode would be altered to the point where it would sound too much like the C major scale.

Play or sing the scales below, and observe that the C major scale, except for the pitch located on scale degree 3, looks and sounds very similar to the ascending form of the C melodic minor scale.

3.86

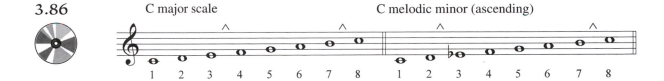

After using the ascending form of the melodic minor in a piece of music, it is necessary to restore the pure minor form in order to convince the "mind's ear" that the music has not shifted to a major mode or to another key. Recall that the descending form of the melodic minor scale lowers scale degrees 6 and 7 in order to restore the pure minor form. The ascending side of the melodic minor scale is the pure minor form with scale degrees 6 and 7 raised one half step. (Refer to examples 3.63–3.74 for a review of this concept.)

The following example illustrates how the C pure minor scale has been restored on the descending side of the C melodic minor scale.

3.87

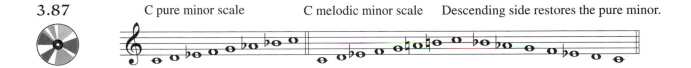

The melodic form of the minor scale is generally used at specific times in a piece of music where it is necessary to assist in "smoothing out" the linear pitches of a musician's vocal or instrumental part. Occasionally, composers will intentionally exploit this scale when they wish to inject its particular musical characteristics into the harmonic and/or melodic fabric of a piece of music, but this must be carried out in a careful manner.

PART III ∞ *Whole-Tone Scales*

The whole-tone scale is a symmetrical scale of six pitches constructed entirely in whole steps within the span of an octave. Because the pitches are equally spaced in whole steps, there is no leading tone to approach the tonic by one half step, which would normally help to establish a clear tonal center.

The whole-tone scale's ambiguity attracted French impressionist composers, such as Claude Debussy (1862–1918) and Maurice Ravel (1875–1937) and others, during the late nineteenth and early twentieth centuries, and continues to be used by modern composers for special effects within a composition. Its unique sound provides composers and performers with an expanded palette of tonal colors that can enhance a listener's interest in a piece of music.

One way to experience this scale is to become familiar with its sound on the piano and then listen to compositions by Claude Debussy, such as *La Mer, Prelude to the Afternoon of a Faun,* and *Nuages.*

Try playing the scales illustrated in example 3.88 on the piano, and observe how they sound entirely different in character. Notice that the C major scale has seven *different* pitches, while the whole-tone scale has only six.

3.88

A whole-tone scale may be constructed on any pitch, but, because it is constructed entirely in whole steps, there can be only two different-sounding whole-tone scales: C and C♯.

3.89

N.B. There are numerous solutions to constructing whole-tone scales; the following method is a recommended approach.

Notice that the two scales in example 3.89, that are written one half step apart, do not have notes on the exact same lines and spaces. The C whole-tone scale omits a note on the second space of the staff, and the C♯ whole-tone scale omits a note on the first line of the staff. (This may seem confusing, but there is a musical reason for it.) Notice that the first and last pitches of both scales are left and approached by one diatonic whole step.

3.90

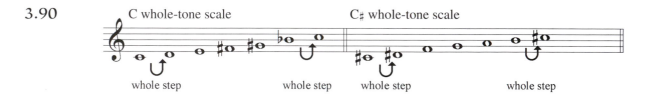

In order to facilitate the playing of the many altered pitches found *between* the first and last pitches of the C♯ whole-tone scale, some pitches are written enharmonically to avoid double sharps and double flats.

If the C♯ whole-tone scale were written with pitches on the same scale degrees as in the C whole-tone scale, it would look as follows.

3.91

Compare both versions of the C♯ whole-tone scale below, and notice how the version on the right simplifies the visual appearance of the scale by using enharmonic equivalents of three of the pitches.

3.92

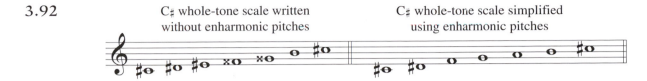

If you were to construct a whole-tone scale beginning on D, you would use the same pitches as for the C whole-tone scale.

3.93a

* = enharmonic equivalent

When constructing a whole-tone scale, it is important to remember that the pitch located on scale degree 1 is left by a diatonic whole step (step 2), and that the pitch located on scale degree 7 is approached by a diatonic whole step (step 6). The remaining pitches between scale degrees 2 and 6 must be written one full diatonic step apart. *As long as you write in the pitches located on scale degrees 2 and 6 first, the remaining pitches may be written enharmonically depending on the specific musical context of the pitches within a piece of music.*

In order to maintain the whole step between scale degrees 7 and 8, there will need to be an enharmonic leap of a **diminished 3rd** somewhere in the scale. The diminished 3rd is a musical distance between pitches and will be addressed in Chapter 6. For now, observe this leap between the pitches located on scale degrees 5 and 6 in both scales in the example below.

3.93b

In the C whole-tone scale in example 3.93b, scale degree 5 is G♯. The distance between G♯ and the next note, B♭, is called a diminished 3rd, if you count G♯ as one, A as two, and B♭ as three. The same is true in the D whole-tone scale between the A♯ and the C. If you count A♯ as one, B as two, and C as three, this distance is also a diminished 3rd. You will understand the concept of a diminished 3rd more clearly after you complete Chapter 6, "Intervals."

The diminished 3rd occurs in all whole-tone scales, but does not necessarily have to occur between scale degrees 5 and 6. The harmonic context within a piece of music will determine the pitches involved in this interval. For example, if the G♯ in the C whole-tone scale were to be written enharmonically as A♭, then the diminished 3rd would be located between scale degrees 4 and 5.

3.93c

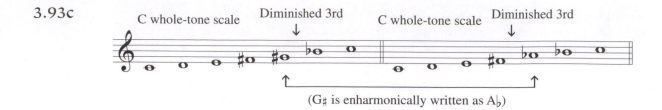

(G♯ is enharmonically written as A♭)

Skill Development

Let's construct the whole-tone scale beginning on F.

Process

Step 1. Place two Fs on the staff one octave apart.

3.94

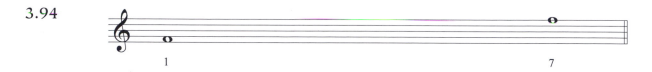

Step 2. Place on the staff the pitches at scale degrees 2 and 6 that are one whole step above scale degree 1 and one whole step below scale degree 7. Refer to the piano keyboard to help compute the correct pitch. Remember, your pitches must be one diatonic whole step away from F.

3.95

Step 3. Now insert the pitch one whole step above scale degree 2, G. This pitch is A.

3.96

Step 4. Now insert the next pitch, which is one whole step above A. This pitch is B.

3.97

Step 5. Now insert the final pitch, which is one whole step above B. This pitch is either C♯ or D♭. If C♯ is used, then the diminished 3rd will occur between scale degrees 5 and 6.

3.98a

If D♭ is used instead of C♯, the diminished 3rd will occur between scale degrees 4 and 5.

3.98b

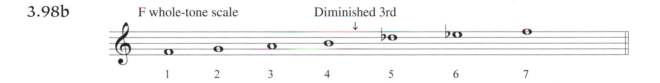

Both versions of the F whole-tone scale in examples 3.98a and 3.98b are correct!

Skill Development

Let's try constructing the A whole-tone scale.

Process

Step 1. Place two A's on the staff one octave apart.

3.99

Step 2. Write pitches one whole step above the pitch on scale degree 1 and one whole step below the pitch on scale degree 7. Remember, both pitches must be one diatonic step away from A.

3.100

Step 3. Now insert the pitch that is one whole step above B. This pitch is C♯.

3.101

Step 4. Now insert the next pitch, one whole step above C♯. This pitch is D♯.

3.102

Step 5. Now insert the final pitch, which is one whole step above D♯. This pitch is either E♯ or F. If E♯ is used, then the diminished 3rd will occur between steps 5 and 6.

3.103a

If F is used instead of E♯, the diminished 3rd will occur between steps 4 and 5.

3.103b

Exercise 6

Construct the following whole-tone scales. For your convenience, the beginning pitch has been placed on the staff.

3.104a   D whole-tone scale

3.104b   E whole-tone scale

3.104c   G whole-tone scale

3.10d   B♭ whole-tone scale

3.104e   E♭ whole-tone scale

PART IV ∾ *Pentatonic Scales*

Throughout the world, different cultures have created folk music based on various types of scales. The five-note **pentatonic scale**, which has many varieties, is prominent in the folk music of Europe, Africa, Asia, eastern Europe (as well as the Far East and Southeast Asia), and in American Indian music. A few examples of this scale include music from the Orient (Chinese and Japanese folk songs), Pacific South Seas vocal and instrumental folk music, and American Indian music (spiritual and dance music). Pentatonic scales were integrated into the compositional styles of the French impressionist composers, as well as serving as a fundamental basis for a number of American folk songs, and the harmonic styles associated with rhythm and blues.

Although there are many variations of the pentatonic scale, the one characteristic common to all of the forms is the lack of any half steps. Music based on this scale does not have a leading tone that would otherwise be extremely helpful in defining a clear key center. Recall that the leading tone is the pitch located on scale degree 7 in both the major and harmonic minor (and the ascending melodic minor) forms, and is located one half step below the tonic (scale degree 1 or 8). The ambiguity arising from the lack of a clearly established key center is one of the most distinctive features of music using the pentatonic scale.

The pentatonic scale may be heard by playing only the black keys on the piano. Try playing the black keys in any order, and sing along with the pitches as they are sounded.

Play the black keys to hear
the pentatonic scale

Two versions of the pentatonic scale seem to be the most popular. Version I *uses only the five pitches of the major scale located on scale degrees 1, 2, 3, 5, and 6.* (Third space C has been added as a sixth note simply to enclose the scale between the two Cs.) Notice that scale degrees 4 (F) and 7 (B) of the C major scale are missing.

3.105   C pentatonic scale: Version I

Version II of this scale omits scale degrees 3 and 7 of the C major scale. If either pitch were there, it would create a half step with the next note above it. Remember, the pentatonic scale does not contain half steps. The scale degrees used in this version are 1, 2, 4, 5, and 6.

3.106   C pentatonic scale: Version II

An easy way to distinguish between the two forms of the pentatonic scale is that Version II replaces scale degree 3 of the major scale with scale degree 4. This is the only difference!

Skill Development

Let's construct the F pentatonic scale using Version I.

Process

Step 1. Construct the F major scale.

3.107 F major scale

1   2   3   4   5   6   7   8

Step 2. Now eliminate the pitches located on scale degrees 4 and 7, and retain the pitches located on the remaining scale degrees (1, 2, 3, 5, and 6) of the F major scale. Remember, all of the pitches of the F pentatonic scale are diatonic in the key of F, so it will not be necessary to alter any pitches chromatically with a sharp or a flat once you determine the correct pitches in the F major scale. Label each pitch with the correct scale degree number.

3.108 F pentatonic scale: Version I

1   2   3   5   6   8

Skill Development

Example 3.108 illustrates the F pentatonic scale using Version I. This is the F major scale *minus* the pitches located on scale degrees 4 and 7. Now create Version II of this scale by replacing scale degree 3 (A) with scale degree 4 (B♭) of the F major scale.

Process

3.109 F pentatonic scale: Version II

1   2   4   5   6   8

Skill Development

Construct both versions of the E pentatonic scale.

Process

Step 1. Place the pitch E on the staff and construct the E major scale. Label each pitch with the correct scale degree number.

3.110

E major scale

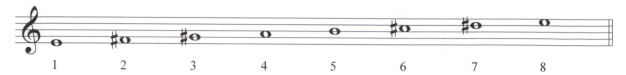

1   2   3   4   5   6   7   8

Step 2. Now eliminate scale degrees 4 and 7. Label each pitch with the correct scale degree number.

3.111   E pentatonic scale: Version I

1   2   3   5   6   8

Now create Version II of this scale by replacing the pitch located on scale degree 3 with the pitch located on scale degree 4 of the E major scale.

3.112   E pentatonic scale: Version II

1   2   4   5   6   8

Exercise 7

Construct the following pentatonic scales in both versions.

3.113a   D pentatonic scale: Version I

3.113b   D pentatonic scale: Version II

3.113c   B♭ pentatonic scale: Version I

3.113d   B♭ pentatonic scale: Version II

3.113e   F♯ pentatonic scale: Version I

3.113f   F♯ pentatonic scale: Version II

PART V ∞ *Chromatic Scales*

At the beginning of this chapter you were introduced to the asymmetrical and symmetrical aspects of scales. Recall that the chromatic scale is a symmetrical scale consisting entirely of half steps.

3.114

Chromatic scales beginning on C

When constructing any chromatic scale, it is important to realize that, in order to avoid enharmonic inconsistencies, chromatic pitches (those that are not diatonic to the scale) must be spelled using *raised diatonic pitches* when ascending, and *lowered diatonic pitches* when descending. For example, if the ascending F major scale were to be rewritten as the F chromatic scale, every chromatic pitch would have to be an alteration of an associated diatonic pitch of the F major scale.

3.115

F major scale

F chromatic scale

Every chromatic pitch is an alteration of an
associated diatonic pitch of the F major scale.

Notice in the F chromatic scale in example 3.115 that the first pitch F moves
to F♯, and not G♭, because the ascending side of the scale must use *raised
diatonic pitches*. If G♭ were to be written instead of F♯, this would be an error,
because G♭ is a *lowered diatonic pitch*.

If the B♭ major scale is to be rewritten as a chromatic scale, it is the diatonic pitches that must be altered to achieve the half step distance between
adjacent pitches.

3.116

B♭ major scale

B♭ chromatic scale ascending

Chromatic scales also may be constructed from any pure minor scale.
Observe in the following example the differences in the C chromatic scale
when it is an alteration first of the C major scale and then of the C minor scale.
Remember that chromatic pitches must be spelled using *raised diatonic
pitches* when ascending and *lowered diatonic pitches* when descending.

3.116a

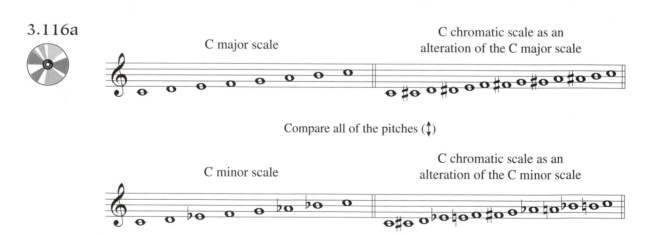

C major scale

C chromatic scale as an
alteration of the C major scale

Compare all of the pitches (↕)

C minor scale

C chromatic scale as an
alteration of the C minor scale

Example 3.116b illustrates the descending side of the scale:

3.116b

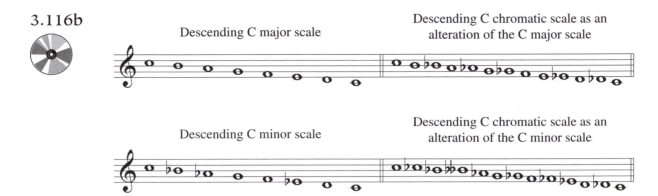

Descending C major scale

Descending C chromatic scale as an alteration of the C major scale

Descending C minor scale

Descending C chromatic scale as an alteration of the C minor scale

Please learn the following principle.

Principle *10*

The altered diatonic pitches in a chromatic scale must be spelled using raised diatonic pitches when ascending and lowered diatonic pitches when descending.

N.B. **Principle 10** is not strictly adhered to. Composers and arrangers frequently write the enharmonic equivalent of a chromatically altered pitch because of its specific harmonic function within the context of a musical composition.

Skill Development

Let's apply **Principle 10** and construct the G chromatic scale as an alteration of the G major scale.

Process

Step 1. Write the G major scale, ascending and descending, on the staff.

3.117

Step 2. Now ascend in half steps. making certain that every non-diatonic pitch is a *raised diatonic pitch* of the G major scale.

3.118

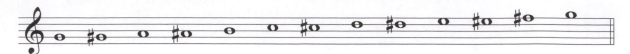

Step 3. Now descend in half steps, making certain that every non-diatonic pitch is a *lowered diatonic pitch* of the G major scale.

3.119

Skill Development

Now let's construct the G chromatic scale as an alteration of the G pure minor scale.

Process

Step 1. Write the G pure minor scale, ascending and descending, on the staff.

3.120

Step 2. Ascend in half steps, making certain that every non-diatonic pitch is a *raised diatonic pitch* of the G minor scale.

3.121

Step 3. Descend in half steps, making certain that every non-diatonic pitch is a *lowered diatonic pitch* of the G minor scale.

3.122

Skill Development

Now let's construct the A chromatic scale as an alteration of the A major scale.

Process

Step 1. Write the A major scale, ascending and descending, on the staff.

3.123

Step 2. Ascend in half steps, making certain that every non-diatonic pitch is a *raised diatonic pitch* of the A major scale.

3.124

Step 3. Descend in half steps, making certain that every non-diatonic pitch is a *lowered diatonic pitch* of the A major scale.

3.125

Skill Development

Let's construct the A chromatic scale as an alteration of the A minor scale.

Process

Step 1. Write the A pure minor scale, ascending and descending, on the staff.

3.126

Step 2. Ascend in half steps, making certain that every non-diatonic pitch is a *raised diatonic pitch* of the A minor scale.

3.127

Step 3. Descend in half steps, making certain that every non-diatonic pitch is a *lowered diatonic pitch* of the A minor scale.

3.128

Exercise 8

Construct the following chromatic scales in both the ascending and descending forms, as alterations of a major scale. Be sure to write the major scale first.

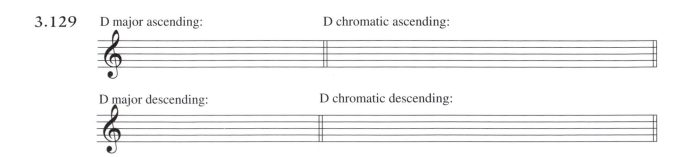

3.129   D major ascending: D chromatic ascending:

D major descending: D chromatic descending:

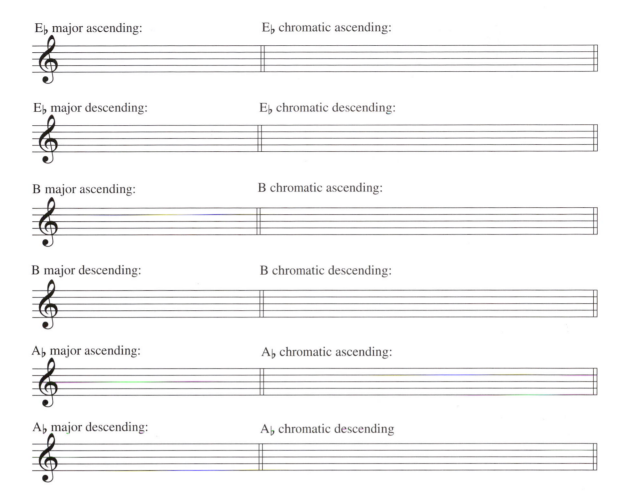

Eb major ascending:

Eb chromatic ascending:

Eb major descending:

Eb chromatic descending:

B major ascending:

B chromatic ascending:

B major descending:

B chromatic descending:

Ab major ascending:

Ab chromatic ascending:

Ab major descending:

Ab chromatic descending

Construct the following chromatic scales, in both the ascending and descending forms, as alterations of the pure form of a minor scale. Be sure to write the pure minor scale first!

Exercise 9

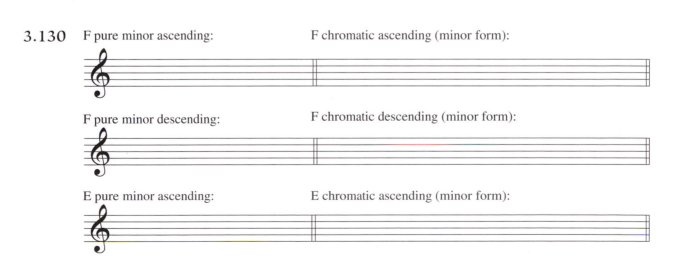

3.130   F pure minor ascending:

F chromatic ascending (minor form):

F pure minor descending:

F chromatic descending (minor form):

E pure minor ascending:

E chromatic ascending (minor form):

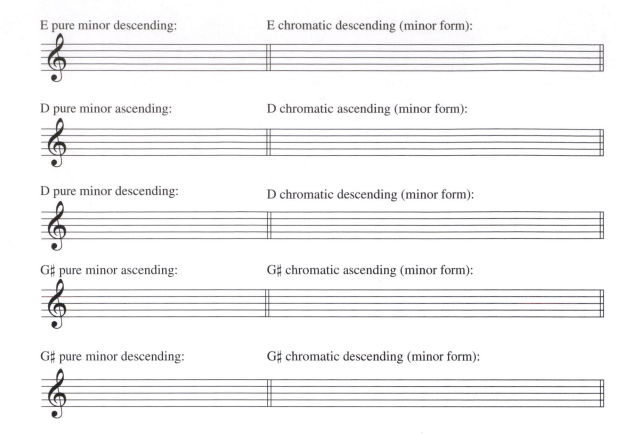

E pure minor descending:

E chromatic descending (minor form):

D pure minor ascending:

D chromatic ascending (minor form):

D pure minor descending:

D chromatic descending (minor form):

G♯ pure minor ascending:

G♯ chromatic ascending (minor form):

G♯ pure minor descending:

G♯ chromatic descending (minor form):

Now that you understand the principles of scale construction, the following chapter will address how the accidentals that occur in both major and minor scales may be expressed as key signatures. Key signatures will be utilized in important ways in subsequent chapters and will assist you in addressing the issues regarding modes, intervals, triads, and the harmonic functions of triads. The following chapter is one of the most important in this textbook!

REVIEW OF PRINCIPLES

Principle 1
A half step is the smallest distance between pitches and may be viewed on the piano keyboard as any two adjacent piano keys.

Principle 2
Two half steps are equal to one whole step.

Principle 3
The distance between E and F, and B and C is one half step.

Principle 4
When constructing a major scale, diatonic half steps must occur between the pitches located on scale degrees 3 and 4, and 7 and 8; all other distances between pitches located on adjacent scale degrees must be one diatonic whole step.

Principle 5
What is true for the key of C major is true for all other major keys.

Principle 6
When constructing a pure minor scale, diatonic half steps must occur between the pitches located on scale degrees 2 and 3, and 5 and 6; all other distances between pitches located on adjacent scale degrees must be one diatonic whole step.

Principle 7
When constructing the harmonic minor scale, first establish the pure minor and then raise the pitch located on scale degree 7 one chromatic half step.

Principle 8
The melodic minor scale is a variation of the pure minor scale in which pitches located on scale degrees 6 and 7 of the pure minor form are raised one chromatic half step while ascending, then lowered to their original pitches when descending (thereby restoring the pure minor).

Principle 9
The leading tone is scale degree 7 of a major scale and the harmonic form of the minor scale, and is one half step below the tonic.

Principle 10
The altered diatonic pitches in a chromatic scale must be spelled using raised diatonic pitches when ascending and lowered diatonic pitches when descending.

ANSWER SHEETS TO CHAPTER 3

Exercise 1

Exercise 2

3.41a B♭ major scale

3.41b D major scale

3.41c E♭ major scale

3.41d F# major scale

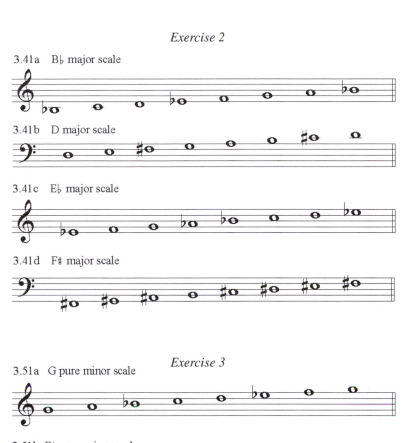

Exercise 3

3.51a G pure minor scale

3.51b B♭ pure minor scale

3.51c F# pure minor scale

3.51d E♭ pure minor scale

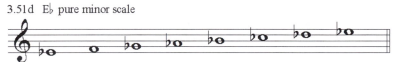

Exercise 4

3.62a D harmonic minor scale

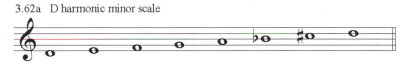

3.62b G# harmonic minor scale

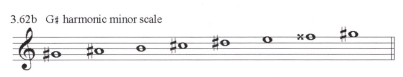

3.62c   C harmonic minor scale

3.62d   A♭ harmonic minor scale

Exercise 5

3.75a   D melodic minor scale

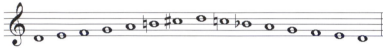

3.75b   C♯ melodic minor scale

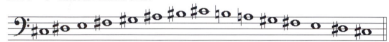

3.75c   G melodic minor scale

3.75d   A melodic minor scale

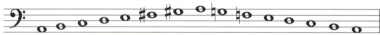

Exercise 6

There is more than one correct solution to contructing the whole-tone scale. Your solution is correct if pitches 1 and 2, and 6 and 7 are one whole step apart and the remaining pitches are enharmonic to the pitches illustrated below.

3.104a   D whole-tone scale

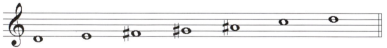

3.104b   E whole-tone scale

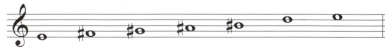

3.104c   G whole-tone scale

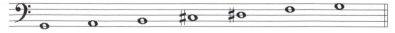

3.104d   B♭ whole-tone scale

3.104e   E♭ whole-tone scale

Exercise 7

3.113a   D pentatonic scale: Version I

3.113b   D pentatonic scale: Version II

3.113c   B♭ pentatonic scale: Version I

3.113d   B♭ pentatonic scale: Version II

3.113e   F♯ pentatonic scale: Version I

3.113f   F♯ pentatonic scale: Version II

Exercise 8

3.129   D major ascending: D chromatic ascending:

D major descending: D chromatic descending:

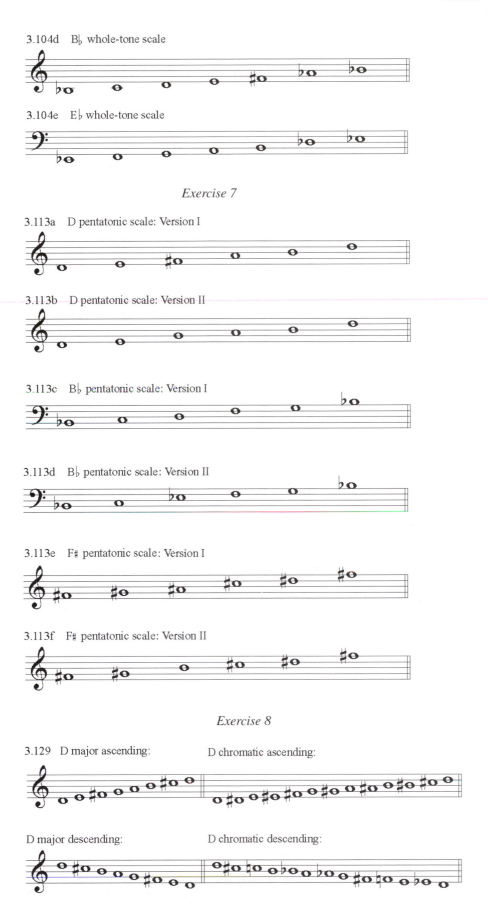

Exercise 9

3.130   F pure minor ascending: F chromatic ascending (minor form):

D pure minor ascending:

D chromatic ascending (minor form):

D pure minor descending:

D chromatic descending (minor form):

G# pure minor ascending:

G# chromatic ascending (minor form):

G# pure minor descending:

G# chromatic descending (minor form):

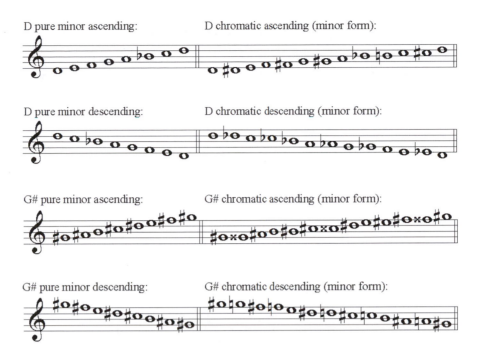

WORKSHEETS FOR CHAPTER 3

Name

1. Write diatonic half steps above each of the following pitches.

2. Write diatonic half steps below each of the following pitches.

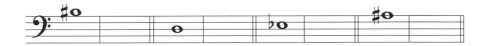

3. Write chromatic half steps above each of the following pitches.

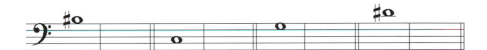

4. Write chromatic half steps below the following pitches.

5. Construct the following major scales.

G major

Name

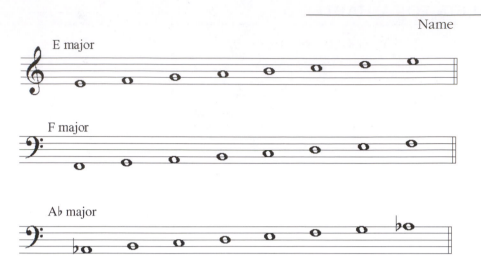

E major

F major

A♭ major

6. Construct the following pure minor scales.

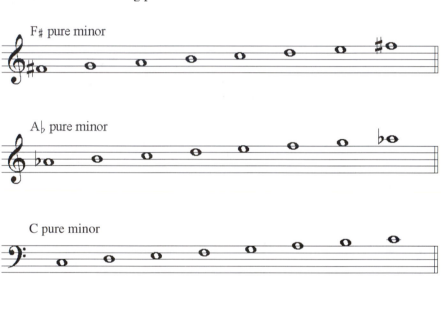

F♯ pure minor

A♭ pure minor

C pure minor

D♯ pure minor

Name _____

7. Construct the following harmonic minor scales.

E harmonic minor

F♯ harmonic minor

C♯ harmonic minor

A harmonic minor

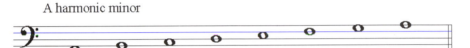

8. Construct the following melodic minor scales.

B♭ melodic minor

B melodic minor scale

E melodic minor scale

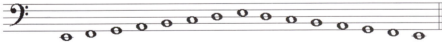

D♯ melodic minor scale

9. Construct the following whole-tone scales.

B whole-tone

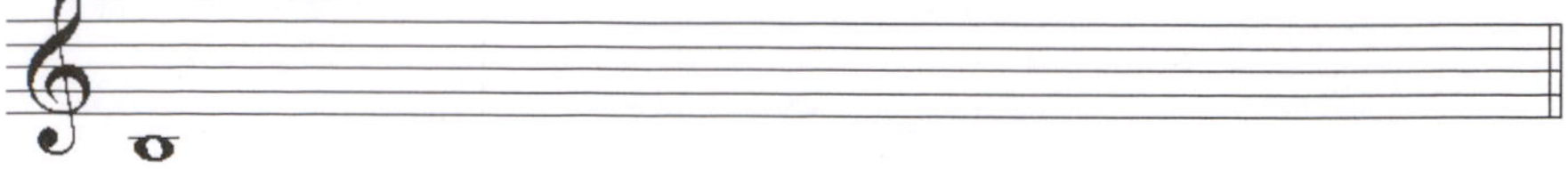

F♯ whole-tone

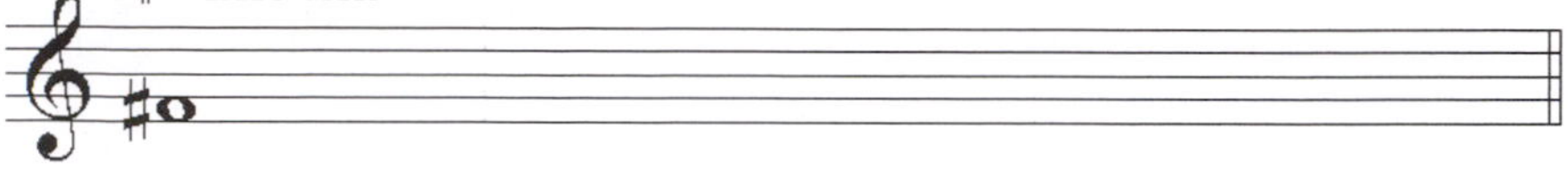

G♭ whole-tone

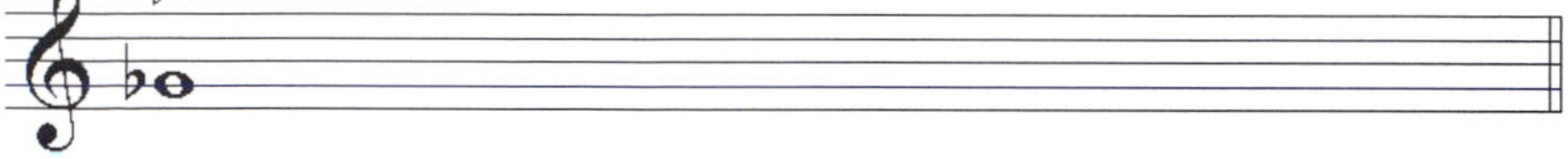

G♯ whole-tone

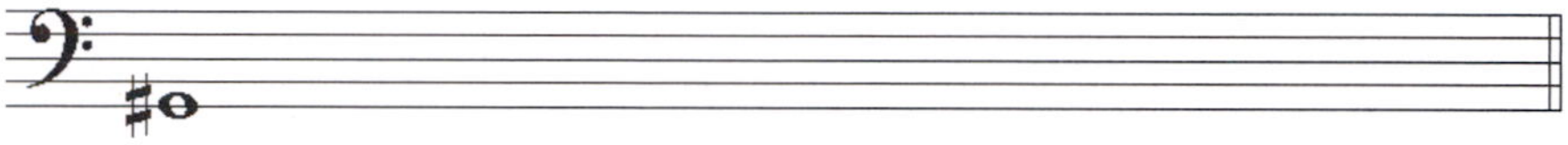

C♭ whole-tone

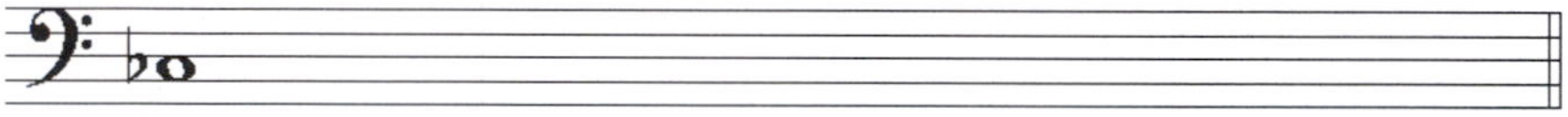

10. Construct the following pentatonic scales in two versions:

A♭ pentatonic: Version I

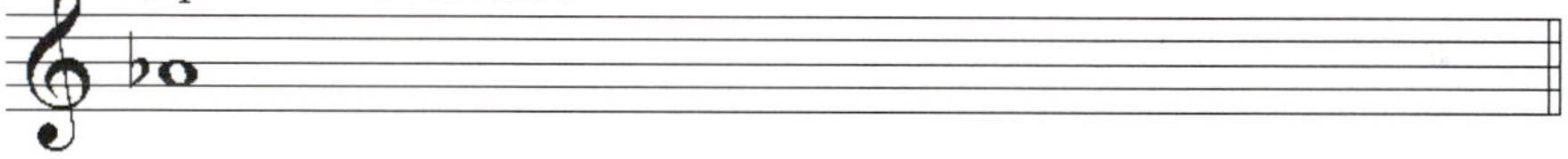

A♭ pentatonic: Version II

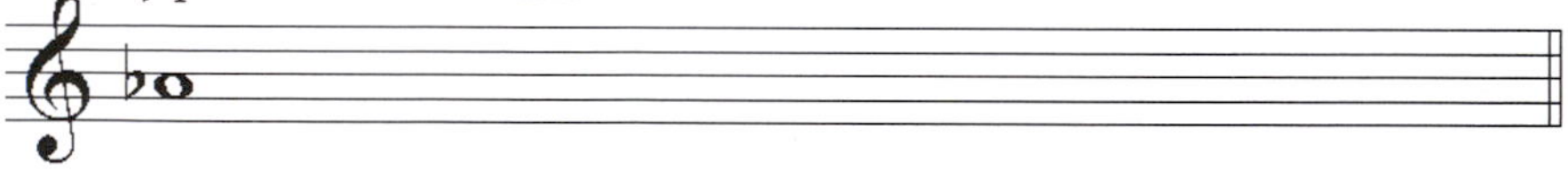

B pentatonic: Version I

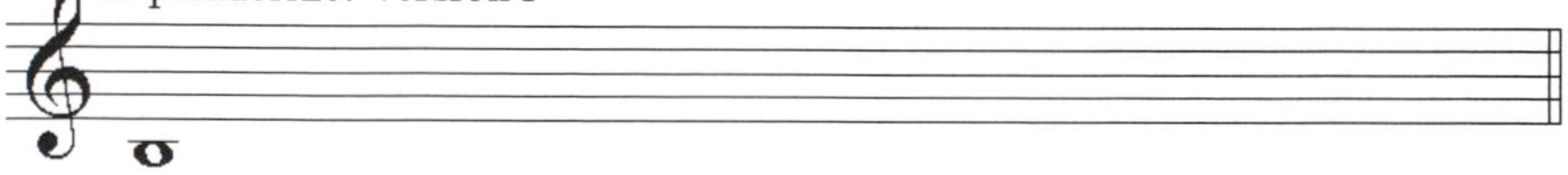

B pentatonic: Version II

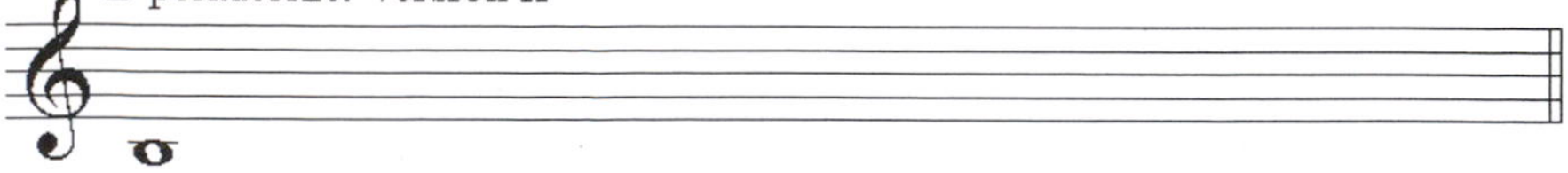

Name _____

G pentatonic: Version I

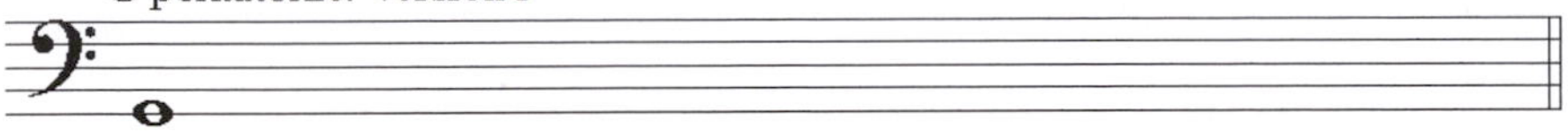

G pentatonic: Version II

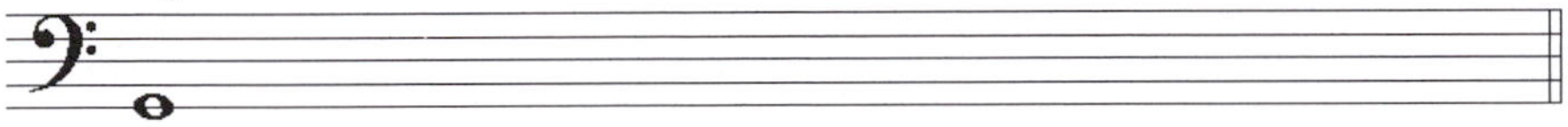

11. Construct each of the following chromatic scales as an altered major scale.

D♭ chromatic ascending.

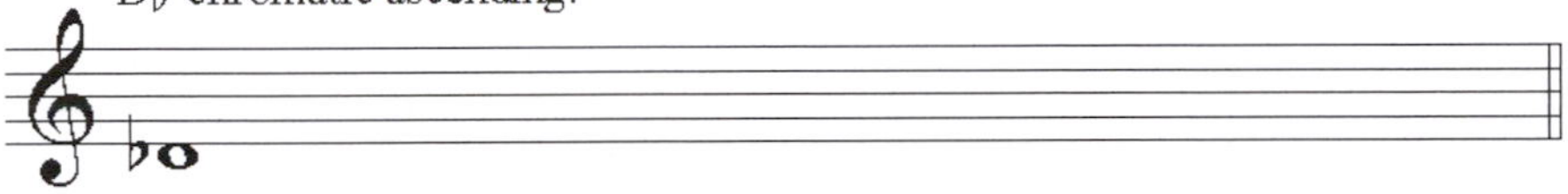

D♭ chromatic descending:

E chromatic ascending:

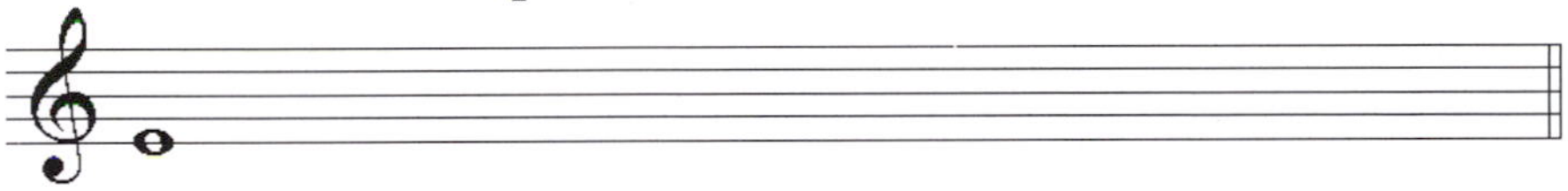

E chromatic descending:

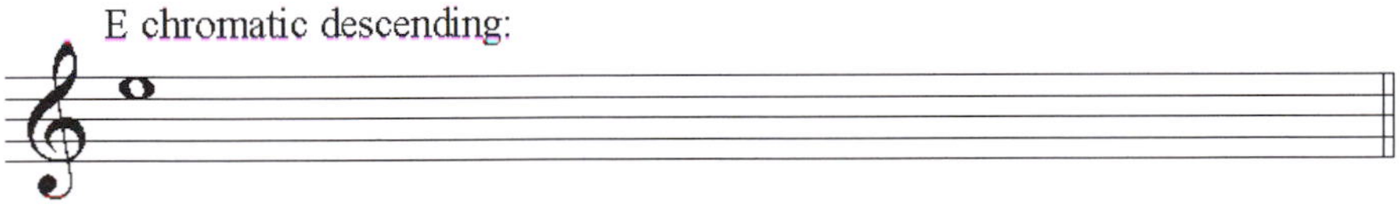

A♭ chromatic ascending:

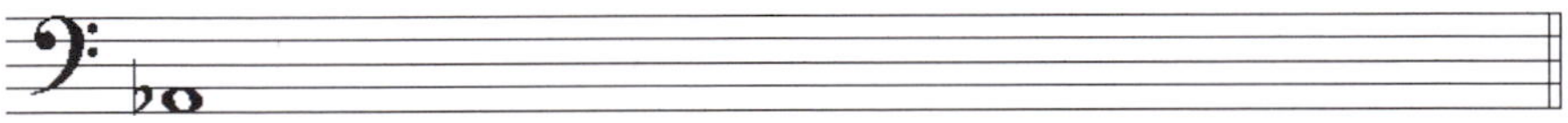

A♭ chromatic descending:

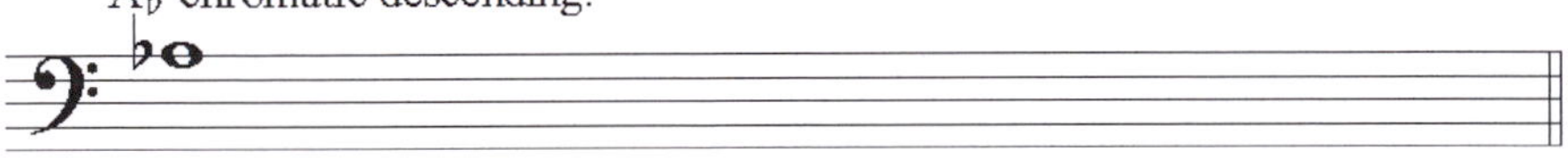

F♯ chromatic ascending:

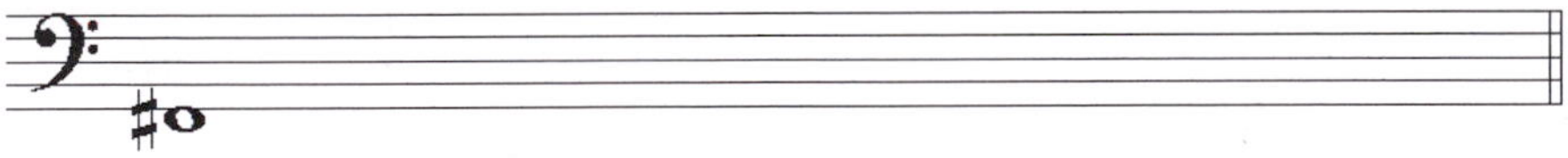

F♯ chromatic descending:

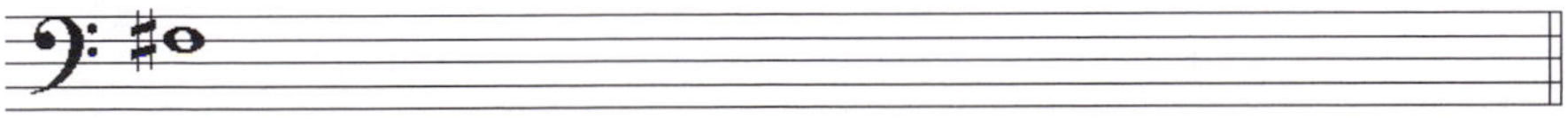

Name

12. Construct each of the following chromatic scales as an altered minor scale.

B chromatic ascending (minor form):

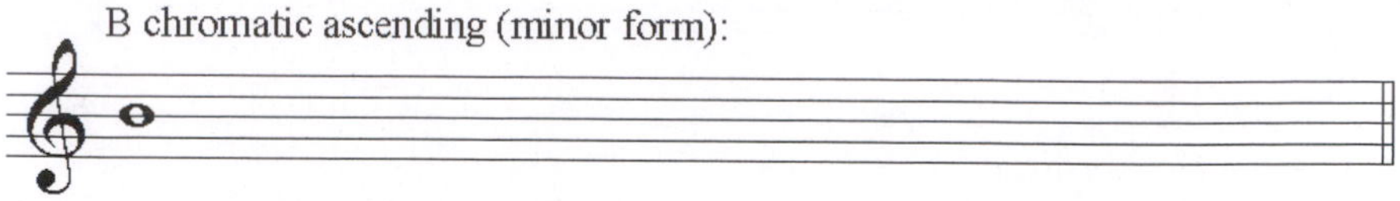

B chromatic descending (minor form):

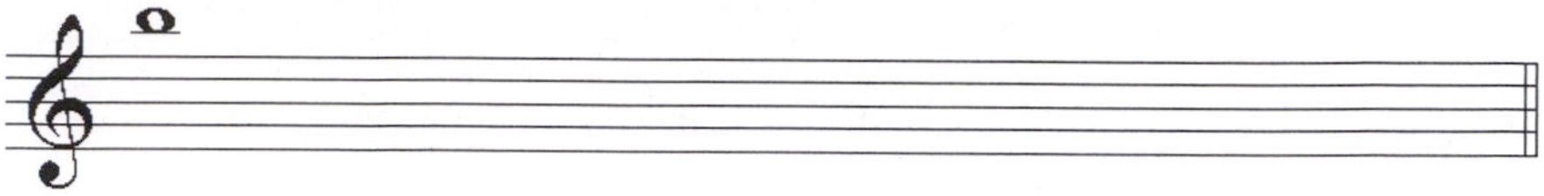

C chromatic ascending (minor form):

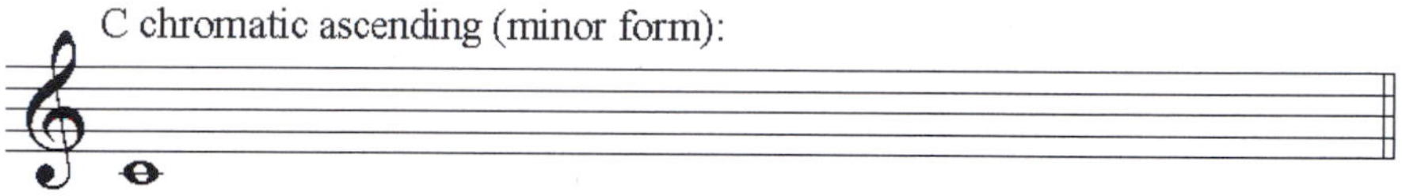

C chromatic descending (minor form):

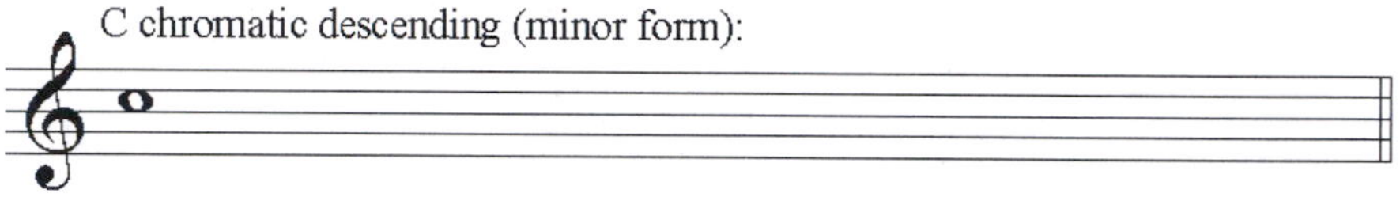

F♯ chromatic ascending (minor form):

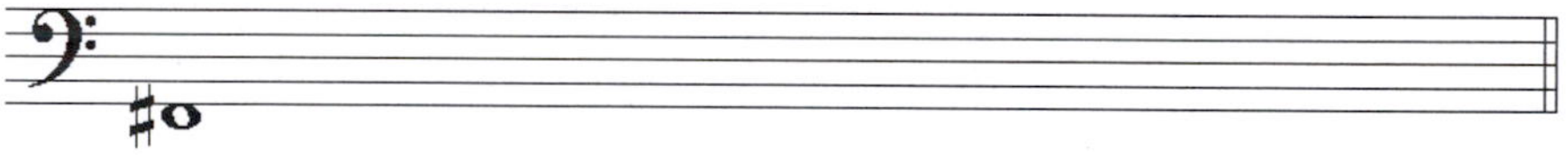

F♯ chromatic descending (minor form):

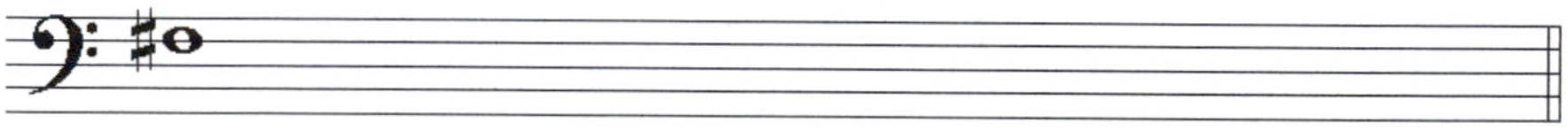

B♭ chromatic ascending (minor form):

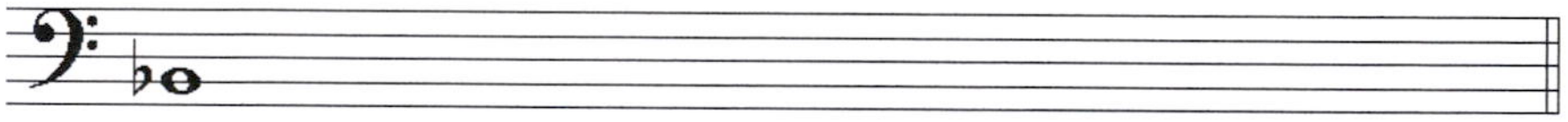

B♭ chromatic descending (minor form):

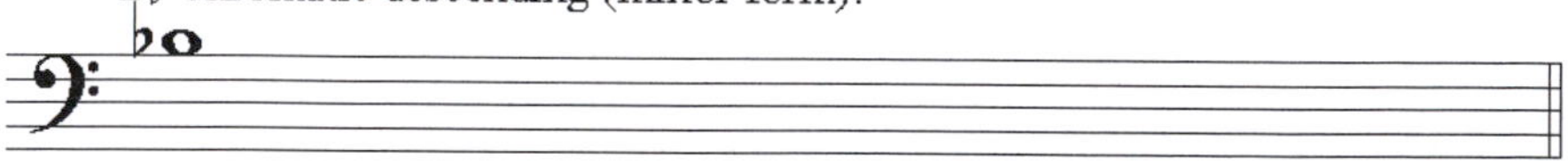

Find additional Skill Development Drills on the accompanying CD-ROM and on the book companion Web site: http://music.wadsworth.com/kinney1e.

4

Key Signatures

When it sounds good, it is good!
—Duke Ellington

Within the collective body of the numerous styles of music available to us, there are many well-known instrumental and vocal compositions that have, at their core, a firmly established and unambiguous tonal center (**key center**). Contemporary music styles written with a key center include classic and current country; rock and roll; Latin American music; rap; reggae; solo vocal and instrumental forms; religious music; Broadway show tunes; movie and television themes; conventional orchestral music; opera; blues; folk music; jazz; and nearly all other idioms of popular music. Even as far back as the fifth century A.D., the sacred music used by the Roman Catholic Church was based on modes that contained a tonal focus toward which all other pitches, albeit weakly, gravitated.

A **key signature** indicates the tonal center of a composition and those pitches of the musical alphabet (A through G) that need to be adjusted by a sharp or flat in order to establish the specific major or minor scale upon which a piece of music is composed. The resulting key center is essential to tonal music and may be an important part of a composition's title, as in Schubert's Mass in G, Beethoven's Symphony no. 5 in C Minor, or Bach's Little Fugue in G Minor.

Although the establishment of a key center is an integral element to the majority of the music to which we listen, there have been successful attempts at composing music that seeks to avoid a clearly defined key. In the late nineteenth and early twentieth centuries, assumptions regarding traditional compositional techniques were dramatically expanded by prominent composers, such as Claude Debussy (1862–1918), Arnold Schoenberg (1874–1951), and Igor Stravinsky (1882–1971). Their immense collective influence challenged the conventional wisdom of their contemporaries and resulted in the creation of musical compositions that lacked a clearly defined key center and any explicit melodic and or harmonic direction. Even though these contributions to musical thought are tremendously important to today's composers, an established key center continues to be a very significant element in most styles of music.

A key signature is indicated in the first measure of a conductor's score, and on a performer's sheet music in a specified pattern of sharps and flats that, very efficiently, provides musicians with the fundamental and necessary information needed to perform, analyze, conduct, and compose a piece of music. In order to illustrate the relationships among the fifteen major and fifteen minor keys, key signatures are arranged into a pattern identified as the **circle of fifths.** The circle is a valuable organizational tool that not only affords a visual map of how keys relate to one another, but also contributes to the ways we conceptualize and articulate some of the basic theoretical constructs of tonal music.

This chapter will focus on identifying and constructing all of the fifteen major and fifteen minor key signatures within the context of the circle of fifths, and understanding their importance to the overall design and structure of music.

THE CIRCLE OF FIFTHS

The circle of fifths is a configuration of the major and minor key signatures that illustrates how the musical interval (the distance between two pitches) of the fifth is used to organize key relationships. This interval is very important to music, and, as you continue to study music theory, you will come to understand its significance to the organization and structure of the tonal system.

Although intervals will be presented in Chapter 6, let's take a moment to learn how the interval of the fifth is used to establish a unique relationship among the key signatures within the circle of fifths.

You are already familiar with the musical alphabet that represents the basic pitches beginning on A and ending on G. The basic interval of the 5th above a pitch may be determined by labeling any starting pitch of the musical alphabet as step 1, and then counting up to step 5. For example, if A is step 1, then a 5th up from it would be E. If F is step 1, a 5th up would be C. This is illustrated in example 4.1a.

4.1a

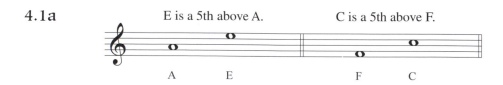

If you needed to determine a 5th below a given pitch, you would count the starting pitch as step 1 and count down the appropriate lines and spaces. The 5th below D would be G, and the 5th below G would be C.

4.1b

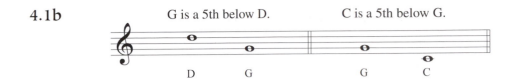

Another interval that will assist you in understanding the tonal relationships within the circle of fifths is the basic interval of the 4th. The 4th is counted in the same manner as the 5th, and is illustrated in the following two examples. Remember, your first note will be counted as step 1.

4.2a

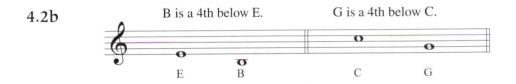

4.2b

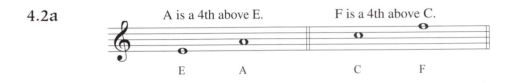

The 5ths in examples 4.1a and 4.1b, and the 4ths in examples 4.2a and 4.2b, are identified as **perfect 5ths** and **perfect 4ths**. Not all 5ths and 4ths are perfect, as you will learn when you study intervals in Chapter 6. For now, so long as you are able to compute these basic intervals, you will be able to understand the 5th and 4th relationships illustrated in the circle of fifths.

The circle of fifths is constructed in a clockwise pattern, beginning on C (at 12 o'clock) and progressing in ascending 5ths through each of the sharp and flat keys, until C is reached once again. In order to continue in 5ths throughout the entire circle, there must be an *enharmonic shift* made somewhere among the keys of B, F♯, and C♯ major. The enharmonic shift allows for the 5th pattern to continue through the flat keys.

On the outside of the circle there are fifteen major key signatures. The seven sharp keys (G, D, A, E, B, F♯, and C♯) are located on the right side, and the seven flat keys (F, B♭, E♭, A♭, D♭, G♭, and C♭) are on the left side. At the top of the circle is the key of C, which has no sharps or flats.

On the inside of the circle are the minor keys that are associated with these major keys. (This will be discussed in detail later on in this chapter.) At the bottom of the circle, the major and minor keys that are enharmonic equivalents are grouped within a bracket.

If you were to play the circle of fifths on the piano, it would make greater musical sense to play it in a counterclockwise motion, because each tonal center would be firmly established by a *descending 5th movement* between keys. Ask a music teacher or friend to play the chords of the circle on a

4.2c

The Circle of Fifths

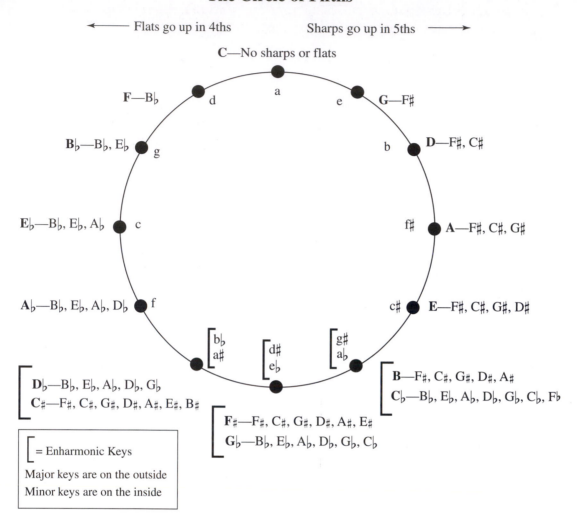

← Flats go up in 4ths   Sharps go up in 5ths →

C—No sharps or flats

F—B♭   d   a   e   G—F♯

B♭—B♭, E♭   g   b   D—F♯, C♯

E♭—B♭, E♭, A♭   c   f♯   A—F♯, C♯, G♯

A♭—B♭, E♭, A♭, D♭   f   c♯   E—F♯, C♯, G♯, D♯

⌈ b♭ ⌉   ⌈ d♯ ⌉   ⌈ g♯ ⌉
⌊ a♯ ⌋   ⌊ e♭ ⌋   ⌊ a♭ ⌋

⌈ D♭—B♭, E♭, A♭, D♭, G♭   B—F♯, C♯, G♯, D♯, A♯
⌊ C♯—F♯, C♯, G♯, D♯, A♯, E♯, B♯   C♭—B♭, E♭, A♭, D♭, G♭, C♭, F♭

⌈ F♯—F♯, C♯, G♯, D♯, A♯, E♯
⌊ G♭—B♭, E♭, A♭, D♭, G♭, C♭

⌈ = Enharmonic Keys

Major keys are on the outside
Minor keys are on the inside

piano or guitar beginning on C and moving in both directions: first clockwise
and then counterclockwise. With some practice and patience you will discover that the circle makes more musical sense when it is played counterclockwise.

At first glance, the circle of fifths may seem complicated and confusing,
but actually it is very simple because every key signature is constructed
using the interval of the 5th. Let's observe this relationship and begin to
understand why the circle is such an invaluable tool!

Principle 1

The key of C major has no sharps or flats, the key of C♯ major has seven
sharps, and the key of C♭ major has seven flats.

Observe in example 4.2c that at the bottom of the circle of fifths there are three major sharp keys (and their associated minors), which are enharmonic with three major flat keys (and their associated minors).

1. B major (g# minor) is enharmonic with C♭ major (a♭ minor)
2. F♯ major (d# minor) is enharmonic with G♭ (e♭ minor)
3. C♯ major (a# minor) is enharmonic with D♭ (b♭ minor)

Although there are a total of fifteen different key signatures, there can be only twelve different-sounding keys because only twelve different pitches exist within the span of an octave on the piano keyboard. The three sharp keys of B, F♯, and C♯ sound exactly the same as their enharmonically equivalent keys of C♭, G♭, and D♭.

PART I ∾ *Major Key Signatures*

THE RIGHT SIDE OF THE CIRCLE OF FIFTHS: MAJOR KEY SIGNATURES REQUIRING SHARPS

Let's apply the method of counting up in 5ths to determine the ordering of the major keys on the right side of the circle of fifths. Locate C at the top of the circle and then the pitch that is a 5th above it. You will need to count as follows: step 1 is C, step 2 is D, step 3 is E, step 4 is F, and step 5 is G.

G is the first sharp key on the right side of the circle. It requires an F♯ in its key signature; you will need to memorize this! The F♯ guarantees the half step required between scale degrees 7 and 8 in the G major scale.

The key signature for the key of G major appears on the staff as follows:

4.3   The key of G major has one sharp.

Please refer to the circle of fifths as each key signature is introduced.

Now let's compute the second *sharp key* in the circle, which will be a fifth above the key of G major. Beginning on G, count up as follows: step 1 is G, step 2 is A, step 3 is B, step 4 is C, and step 5 is D. You will arrive on D, which is the second sharp key on the right side of the circle.

Now you must determine the key signature for the key of D major. Since it is the second key on the right side of the circle, it will require two sharps. The first sharp will be the same F♯ required for the key of G major, and the second sharp will be a 5th above it. To compute the second sharp, count up a 5th from F♯ (or alphabet letter F). You will arrive on C, which will need to be changed to C♯. D major requires two sharps: F♯ and C♯, and they are placed on the staff as follows.

4.4   The key of D major has two sharps.

Now let's compute the third sharp key. Because D major is the second sharp key on the right side of the circle, the next major key will be located a 5th above it, and will be the third key in the circle. The key located a 5th above D major is A major.

Since the key of A major is the *third key* on the right side of the circle, it will need *three sharps*. It will require the F♯ and C♯, which were already used for the key of D, plus one more sharp, located a fifth above C♯ (or alphabet letter C). A fifth above C♯ is G♯. The sharps required for the key signature of A major are F♯, C♯, and G♯, and they are placed on the staff as follows.

4.5   The key of A major has three sharps.

The next major key in the circle will be the fourth key, and will be located a 5th above A major. This key is E major, and it will need four sharps.

The key of E major requires the three sharps of A major: F♯, C♯, and G♯, plus an additional sharp located a fifth above G♯ (or alphabet letter G). The sharp located a fifth above G♯ is D♯. When placed on the staff, the key signature for E major will appear as follows:

4.6   The key of E major has four sharps.

The next major key is B, which is the fifth key in the circle, and a 5th above E major.

The key of B major requires the four sharps needed in the key of E, plus one more, a 5th above the last sharp, D♯. A 5th above D♯ is A♯. The key signature for the key of B major is illustrated below.

4.7   The key of B major has five sharps.

The next sharp key signature requires six sharps and is located a 5th above B. Count B as step 1 and ascend to step 5, which is F. At this point, you will need to adjust this pitch to F♯ because, although alphabetically F is a 5th above B, *its exact musical distance is smaller than the previous fifth distances* among the keys; the distance between the keys G and D, D and A, A and E, and E and B is larger than that from B to F. In addition, please notice that F♯ has occurred in every prior key. F♯ was the first sharp to be added in the circle and eventually will occur in all of the seven sharp keys. Therefore, the key that is a 5th above B major is F♯ major. This issue will become clearer when you study intervals in Chapter 6. Also, later on, you will learn that the key of *F major is a flat key* located on the left side of the circle.

In the example below, notice that F♯ is in every key signature studied up to this point.

4.8

The key of F♯ major is the sixth key on the right side of the circle. It uses all of the sharps in the key of B major, plus one more sharp located a 5th above the last sharp, A♯. A 5th above A♯ is alphabet letter E, which must be changed to E♯. The key signature for F♯ major is illustrated below.

4.9   The key of F♯ major has six sharps.

Since there can be only seven sharped pitches in a major key (C♯ major), another way to think about the key signature for F♯ major is to recognize that every note of the F♯ major scale will be sharped except for B!

The last sharp key is C♯ major, which has seven sharps. This means that, in this key, every pitch will be sharped. (This reflects **Principle 1**.) C♯ major will require the six sharps of F♯ major, plus one more sharp located a 5th above the last sharp, E♯. A 5th above E♯ is B♯. C♯ major is the seventh sharp key in the circle, and its key signature is illustrated below.

4.10   The key of C♯ major has seven sharps.

All of the seven major sharp key signatures are located on the right side of the circle and are written as follows.

4.11   The seven sharp keys and their key signatures

THE LEFT SIDE OF THE CIRCLE OF FIFTHS: MAJOR KEY SIGNATURES REQUIRING FLATS

The order of the flat keys and their respective key signatures may be computed using nearly the same process as for determining the sharp keys and their respective key signatures. When you were calculating the key signatures for the major sharp keys located on the right side of the circle of fifths, you were required to do two things: (1) count up five steps from each sharp key to determine the next new sharp key, and (2) count up five steps from the last sharp of the key signature to ascertain the next sharp needed for the new key signature. Now you will be working on the left side of the circle in a similar manner.

Although the flat key signatures located on the left side of the circle have the same fifth relationship as do the sharp key signatures, when computing their order and their associated flats, instead of counting up in 5ths, as you did for determining the order of the sharp keys, you will always count up in 4ths to locate the next flat key and the additional flat needed to complete the key signature.

For a number of theoretical reasons, the movement from C to the first flat key is more appropriately identified as a movement of C major moving *down a 5th* to F major rather than a movement of C moving *up a 4th* to F. Musicians generally think of pitch relationships in 5ths rather than in 4ths; the circle of fifths is *not* known as the circle of fourths! However, when learning how to compute the flat keys and their key signatures on the left side of the circle, it is more practical and efficient to think in terms of 4ths. Eventually, if you choose to study music theory more deeply, you will need to be able to think about pitch relationships in terms of 4ths and 5ths. The following example illustrates the process of counting down a 5th and up a 4th from B♭.

4.11a

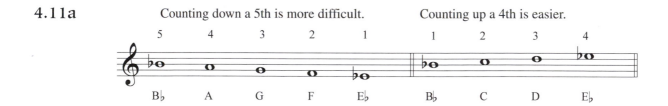

For now, simply remember that on the circle, the sharp keys and their associated sharps are counted up in 5ths, and the flat keys and their associated flats may be counted up in 4ths!

Let's apply the method of counting up in 4ths to determine the ordering of the flat keys on the left side of the circle of fifths. Using the musical alphabet A through G, at the top of the circle locate C and then the pitch that is a 4th above it. You will need to count as follows: step 1 is C; step 2 is D; step 3 is E; and step 4 is F. F major, therefore, is the first flat key on the left side of the circle and requires a B♭ in its key signature. (You will need to memorize this.) The B♭ guarantees the half step needed between scale degrees 3 and 4 in the F major scale!

The Circle of Fifths

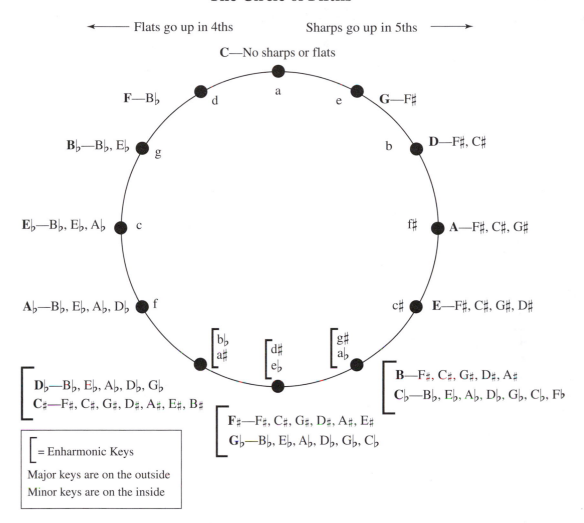

⟵ Flats go up in 4ths   Sharps go up in 5ths ⟶

C—No sharps or flats

F—B♭   d   a   e   G—F♯

B♭—B♭, E♭   g   b   D—F♯, C♯

E♭—B♭, E♭, A♭   c   f♯   A—F♯, C♯, G♯

A♭—B♭, E♭, A♭, D♭   f   c♯   E—F♯, C♯, G♯, D♯

[b♭ / a♯]   [d♯ / e♭]   [g♯ / a♭]

D♭—B♭, E♭, A♭, D♭, G♭
C♯—F♯, C♯, G♯, D♯, A♯, E♯, B♯

B—F♯, C♯, G♯, D♯, A♯
C♭—B♭, E♭, A♭, D♭, G♭, C♭, F♭

F♯—F♯, C♯, G♯, D♯, A♯, E♯
G♭—B♭, E♭, A♭, D♭, G♭, C♭

[= Enharmonic Keys

Major keys are on the outside
Minor keys are on the inside

If you were to place this key signature on the staff, it would be written as follows.

4.12   The key of F major has one flat.

Now let's compute the second flat key in the circle, which will be a 4th above F major. Beginning on F, count up a 4th as follows: step 1 is F, step 2 is G, step 3 is A, and step 4 is B. At this point you must change B to B♭, because *each of the seven flat keys will be identified with a flat except for the key of F major.*

Principle 2

F major is the only flat key in which there is a flat in the key signature that is not expressed in the name of the key.

This principle will become clearer as you progress through this section. B♭ major is the second flat key on the left side of the circle.

Now you must determine the *key signature* for the key of B♭ major. Because it is the second key on the left side of the circle, it will require two flats. The first flat will be the same B♭ required for the key of F major, and the second flat will be located a 4th above it. To compute the second flat, use the musical alphabet and count up a 4th from B♭. You will arrive on alphabet letter E, which will need to be changed to E♭. B♭ major requires two flats (B♭ and E♭), which are written as follows.

4.13   The key of B♭ major has two flats.

Because B♭ major is the second flat key on the left side of the circle, the next key will be located a 4th above it. A 4th above B♭ is the alphabet letter E, which you must change to E♭ because, as previously stated, each of the seven flat keys will be identified with a flat, except for the key of F major (see **Principle 2**). The key of E♭ major is the third flat key on the circle and will require three flats. It will take the B♭ and E♭ already used for the key of B♭, plus one more flat, located a 4th above E♭ (or alphabet letter E). A 4th above E♭ is A♭. The key signature for the key of E♭ major is B♭, E♭, and A♭, and is written as follows.

4.14   The key of E♭ major has three flats.

The next major key will be the fourth flat key in the circle, located a 4th above E♭ major. This key is A♭ major and will require four flats.

The key of A♭ major will use the three flats of E♭ major—B♭, E♭, and A♭—plus an additional flat located a 4th above A♭ (or alphabet letter A). The flat located a fourth above A♭ is D♭. The key signature for A♭ major is written as follows.

4.15   The key of A♭ major has four flats.

The next flat key is the fifth in the circle, and it is located a 4th above A♭ major. The fifth flat key in the circle is D♭, and it requires five flats. D♭ major will require the four flats used in the key of A♭—B♭, E♭, A♭, and D♭—plus one more, located a 4th above D♭. A 4th above D♭ is G♭. The key signature for the key of D♭ major is illustrated in the following example.

4.16   The key of D♭ major has five flats.

The next key signature is the sixth flat key on the left side of the circle, located a 4th above D♭: G♭. The key of G♭ major will require all of the flats used in D♭ major, plus one more located a 4th above the last flat, G♭. A 4th up from G♭ is C♭, and this will be needed to complete the key signature for G♭ major, which is illustrated below.

4.17   The key of G♭ major has six flats.

Since there can be no more than seven flatted pitches in a major key, another way to think about the key signature for the key of G♭ major is to recognize that every note of the G♭ major scale will be flatted except for F!

The last flat key is a 4th above G♭ major, and is the seventh flat key in the circle. This key is C♭ major, and it has seven flats. In the key of C♭ major, every note will have a flat (recall **Principle 1**). C♭ major will use the six flats of G♭ major, plus one more flat located a 4th above the last flat, C♭. A 4th above C♭ is F♭. The key signature for C♭ major is written as follows.

4.18   The key of C♭ major has seven flats.

All of the seven major flat key signatures are located on the left side of the circle and are written as follows.

4.19   The seven flat keys and their key signatures

Observe in example 4.19 that the only flat key that is not identified with a flat is F major. There is no key signature for the key of F♭ major! Recall **Principle 2**, which states that F major is the only flat key in which there is a flat in the key signature that is not expressed in the name of the key.

Principle 2 is important because it provides you with information which will help you memorize the ordering of the flat keys.

If you now wish to recall the correct order of the flat keys, begin with C major and count up in 4ths. You must memorize that the first flat key, F, requires B♭ in its key signature, and that all of the other keys will have a flat associated with the name of their key. Counting up in 4ths from F will give you B♭, then E♭, A♭, D♭, G♭, and C♭. These are the seven major flat keys illustrated on the left side of the circle of fifths.

APPLYING THE CIRCLE OF FIFTHS

Skill Development

Let's review and see what you have learned up to this point. What is the key signature for the key of E major?

Process

Step 1. Identify the side of the circle where E major is located. It is located on the right side and *cannot* be on the left side because that is where all of the *flat keys* are placed.

Step 2. Determine the position of E major in the circle. Is it the third, fourth, or fifth key on the right side? This is important, because its position will indicate the number of sharps it requires. Beginning with C at the top of the circle, count up in 5ths until you reach E. (If you are unsure of how to count in 5ths, please review example 4.1a.) The first key up a 5th from C major is G major, followed by D major, A major, and then E major. E major is the fourth key in the circle, and it requires four sharps.

Step 3. The four sharps needed for the key of E major may be determined by counting up in 5ths from the first sharp required in the key of G major, F♯. Count up in 5ths until you have a total of four sharps: A 5th above F♯ is C♯, then up a fifth to G♯, and then D♯. The four sharps required in the key of E major are F♯, C♯, G♯, and D♯, and are written as follows.

4.20　　　The key of E major has four sharps.

The Circle of Fifths

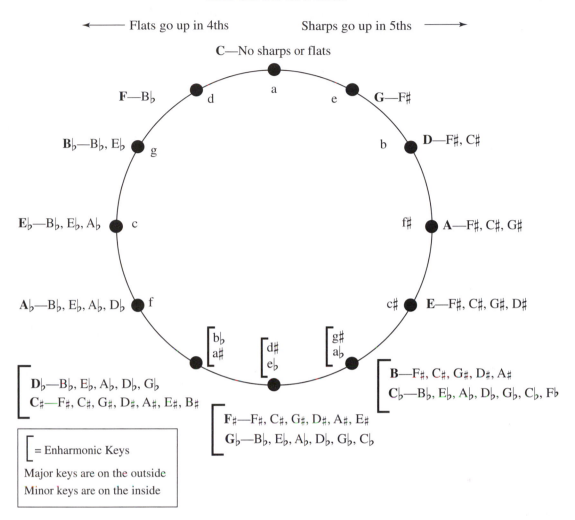

← ——— Flats go up in 4ths   Sharps go up in 5ths ———→

C—No sharps or flats

F—B♭

B♭—B♭, E♭

E♭—B♭, E♭, A♭

A♭—B♭, E♭, A♭, D♭

D♭—B♭, E♭, A♭, D♭, G♭
C♯—F♯, C♯, G♯, D♯, A♯, E♯, B♯

F♯—F♯, C♯, G♯, D♯, A♯, E♯
G♭—B♭, E♭, A♭, D♭, G♭, C♭

B—F♯, C♯, G♯, D♯, A♯
C♭—B♭, E♭, A♭, D♭, G♭, C♭, F♭

E—F♯, C♯, G♯, D♯

A—F♯, C♯, G♯

D—F♯, C♯

G—F♯

d   a   e
g   b
c   f♯
f   c♯
b♭   d♯   g♯
a♯   e♭   a♭

⌈ = Enharmonic Keys
Major keys are on the outside
Minor keys are on the inside

Skill Development

Let's try another. What is the key signature for the key of D♭ major?

Process

Step 1. Identify the side of the circle where D♭ major is located. It is on the left side, because this is where all of the keys containing flats are placed.

Step 2. Determine the position of D♭ major in the circle. Is it the second, third, fourth, or fifth key on the left side? This is important because its position will indicate the number of flats its key signature requires. Beginning with C major at the top of the circle, count up in 4ths until you reach D♭. (Refer to example 4.2a if you are uncertain of how to count in 4ths.)

The first flat key up a 4th from C major is F major (all of the remaining six flat keys will be identified with a flat), then B♭, E♭, A♭, and D♭. D♭ major is the fifth key in the circle, and therefore it requires five flats.

Step 3. The five flats required for the key of D♭ major may be determined by counting up in 4ths from B♭, which is required in the first flat key of F major, until you have a total of five flats: B♭ up a 4th to E♭, then up a 4th to A♭, up a 4th to D♭, and up a 4th to G♭. The five flats required in the key of D♭ major are B♭, E♭, A♭, D♭, and G♭.

4.21   The key of D♭ major has five flats.

The Circle of Fifths

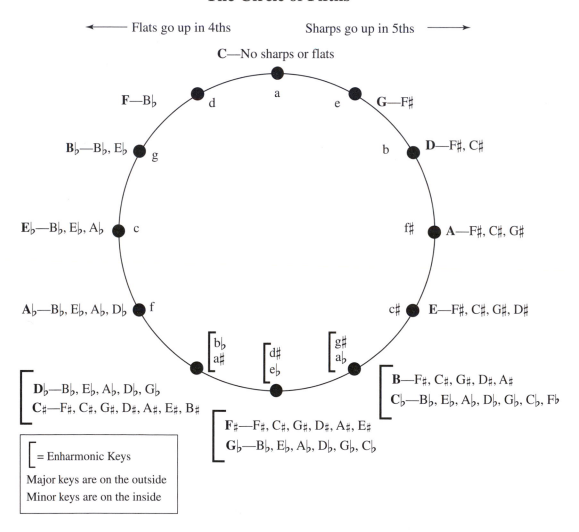

Exercise 1

Indicate, in the correct order, the sharps and flats needed for the following major key signatures. The answers are at the end of this chapter.

4.21a

1. A major: _____
2. E♭ major: _____
3. B major: _____
4. F♯ major: _____
5. A♭ major: _____

6. G♭ major: _____
7. D major: _____
8. C♯ major: _____
9. C♭ major: _____
10. F major: _____

CONSTRUCTING MAJOR KEY SIGNATURES USING SHARPS

Now that you are familiar with the layout of the circle of fifths, let's study the logic of how the sharps and flats are placed on the staff.

In this chapter you have learned that the sharp keys and their respective key signatures are determined by counting up in 5ths, beginning with the key of C major, which has no flats or sharps in its key signature. When the sharps are written on the staff, the 5th pattern applies to their placement, but it must be modified in order to keep all of the sharps on the staff.

If the sharps were written on the staff in ascending 5ths, they would need numerous ledger lines. If all of the seven sharps or flats were written in this way, they would eventually be too difficult to read because they would be placed far above the staff! The key of E major, which has four sharps, would look as follows:

4.22   The key signature for   The key signature
        E major written   for E major written
        incorrectly with the   *correctly*
        sharps placed in   ☺
        ascending 5ths ☹

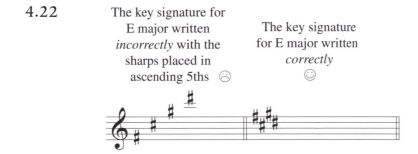

Principle 3

Key signatures are never written using ledger lines.

Let's observe the pattern of how sharps are placed on the staff.

The first sharp key is G major, which requires an F♯. This sharp will be your starting point and must be placed on the top line of the staff.

4.23 The key signature for G major

The next sharp key located a 5th above G is D major and it requires the F♯ and the sharp located a fifth above it, C♯. This sharp will be placed below the F♯ in order to keep it on the staff.

4.24 The key signature for D major

The next sharp key, A major, is a 5th above D and requires F♯ and C♯ and another sharp located a 5th above C♯; G♯. This sharp is written as follows:

4.25 The key signature for A major

The 5th pattern continues for the remaining sharp keys and results in key signatures in the treble and bass clefs as follows:

4.26a

Notice in the treble clef in example 4.26a that the last sharp in the key of F♯ major, E♯, could have been placed one octave lower, on the bottom line, instead of the top space. It is written on the top space to maintain the visual continuity of the descending left to right pattern of the sharps. Once you practice writing the sharp key signatures a few times, you will find it to be a simple task.

Exercise 2

Beginning with the key of G major, write each major sharp key signature on the staff below, as illustrated in example 4.26a, and indicate its respective key. Do this three times *from memory*!

4.26b

CONSTRUCTING MAJOR KEY SIGNATURES USING FLATS

The placement of the flats in key signatures is similar to that of sharps, in that they, too, must be written without the use of ledger lines. Although the flat keys and their respective key signatures are computed by counting in 4ths, they follow a more consistent pattern than do the sharp key signatures.

Begin at the top of the circle of fifths and count up a 4th from C major. You will arrive on F major, which is the first flat key whose key signature requires a B♭. Place this flat on the middle line of the staff.

4.27   The key signature for F major

The next flat key, B♭ major, is the second key located a 4th above F major on the left side of the circle. Its key signature includes the B♭ required for F major and adds the flat a 4th above it, which is E♭. E♭ is placed on the top space.

4.28   The key signature for B♭ major

The next major flat key in the circle is E♭ major. Since it is the third key in the circle, its key signature requires three flats: B♭, E♭, and A♭. Although A♭ is located a 4th above the last flat, E♭, it will be placed below it, on the second space.

4.29   The key signature for E♭ major

The next flat key, A♭, requires four flats. The additional flat will be located a 4th above the last flat in the key of E♭ major. D♭ is placed on the fourth line of the staff as follows.

4.30   The key signature for A♭ major

At this point, a left-to-right pattern of descending flats is beginning to emerge. Notice that the last flat added, D♭, is located to the right of E♭ and is on the line below it.

4.31

Notice that the previously written A♭, is placed on the space to the lower right side of the B♭.

4.32

The next flat key, which is a 4th above A♭ major, is D♭. Its key signature requires all of the flats of A♭ major (B♭, E♭, A♭, and D♭), plus a 4th above the last flat, D♭, which is G♭. Because the process of placing flats on the staff moves in a descending order from left to right, the next flat must continue this downward pattern. G♭ is therefore placed on the second line of the staff, as indicated in example 4.33.

4.33   The key signature for D♭ major.

The process of placing flats on the staff will continue in a left-to-right descending pattern until there is a total of seven flats (C♭ major). The next flat key, which is located a 4th above D♭ major, is G♭. Its key signature requires all of the flats of D♭ major (B♭, E♭, A♭, D♭, and G♭), plus a 4th up from G♭, which is C♭.

4.34   The key signature for G♭ major.

The final flat key of C♭ major is a 4th above G♭ and requires seven flats (recall **Principle 1**). The last flat to be added is F♭, which will complete the descending left-to-right pattern in the placement of flats.

4.35   The key signature for C♭ major.

Please observe the left-to-right descending placement of the flat key signatures in both the treble and bass clefs, illustrated in example 4.36a.

4.36a   The left-to-right descending pattern of the flats for the major flat key signatures

Exercise 3

Beginning with the key of F major, write each major flat key signature on the staff below, as illustrated in example 4.36a, and indicate its respective key. Do this three times *from memory*!

4.36b

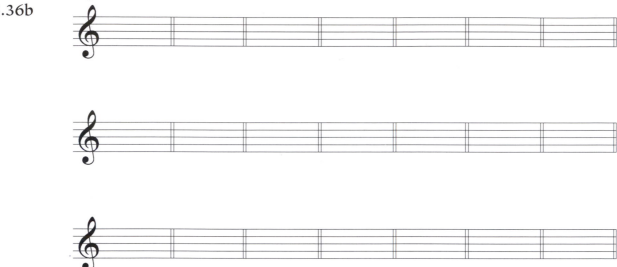

IDENTIFYING MAJOR KEY SIGNATURES WRITTEN IN SHARPS

Now that you know how to place all of the sharp and flat major key signatures on the staff, let's learn how they are identified in a piece of music.

Principle 4

A major key signature written in sharps is identified by the pitch that is one diatonic half step above the last sharp to the right.

Skill Development

Identify the following key signature.

4.37

Process

Step 1. Apply **Principle 4** and locate the last sharp to the right in the key signature. This sharp is D♯.

4.38

Step 2. Now let's apply the second part of **Principle 4** and locate the pitch that is one diatonic half step above D♯. Refer to the piano keyboard below if needed. The pitch that is one diatonic half step above D♯ is E. Four sharps, therefore, represent the key of E major.

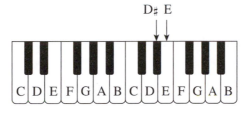

4.39   Key of E major

Skill Development

Identify the following key signature.

4.40

Process

Step 1. Apply **Principle 4** and locate the last sharp to the right in the key signature. The last sharp to the right is A♯.

4.41

Step 2. Now let's apply the second part of **Principle 4** and locate the pitch that is one diatonic half step above A♯. Please refer to the piano keyboard

below if needed. The pitch that is one diatonic half step (semitone) above A♯ is B. Five sharps, therefore, represent the key of B major.

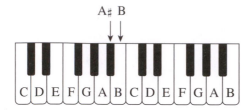

4.42   Key of B major

This process for the identification of major key signatures written in sharps is consistent for all of the sharp keys.

Exercise 4

Identify the following major key signatures.

4.43

_____   _____   _____   _____   _____   _____   _____

IDENTIFYING MAJOR KEY SIGNATURES WRITTEN IN FLATS

Now let's address the flat key signatures. Please learn the following principle.

Principle 5

A major key signature written in flats is identified by the next to the last flat from the right. The only exception is when there is one flat; this indicates the key of F.

Skill Development

Identify the following key signature.

4.44

Process

Step 1. Apply **Principle 5** and first locate the last flat to the right in the key signature. This flat is G♭.

4.45   G♭ is the last flat to the right.

Step 2. Now apply the second part of **Principle 5** and locate the next to the last flat from G♭. This flat is D♭, and it identifies this key signature as D♭ major.

4.46   D♭ is the next to the last flat from the right. It identifies this key signature as D♭ major.

Skill Development

Let's try one more. Identify the following key signature.

4.47

Process

Step 1. Apply **Principle 5** and first locate the last flat to the right in the key signature. This flat is F♭.

4.48   F♭ is the last flat to the right.

Step 2. Now let's apply the second part of **Principle 5** and locate the next to the last flat from F♭. This flat is C♭, and it identifies this key signature as C♭ major.

4.49   C♭ is the next to the last flat from the right. It identifies this key signature as C♭ major.

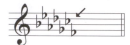

A quicker method of identifying the key signature in example 4.49 would have been to recall **Principle 1**, which states that the key of C major has no sharps or flats. The key of C♯ major has seven sharps and the key of C♭ major has seven flats. The process used to identify major key signatures written in flats will be consistent for all of the flat keys except when encountering only one flat. One flat is the key of F major (this is stated in **Principle 5**).

Exercise 5

Identify the following major key signatures.

4.50

_____ _____ _____ _____ _____ _____

PART II   ∽   *Minor Key Signatures*

IDENTIFYING THE MINOR KEY SIGNATURES

Each of the fifteen major keys shares its key signature with a specific minor key. Because of this special relationship, minor keys are identified as "relatives" of major keys and are commonly referred to as **relative minors**.

The key signature for B♭ major has an associated relative minor key.

4.51

To identify the relative minor key that shares its key signature with B♭ major, please learn the following principle.

Principle 6

A major key's associated relative minor is located on scale degree 6 of its scale.

Scale degree 6 of the B♭ major scale is G. G minor therefore is the relative minor to B♭ major and shares its key signature.

4.52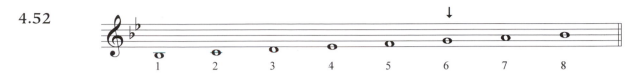

The key signature for G minor appears on the staff as follows.

4.53 The key signature for
G minor has two flats.

Skill Development

What is the relative minor key to the key of A major?

Process

Step 1. Write the A major scale and its key signature on the staff and locate scale degree 6. F♯ is the 6th scale degree of the A major scale and is the relative minor key that will share A major's key signature.

4.54

The key signature for F♯ minor would appear on the staff as follows.

4.55 The key signature for F♯
minor has three sharps.

A quicker method of locating scale degree 6 of a major scale is to count down to it from scale degree 8. This is illustrated for the case of A major in the second measure of example 4.56.

4.56

F♯ is located by counting
up to scale degree 6.

F♯ is located by counting
down to scale degree 6.

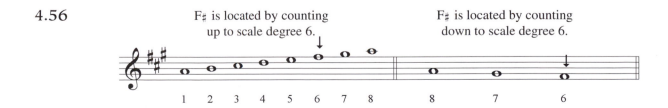

Counting down from scale degree 8 to scale degree 6 to locate the relative minor key is quicker than counting up to it! Another way to think about this is first to place both the key signature and the pitch A on the staff and then locate the diatonic pitch that is on the space directly below. This is scale degree 6!

4.57   Scale degree 6 is located
            on the space below A.

Principle 6 states that the relative minor key of a major key is located on scale degree 6 of a major scale. F♯ is the relative minor to the key of A major!

4.58   This is the key
        signature for F♯ minor.

Skill Development

Let's apply this process to identifying the relative minor key of B major.

Process

Step 1. Place the key signature for B major and the note B on the staff.

4.59

Step 2. Place on the staff the note that is on the line below B. This is scale degree 6 of the B major scale.

4.60   The arrow indicates scale
        degree 6 of the B major scale.

Step 3. Now check the key signature for B major to see if G is sharped. Remember that **Principle 6** states that the relative minor must be scale degree 6 of the major scale! The key signature for B has five sharps, one of which is G♯.

4.61   G is sharped in the
key of B major.

Step 4. G♯ is the relative minor to B major.

4.62   The key signature for
G♯ minor has five sharps.

Skill Development

Use the same method and determine the relative minor key to A♭ major.

Process

Step 1. Place the key signature for A♭ major and the note A♭ on the staff.

4.63

Step 2. Write the pitch that is on the space below A♭.

4.64   The arrow indicates scale
degree 6 of the A♭ major scale.

Step 3. Now check the key signature for A♭ major to see if F is altered in any way. Remember that **Principle 6** states that the relative minor must be scale degree 6 of the major scale! The key signature for A♭ major has four flats, none of which alter the note F.

4.65

The relative minor key to A♭ major, therefore, is F minor.

4.66   The key signature for
F minor has four flats.

Exercise 6

Identify the following minor keys using the process you have just learned. When indicating a minor key signature, it is customary to write a lowercase letter, such as "f", to indicate F minor.

4.67

4.68

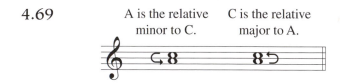

CONSTRUCTING THE MINOR KEY SIGNATURES

In the previous section, the process of identifying a minor key signature involved first determining the major key signature illustrated on the staff, then locating the pitch on scale degree 6. The pitch on scale degree 6 was identified as the relative minor because it shared the same key signature with the major scale of which it was a part. Now you must learn to *reverse this process* when constructing a minor key signature, because you will need to identify the relative major with which it is associated. Example 4.69 illustrates this relationship.

4.69

A is the relative   C is the relative
minor to C.   major to A.

The important association that a minor key has with its relative major key may be illustrated by observing their shared pitches. Example 4.70a demonstrates how the A minor scale is contained within the C major scale (its relative major), while example 4.70b illustrates how the C major scale is contained within the A minor scale (its relative minor). It is because of this relationship that they share exactly the same key signature, with no sharps or flats.

4.70a

A minor is the relative minor of the C major scale.

4.70b

C major is the relative major of the A minor scale.

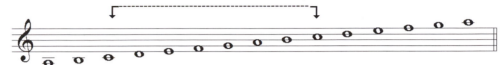

To construct the key signature for a minor key, please learn the following principle.

Principle 7

A minor key signature uses the key signature of its relative major. To locate the relative major, label the minor key as scale degree 6 of a major scale, then count up to locate scale degree 8. Apply the relative major's key signature to the minor key.

Skill Development

Let's apply **Principle 7** and construct the key signature for E minor.

Process

Step 1. Place E on the staff and label it as scale degree 6 of a major scale.

4.71

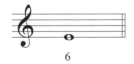

Step 2. Now identify its relative major by ascending to scale degree 8, as if you were constructing a major scale. (Remember, in major scales, half steps occur at scale degrees 7 and 8.) G major is the relative major to E minor.

4.72   G is the relative major of E minor.

Step 3. Now apply the key signature for G major to the key of E minor. G major has one sharp, as does E minor.

4.73   The key signature for
E minor has one sharp.

Skill Development

Let's construct the key signature for A♭ minor.

Process

Step 1. Place A♭ on the staff and label it as scale degree 6 of a major scale.

4.74

Step 2. Now locate its relative major by ascending to scale degree 8, as if you were constructing a major scale. (Remember, in major scales, half steps occur at scale degrees 7 and 8.) C♭ major is the relative major to A♭ minor.

4.75   C♭ is the relative major of A♭ minor.

Step 3. Now apply the key signature for C♭ major to the key of A♭ minor.

4.76   The key signature for
Ab minor has seven flats.

Skill Development

Now let's construct the key signature for C♯ minor.

Process

Step 1. Place C♯ on the staff and label it as scale degree 6 of a major scale.

4.77

Step 2. Locate its relative major by ascending to scale degree 8, as if you were constructing a major scale.

4.78   E is the relative major to C♯ minor.

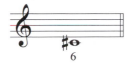

Step 3. Now apply the key signature of E major to the key of C♯ minor. E major has four sharps, as does C♯ minor.

4.79   The key signature for
C♯ minor has four sharps.

Exercise 7

Construct the following minor key signatures using the process you have just learned.

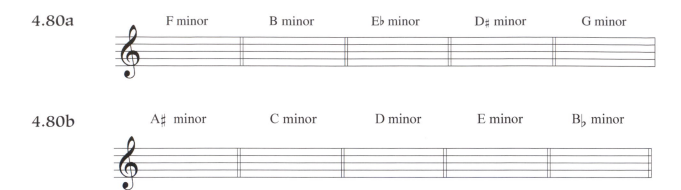

PARALLEL MAJOR AND MINOR KEYS

Composers and songwriters have at their disposal numerous ways to make compositions interesting. Frequently they change keys in a piece of music to enhance the overall effect of a tune or write beautiful, memorable melodies that linger in one's mind. They may also inject an unforgettable melodic or rhythmic **hook** that captivates the attention of listeners and makes them want to sing or tap their foot or dance to the music.

One musical effect in which the *tonal center of a piece remains the same* but the **mode** is switched from major to minor or vice versa results from the use of **parallel minor** and **parallel major** keys. For example, the parallel minor key related to C major is C minor, and the parallel major key related to C minor is C major. In both instances, although the tonal centers remain the same, the modes and key signatures have changed.

Relative minor keys, which were presented earlier in this chapter, differ from parallel minor keys because, although they *share their key signatures* with major keys, they have different tonal centers. Parallel major and minor keys share the same tonal center but have *different key signatures*! The following example illustrates this concept:

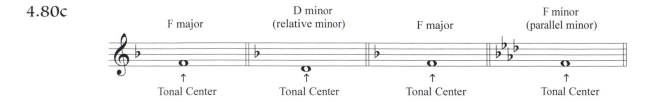

Only twelve of the fifteen major keys have an associated parallel minor key. The three flat keys, D♭, G♭, and C♭, *do not* have associated parallel minor keys, because they would require double flats in their key signatures. For example, the relative major key signature associated with D♭ minor would be F♭ major (a flat key that does not exist!), which would contain a B♭♭. Double-flat and double-sharp key signatures in both the major and minor modes are avoided.

There are also three sharp minor keys that do not have an associated parallel major key, because this would require using double sharps in their key signatures. These keys are G♯ minor, D♯ minor, and A♯ minor.

Exercise 8

Write the parallel minor key associated with each of the following major keys.

4.81

1. F major _____   7. D major _____

2. B♭ major _____   8. A major _____

3. E major _____   9. B major _____

4. G major _____   10. F♯ major _____

5. A♭ major _____   11. C♯ major _____

6. E♭ major _____   12. C major _____

ANOTHER METHOD FOR CONSTRUCTING MINOR KEY SIGNATURES

Here is a quick method of determining the key signature for all minor keys, if you are able to quickly recall the major key signatures.

Principle 8

To determine the key signature for a minor key, apply three flats to its associated parallel major key signature.

To determine the key signature for the key of B♭ minor, all you need to do is add three flats to its parallel major, B♭ major.

4.82   B♭ major   B♭ minor

Remember that *the most flats or sharps a key signature can have is seven.* You *must not* add three flats to a key signature with five or more flats! This is illustrated in example 4.83.

4.83

D♭ major ☺   INCORRECT! ☹
                                              D♭ minor does not exist!

When computing the key signatures for minor keys in which the parallel major keys are written in sharps, adding three flats means that sharps will be canceled, *beginning with the farthest sharp to the right.* In example 4.84, the key signature for E minor was determined by adding three flats to the key signature of E major (its parallel major), thereby negating three of its sharps.

4.84

                                              E minor (adding three flats
        E major   canceled the last three sharps)

If you begin with fewer than three sharps to negate, then the key signature will be represented in flats. Remember, your goal is to apply three flats to the major key signature (**Principle 8**). In the example below, three flats have been applied to each major key signature to create the key signature for its associated parallel minor key.

4.85

    D major   D minor   G major   G minor   C major   C minor
               (parallel minor)   (parallel minor)   (parallel minor)

Skill Development

Let's use this method to determine the key signatures for three minor keys. What is the key signature for E♭ minor?

Process

Step 1. Identify the key signature for E♭ minor's parallel major key. E♭ major is the parallel major key, and it has three flats in its key signature.

4.86   E♭ major

Step 2. Now add three flats to the key signature. (If you need to review the correct pattern for placing flats on the staff, see examples 4.27–4.36a.) The key signature for E♭ minor is six flats.

4.87

Skill Development

What is the key signature for F♯ minor?

Process

Step 1. Identify the key signature for F♯ minor's parallel major key. F♯ major is the parallel major key, and it has six sharps in its key signature.

4.88

Step 2. Now add three flats to cancel three of these sharps. Remember, *the flats negate the sharps, beginning with the farthest from the right!* There will be three sharps remaining to indicate the key signature for F♯ minor.

4.89

Skill Development

What is the key signature for G minor?

Process

Step 1. Identify the key signature for G minor's parallel major key. G major is the parallel major key, and it has one sharp in its key signature.

4.90

Step 2. Now add three flats to the key signature. The first flat will cancel the one sharp and leave two remaining flats in the key signature for G minor.

4.91

Exercise 9

On the staff, write the key signatures for the following parallel minor keys.

4.92

Review

The minor key signatures for all of the fifteen minor keys are located in the inner part of the circle of fifths with the sharps and flats computed in exactly the same pattern as the major key signatures. On the right side of the circle, the minor sharp key signatures are located a 5th away from one another as you travel clockwise around the circle. On the left side, the minor flat keys are located a 4th away from one another as you travel counterclockwise around the circle.

The Circle of Fifths

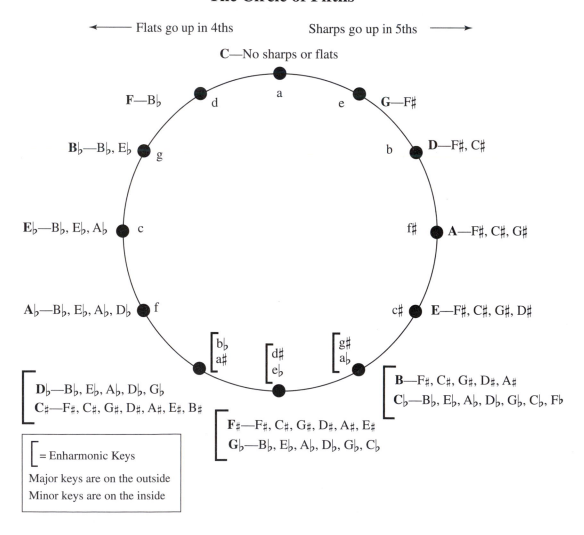

The key signatures for the seven minor sharp keys are written in lower-case letters and are illustrated in the following example.

4.93   The key signatures for each minor sharp key

The key signatures for the seven minor flat keys are also written in lowercase letters and are illustrated in the following example.

4.94   The key signatures for each minor flat key

At the top of the circle of fifths, the remaining key of A minor shares its key signature with that of C major, which requires no sharps or flats.

4.95   A minor

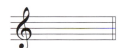

It is a good idea to commit the major key signatures to memory. In the remaining chapters the key signatures will be applied to understanding modes (Chapter 5), intervals (Chapter 6), triads (Chapter 7), and the harmonic functions of triads (Chapter 8).

REVIEW OF PRINCIPLES

Principle 1
The key of C major has no sharps or flats, the key of C♯ major has seven sharps, and the key of C♭ major has seven flats.

Principle 2
F major is the only flat key in which there is a flat in the key signature that is not expressed in the name of the key.

Principle 3
Key signatures are never written using ledger lines.

Principle 4
A major key signature written in sharps is identified by the pitch that is one diatonic half step above the last sharp to the right.

Principle 5

A major key signature written in flats is identified by the next to the last flat from the right. The only exception is when there is one flat; this indicates the key of F.

Principle 6

A major key's associated relative minor is located on scale degree 6 of its scale.

Principle 7

A minor key signature uses the key signature of its relative major. To locate the relative major, label the minor key as scale degree 6 of a major scale, then count up to locate scale degree 8. Apply the relative major's key signature to the minor key.

Principle 8

To determine the key signature for a minor key, apply three flats to its associated parallel major key signature.

ANSWER SHEETS TO CHAPTER 4

Exercise 1

4.21a

1. A major: F♯, C♯, G♯

2. E♭ major: B♭, E♭, A♭

3. B major: F♯, C♯, G♯, D♯, A♯

4. F♯ major: F♯, C♯, G♯, D♯, A♯, E♯

5. A♭ major: B♭, E♭, A♭, D♭

6. G♭ major: B♭, E♭, A♭, D♭, G♭, C♭

7. D major: F♯, C♯

8. C♯ major: F♯, C♯, G♯, D♯, A♯, E♯, B♯

9. C♭ major: B♭, E♭, A♭, D♭, G♭, C♭, F♭

10. F major: B♭

Exercise 2

4.26b

Exercise 3

4.36b

Exercise 4

4.43

Exercise 5

4.50

Exercise 6

4.67

4.68

Exercise 7

4.80a

4.80b

Exercise 8

4.81

1. F minor	7. D minor
2. B♭ minor	8. A minor
3. E minor	9. B minor
4. G minor	10. F♯ minor
5. A♭ minor	11. C♯ minor
6. E♭ minor	12. C minor

Exercise 9

4.92

WORKSHEETS FOR CHAPTER 4

Name _____

1. Identify the major key signatures.

_____ _____ _____ _____ _____ _____

_____ _____ _____ _____ _____ _____

2. Construct the following major key signatures.

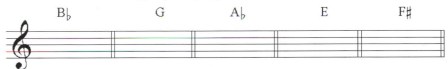

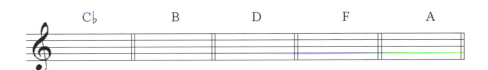

3. Identify the following minor key signatures.

_____ _____ _____ _____ _____ _____

_____ _____ _____ _____ _____ _____

Name _____

4. Construct the following minor key signatures.

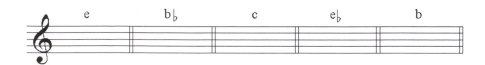

f♯   d   c♯   g   f

e   b♭   c   e♭   b

a♭   g♯   d♯   a♯

5. Construct the parallel minor key signature next to its parallel major.

Name _____

6. Write each of the major sharp key signatures in the bass clef.

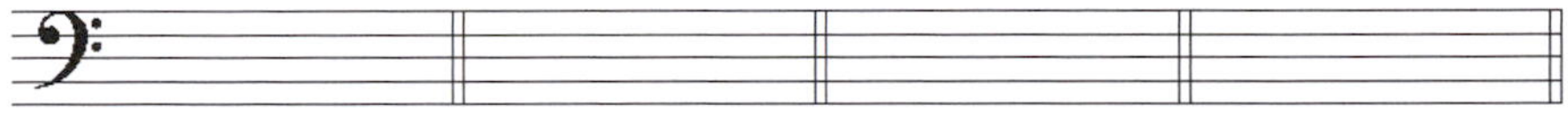

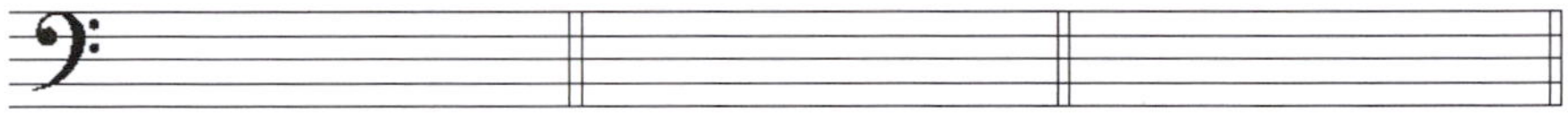

7. Write each of the major flat key signatures in the bass clef.

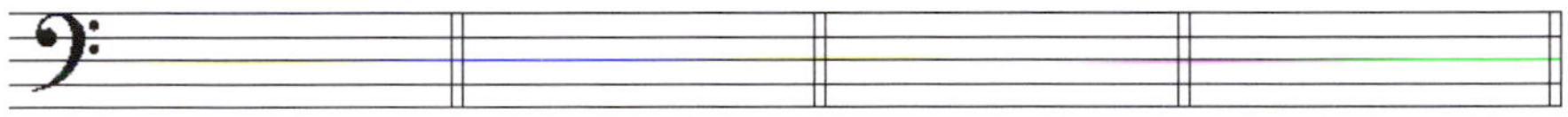

8. Which major keys do not have an associated parallel minor key?

_____

_____

Find additional Skill Development Drills on the accompanying CD-ROM and on the book companion Web site: http://music.wadsworth.com/kinney1e.

5

∞

Modes

Oh, Mozart, immortal Mozart, how many, how infinitely many inspiring suggestions of a finer, better life have you left in our souls!

—Franz Schubert

The development of the church modes has a long and complex history that began around 450 A.D. and lasted over 1100 years. The seven **church modes** of ancient Europe may be thought of as scales in which the placement of the diatonic half and whole steps, commonly found in a major or a minor scale, have been shifted to other scale degrees. The major and minor scales you studied in Chapter 3 are also known as the Ionian and Aeolian modes. These are two of the seven church modes that, over the last four hundred years, have gained widespread popularity.

The specific placement of the whole and half steps contained within the modes produces a distinctive overall musical effect that is strangely hypnotic and unique to each mode. Even though the historical development of the modes dates back to the fifth century A.D., modal music continues to attract contemporary songwriters of all styles and composers of large-scale instrumental and vocal music.

One of the most accessible ways of experiencing modal music is to listen to the beautifully haunting and inspiring sacred music by Medieval (450–1450) and Renaissance (1450–1600) composers such as Giovanni Palestrina, Orlando di Lasso, Heinrich Schütz, and Josquin Desprez. You will be able to locate a "classical music" section at most music stores that sell recordings containing well-known compositions by these composers. While you are at the music store, take time to look through the jazz section and locate a few recordings of trumpeter Miles Davis, such as *Kind of Blue* and *Milestones*. After listening to them a few times you will be able to recognize the influence of modal music in this idiom. In addition, the music of rock star Carlos Santana, the Afro-Cuban music of Dizzy Gillespie, and the Latino jazz compositions of Tito Puente, Eddie Palmieri, and Paquito D'Rivera reflect a modal influence, particularly during the solo sections, when musicians improvise over a "**montuno**" (a repetition of specific chords). The modes you now will study are seven of the most popular versions used by today's musicians in a variety of musical styles and still may be found in numerous examples within the music of the Roman Catholic Church.

MAJOR KEY SIGNATURES

The major key signatures will be useful in constructing the various modes because they will provide you with an efficient means of quickly determining if any pitches need to be altered by a sharp or a flat. For your convenience, the key signatures are illustrated below, but you should work on memorizing them until you are able to recall them with ease.

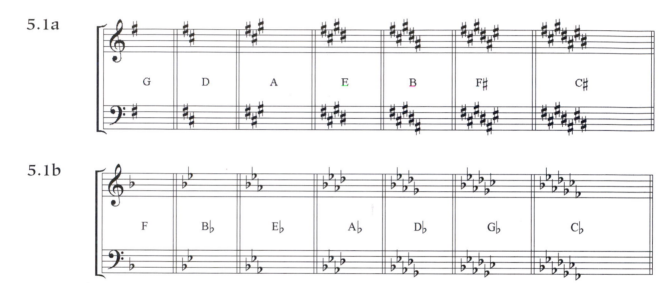

THE SEVEN CHURCH MODES

The seven church modes are known by the following names: Ionian, Dorian, Phrygian, Lydian, Mixolydian, Aeolian and Locrian.

Although the modes may be constructed on any note of the chromatic scale, initially they are most easily understood within the context of the white keys of the piano keyboard. If you start on any pitch of the musical alphabet (A through G) and play all of the white keys within the span of one octave, you will have played one of the modes. Since each of the seven modes may be played on the piano keyboard with relative ease, you should not hesitate to locate a piano keyboard and experience their unique sounds.

Ionian Mode

The Ionian mode is the major scale you learned to write in Chapter 3. It may be played on the piano keyboard using the notes C–C. It is illustrated on the piano keyboard on the next page and on the staff in example 5.2a.

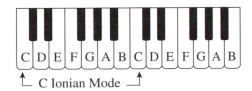

L C Ionian Mode ⌐

5.2a

Aeolian Mode

The Aeolian mode is the pure minor scale you studied in Chapter 3 and may be played on the white keys of the piano using the notes A–A. It is illustrated on the piano keyboard below and on the staff in example 5.2b.

L A Aeolian Mode ⌐

5.2b

If each of the seven church modes were performed on the piano keyboard using only the white keys, they would be played by depressing each white key within the span of one octave as follows.

D Dorian Mode

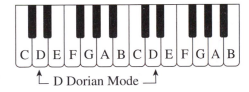

L D Dorian Mode ⌐

5.3

E Phrygian Mode

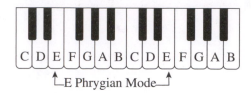

5.4

F Lydian Mode

5.5

G Mixolydian Mode

5.6

A Aeolian Mode

5.7

B Locrian Mode

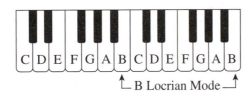

C D E F G A B C D E F G A B

⌐ B Locrian Mode ¬

5.8

While playing each of the modes on the white keys of the piano keyboard, it is very easy to see where half and whole steps occur. You already know that the white keys on the piano keyboard are one whole step apart except between E and F, and B and C, in which cases the distance is one half step. If you begin on the note C, and memorize the names of the modes in an ascending diatonic fashion, you will quickly be able to construct any mode!

5.9

Ionian   Dorian   Phrygian   Lydian   Mixolydian   Aeolian   Locrian   Ionian

Once the order of the modes is memorized, simply look at the keyboard as presented in examples 5.2a–5.8 and determine the scale degrees at which half steps occur. To illustrate this, let's determine where the half steps occur in the Phrygian mode.

You have learned that the Phrygian mode may be played on the piano by depressing all of the white keys from E to E. On the keyboard, *identify the scale degrees* at which the half steps E and F, and B and C occur. When you locate these scale degrees, you will know where the half steps are in this mode. (Recall that the remaining adjacent white keys on the piano keyboard are one full step apart!)

E Phrygian Mode

C D E F G A B C D E F G A B

Scale degrees: 1 2 3 4 5 6 7 8

You will notice on the keyboard on page 221 that if you begin counting the note E as scale degree 1, half steps in the Phrygian mode will occur between scale degrees 1 and 2 (E and F) and 5 and 6 (B and C). This is indicated by the carets on the staff as follows.

5.10   E Phrygian mode

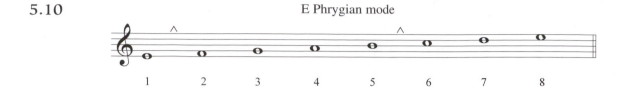

Now let's look at the Lydian mode and determine where the half steps occur. You have learned that this mode is F–F on the piano keyboard, so now try to identify the scale degrees at which the pitches E and F, and B and C occur. When you locate these scale degrees, you will know where the half steps are in this mode.

F Lydian Mode

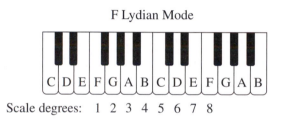

Notice that if you count the note F as scale degree 1, half steps in the Lydian mode will occur between scale degrees 4 and 5 and between scale degrees 7 and 8. This is illustrated on the staff as follows.

5.11   F Lydian mode

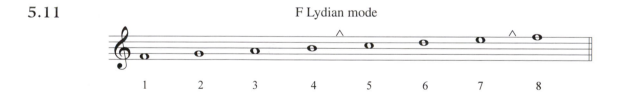

If you were to carry out this process with each mode, you would generate the information shown in Mode Table I (page 223).

Mode Table I provides information that is very important to musicians writing and performing in modes, but it is highly impractical to commit it to memory. There is, however, a more efficient way to think about modes, particularly when composing or **improvising** music based on one or more of the modes.

Mode Table I

Mode	Half Steps between Scale Degrees
Ionian	3, 4 and 7, 8
Locrian	1, 2 and 4, 5
Aeolian	2, 3 and 5, 6
Mixolydian	3, 4 and 6, 7
Lydian	4, 5 and 7, 8
Phrygian	1, 2 and 5, 6
Dorian	2, 3 and 6, 7

Let's take a close look at example 5.12 and see how the modes are associated with the scale degrees of the C major scale. Scale degree 8 has been omitted because it is C, which is the same pitch located on scale degree 1.

5.12

Example 5.12 illustrates how each of the seven modes may be associated with a scale degree of the C major scale (the white keys on the piano keyboard). If you play the pitches beginning and ending on E within the C scale, you will be playing the notes comprising the E Phrygian mode.

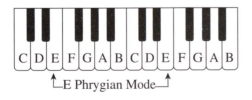

To illustrate this on the staff, we need to look at the C scale in two octaves and play, beginning on E, all the notes up to the E one octave above it. This will be the Phrygian mode beginning on E.

5.13

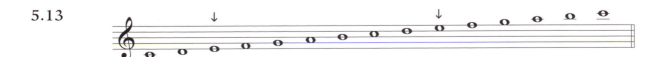

Now look at example 5.14a and notice that the C scale, which is written in two octaves, reflects only the scale degree numbers 1 through 7. The number 8 has been replaced by 1, because the scale degree pitches keep repeating in octaves! For example, the three Cs all are labeled as scale degree 1, both Ds are labeled as scale degree 2, both Es are labeled as scale degree 3, both Fs are labeled as scale degree 4, and so on.

5.14a

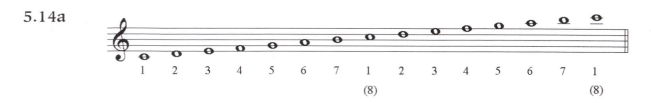

In example 5.14b, observe that the E Phrygian mode begins and ends on scale degree 3 of the C major scale.

5.14b

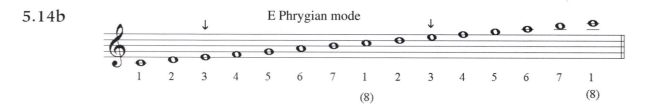

Recall from example 5.2a that the C major scale was used to illustrate the Ionian mode. Since the C major scale *is* the Ionian mode, *all major scales* may be identified as Ionian! Observe that the C Ionian mode written within one octave will use the numbers 1 to 1.

5.15

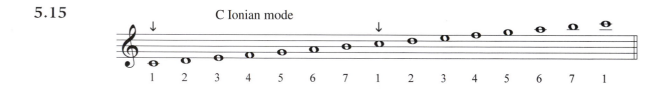

We now are able to look at each mode and observe the scale degree numbers assigned to it. The Dorian mode associated with the C major scale comprises the pitches D–D and uses scale degree numbers 2–2.

5.16

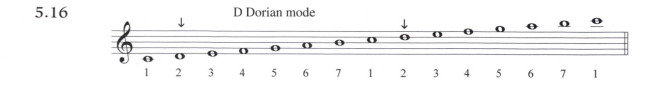

The Phrygian mode associated with the C major scale comprises the pitches from E–E and uses scale degrees 3–3.

5.17

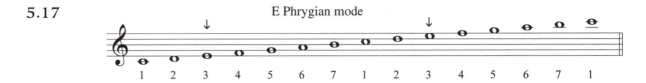

The Lydian mode associated with the C major scale comprises the pitches F–F and uses scale degrees 4–4.

5.18

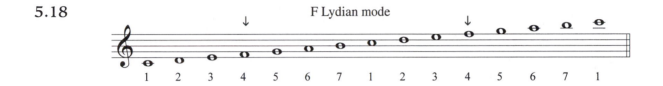

The Mixolydian mode associated with the C major scale comprises the pitches G–G and uses scale degrees 5–5.

5.19

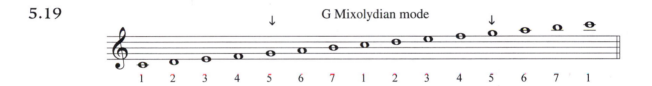

The Aeolian mode associated with the C major scale comprises the pitches A–A and uses scale degrees 6–6. The Aeolian mode *is* the pure minor scale!

5.20

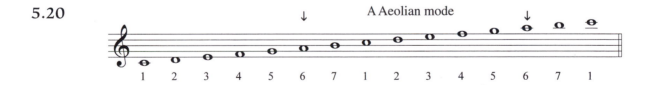

The Locrian mode associated with the C major scale comprises the pitches B–B and uses scale degrees 7–7.

5.21

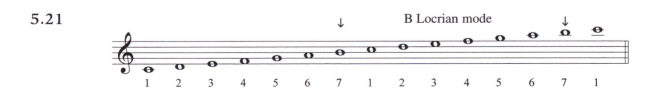

We now are able to represent all of the scale degree numbers associated with each mode, as shown in Mode Table II.

Mode Table II

Mode	*Major Scale Degree Numbers Associated with Each Mode*
Ionian	1 to 1
Locrian	7 to 7
Aeolian	6 to 6
Mixolydian	5 to 5
Lydian	4 to 4
Phrygian	3 to 3
Dorian	2 to 2

USING THE C MAJOR SCALE TO COMPUTE HALF-STEP LOCATIONS IN THE MODES

Once you have memorized Mode Table II, you will be able to locate the half steps within each mode with ease. Let's identify where the half and whole steps occur within any Lydian mode by first observing how it appears in the C major scale.

You have already observed in example 5.18 that the F Lydian mode is located on step 4 of the C major scale. The Lydian mode is therefore assigned the numbers 4–4, with half steps occurring *where the numbers 3 and 4, and 7 and 8 (1) are placed (indicated by carets) within a major scale.*

5.22

F Lydian mode as it occurs within the C major scale

4　　5　　6　　7　　8　　2　　3　　4
(1)

This means that if you play the pitches beginning and ending on step 4 of any major scale, you will be playing the Lydian mode associated with that scale. Remember that when constructing modes in this manner, except for the Ionian mode, the number 8 will always be counted using the number 1. This simplifies locating the half steps in each mode, as illustrated in Mode Table II, because each mode will begin and end on the same number.

Principle **1**

Modes associated with major scales will have half steps where the numbers 3 and 4, and 7 and 8 (1) are placed. All other distances between adjacent scale degrees will be whole steps.

The D Dorian mode occurs within the C major scale, using the numbers 2–2 with half steps between 3 and 4, and 7 and 8. Please observe **Principle 1** in the following example.

5.23

D Dorian mode as it occurs within the C major scale

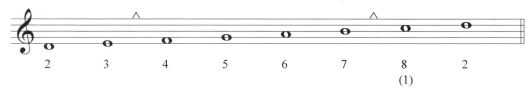

2   3   4   5   6   7   8   2
                        (1)

MODE CONVERSION TECHNIQUE

Now that you are familiar with assigning each scale degree of a mode with an associated number of the C major scale, let's renumber all of the modes and identify *the exact scale degrees* at which half and whole steps occur in the modes. Compare examples 5.24a and 5.24b and observe the renumbering of the F Lydian mode.

5.24a

F Lydian mode as it occurs within the C major scale

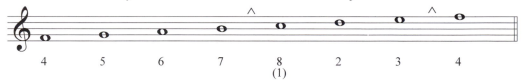

4   5   6   7   8   2   3   4
                    (1)

5.24b

F Lydian mode converted to its correct numbering

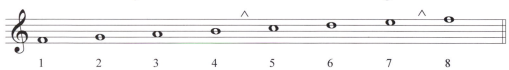

1   2   3   4   5   6   7   8

Observe that when the F Lydian mode is renumbered using the scale degree numbers 1 through 8, half steps occur between scale degrees 4 and 5, and 7 and 8. (Please refer to Mode Table I illustrated on page 223.)

Let's observe this conversion in the Locrian mode. Example 5.25a illustrates the Locrian mode as it appears in the C major scale with half steps occurring between the numbers 3 and 4, and 7 and 8.

5.25a

B Locrian mode as it occurs within the C major scale

7   8   2   3   4   5   6   7
    (1)

Example 5.25b illustrates how each pitch of the scale has been renumbered to represent scale degree numbers 1–8. (The carets indicating where the half steps occur in this mode must remain unmoved.)

5.25b

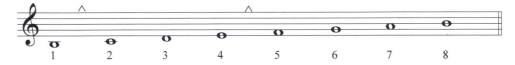

B Locrian mode converted to its correct numbering

1   2   3   4   5   6   7   8

Observe in example 5.25b that once the scale is renumbered, the half steps of the B Locrian mode actually are at scale degrees 1 and 2, and 4 and 5. Refer to Mode Table I to verify this (see page 223).

Principle 2

To determine the actual scale degrees at which half steps occur in a mode, first construct the mode according to Mode Table II and then renumber it in ascending order using the numbers 1 through 8.

Let's apply **Principles 1** and **2** and the information in Mode Table II (page 226) to determine the scale degrees between which half steps occur in the G Mixolydian mode.

Recall that the G Mixolydian mode begins and ends on scale degree 5 of the C major scale.

5.26

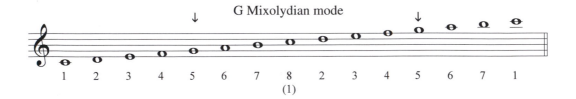

G Mixolydian mode

1   2   3   4   5   6   7   8   2   3   4   5   6   7   1
                        (1)

Example 5.27 has isolated the G Mixolydian mode section from example 5.26.

5.27

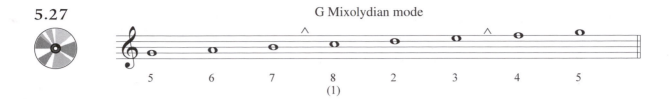

G Mixolydian mode

Notice in example 5.27 that carets have been placed to indicate that half steps occur in this mode between 3 and 4, and 7 and 8. This reflects **Principle 1**, which states that modes associated with major scales have half steps where the numbers 3 and 4, and 7 and 8 (1) are placed. All other distances between adjacent scale degrees will be whole steps.

The Mixolydian mode is numbered 5–5 to indicate it is part of a major scale beginning and ending on scale degree 5. Now you must remove these numbers and write in the numbers 1 through 8 to determine the actual scale degrees between which half steps occur in this mode.

5.28

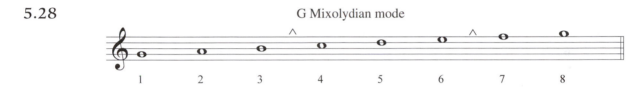

G Mixolydian mode

It is now clear that half steps in the Mixolydian mode occur at scale degrees 3 and 4, and 6 and 7. This reflects the information in Mode Table I.

Let's apply the mode conversion technique to the process of constructing modes.

CONSTRUCTING MODES, METHOD ONE: LOCATING HALF STEPS

Although the modes you have been studying up to this point have been associated with the C major scale, they may be constructed on any note. The process of relating modes to the various scale degrees of the C major scale may be applied to all other modes because, as you may recall from Chapter 3, **Principle 5** states "what is true for the key of C major is true for all other major keys."

The first method of constructing modes is similar to the one you learned when constructing scales in Chapter 3. This method will use Mode Table II (page 226) as a basis for determining where half steps occur in each mode. Once the ordering of the modes in Mode Table II is memorized, apply **Principle 1**, and you will know that half steps are placed where the numbers 3 and 4, 7 and 8 (1) occur. **Principle 1** states that modes associated with major scales have half steps where the numbers 3 and 4, and 7 and 8 (1) are placed. All other distances between adjacent scale degrees will be whole steps.

Skill Development

Let's construct the B♭ Dorian mode.

Process

Step 1. Place on the staff the pitches of the musical alphabet beginning and ending on B♭.

5.29

Step 2. Using the information in Mode Table II (page 226), place the numbers associated with the Dorian mode under each appropriate scale degree. The numbers associated with the Dorian mode are 2–2. Recall that the number 8 must be changed to the number 1.

5.30

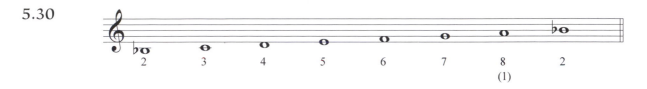

Step 3. Next, place carets where half steps occur by applying **Principle 1**, modes associated with major scales have half steps where the numbers 3 and 4, and 7 and 8 (1) are placed. All other distances between adjacent scale degrees will be whole steps.

5.31

Step 4. Now construct this scale as you would any major or pure minor scale by adjusting, where necessary, the distance between adjacent pitches. All distances will be one whole step except where indicated by the carets, at which point there must be one half step. The keyboard diagram below may help you compute the distances between pitches. If you have difficulty with this process, review Chapter 3, "Scales."

The B♭ Dorian mode appears as follows:

5.32

B♭ Dorian mode

Step 5. Now that you have the correct notes of the scale, convert the numbers under each scale degree to reflect scale degrees 1–8.

5.33

Bb Dorian mode

Observe in example 5.33 that the half steps in the Dorian mode occur between scale degrees 2 and 3, and 6 and 7, as represented in Mode Table I (see page 223).

Skill Development

Let's construct the F♯ Phrygian mode.

Process

Step 1. Write on the staff the pitches of the musical alphabet beginning and ending on F♯.

5.34

Step 2. Now using the information in Mode Table II (page 226), place the numbers associated with the Phrygian mode under the notes. The numbers associated with the Phrygian mode are 3–3.

5.35

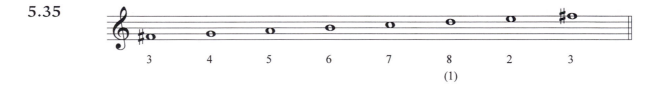

Step 3. Place carets where half steps occur by applying **Principle 1**, modes associated with major scales have half steps where the numbers 3 and 4, and 7 and 8 (1) are placed. All other distances between adjacent scale degrees will be whole steps.

5.36

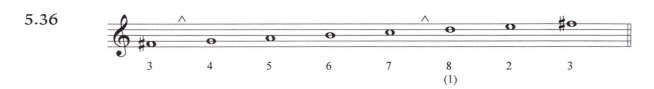

Step 4. Now construct this scale as you would any major or pure minor scale by adjusting, where necessary, the distance between adjacent pitches. All distances will be one whole step except where the carets indicate that there must be one half step.

5.37

F♯ Phrygian mode

Step 5. Now that you have the correct pitches of the scale, convert the numbers under the notes to reflect scale degrees 1–8.

5.38

F♯ Phrygian mode

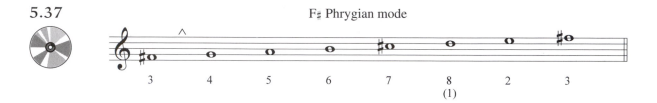

Observe in example 5.38 that the half steps in the Phrygian mode occur between scale degrees 1 and 2, and 5 and 6, as represented in Mode Table I.

Skill Development

Now let's construct the C Locrian mode.

Process

Step 1. Write the pitches of the musical alphabet beginning and ending on C.

5.39

Step 2. Now use the information in Mode Table II (page 226) and place the numbers associated with the Locrian mode under the notes. The numbers associated with the Locrian mode are 7–7.

5.40

7   8   2   3   4   5   6   7
     (1)

Step 3. Next, place carets where half steps occur by applying **Principle 1**, which states that modes associated with major scales have half steps where the numbers 3 and 4, and 7 and 8 (1) are placed. All other distances between adjacent scale degrees will be whole steps.

5.41

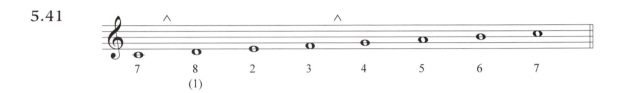

7   8   2   3   4   5   6   7
     (1)

Step 4. Now construct this scale as you would any major or pure minor scale by adjusting the distance between adjacent pitches as necessary. All distances will be one whole step except where the carets indicate that there must be one half step. The keyboard diagram below is for your use to help compute the distances between pitches. If you have difficulty with this process, review Chapter 3, "Scales."

5.42

C Locrian mode

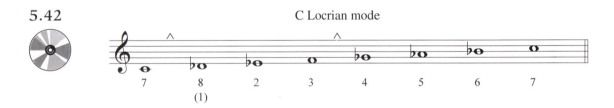

7   8   2   3   4   5   6   7
     (1)

Step 5. Now that you have the correct notes of the scale, convert the numbers under the notes to reflect scale degrees 1–8.

5.43

C Locrian mode

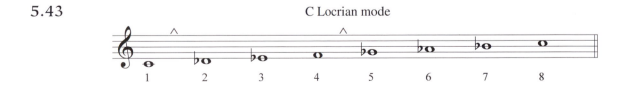

1   2   3   4   5   6   7   8

Observe in example 5.43 that the half steps in the Locrian mode occur between scale degrees 1 and 2, and 4 and 5, as represented in Mode Table I.

Exercise 1

Construct the following modes.

5.44a   D Phrygian mode

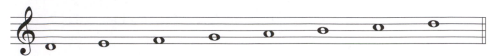

5.44b   E♭ Mixolydian mode

5.44c   F Locrian mode

5.44d   A Lydian mode

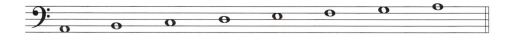

5.44e   B♭ Aeolian mode

5.44f   C♯ Dorian mode

5.44g   D♭ Lydian mode

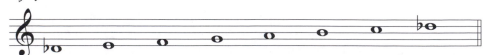

CONSTRUCTING MODES, METHOD TWO: UTILIZING KEY SIGNATURES

Method One for constructing modes is effective, but it involves too many steps if you are trying to determine the pitches of a particular mode quickly. A faster and more efficient way to determine a mode's correct pitches is to associate it with a key signature. The only information you will need to have memorized to assist you with this process is Mode Table II and the major key signatures located on page 218.

Let's look more closely at Mode Table II and interpret the numbers associated with each mode in a new way.

Notice that the first column lists the modes and the second column lists the major scale degree numbers associated with each mode. What this means is that the Ionian mode is constructed on scale degrees 1–1 (8) of a major scale. The Dorian mode is constructed on scale degrees 2–2 of a major scale. The Phrygian mode is constructed on scale degrees 3–3 of a major scale, and so on.

Mode Table II

Mode	Major Scale Degree Numbers Associated with Each Mode
Ionian	1 to 1
Locrian	7 to 7
Aeolian	6 to 6
Mixolydian	5 to 5
Lydian	4 to 4
Phrygian	3 to 3
Dorian	2 to 2

Principle 3

To identify the major key signature associated with a mode, establish the scale degree number for the first and last note of the mode, as illustrated in Mode Table II. Next, count up or down to locate scale degrees 1 or 8 of the major scale associated with the mode and apply its key signature to the mode.

For instance, to construct the D Phrygian mode, notice that it is constructed on scale degree 3 of an associated major scale. (Remember, since Mode Table II lists the major scale degree numbers associated with each mode, all modes may be considered sections of major scales.)

Which major scale has D on scale degree 3? To determine this, label D as scale degree 3 of a major scale and *count down and locate scale degree 1*. Step 1 is B♭, and its key signature is associated with the D Phrygian mode.

5.45a

D is step 3 of the B♭ major scale

3   2   1

It is possible to determine the scale of which D is scale degree 3 by counting *up* and locating scale degree 8, but it is more time-consuming to do this than simply counting down to scale degree 1. However, if it is easier for you to count upward, then do not hesitate to count in this manner.

5.45b

D has been determined to be scale degree 3 of the B♭ major scale, by counting up to scale degree 8.

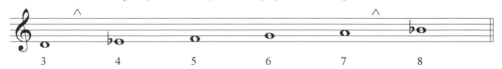

3   4   5   6   7   8

Since you have determined that the major scale associated with the D Phrygian mode is B♭ major, place on the staff the pitches D–D and apply the key signature of B♭ major.

5.46

The D Phrygian mode uses the key signature of B♭ major.

This method avoids having to construct the scale in whole and half steps because the key signature indicates which pitches need to be adjusted chromatically.

Skill Development

Let's use the same method to construct the E Dorian mode.

Process

Step 1. Place on the staff, in ascending order, the pitches of the musical alphabet beginning and ending on E.

5.47

Step 2. You know that the Dorian mode uses the numbers 2–2, as displayed in Mode Table II. Label E as scale degree 2 of a major scale and then locate scale degree 1 by counting down one full step. Scale degree 1 is D.

5.48

E is scale degree 2 of
the D major scale.

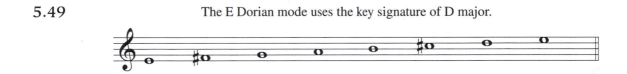

Since you have determined that the major scale associated with the E Dorian mode is D major, apply its key signature of two sharps to the pitches you placed on the staff in example 5.47.

5.49

The E Dorian mode uses the key signature of D major.

Skill Development

Let's construct the F Aeolian mode.

Process

Step 1. Place on the staff, in ascending order, the pitches of the musical alphabet beginning and ending on F.

5.50

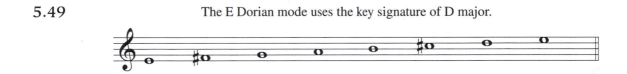

Step 2. Refer to Mode Table II and determine that the Aeolian mode uses the numbers 6–6. Label F as scale degree 6 of a major scale and then locate scale degree 1 by counting down or up. (Counting up to 8 is preferred because it is the shorter distance.) Remember, you are in a major scale, so you must not forget that half steps occur between scale degrees 3 and 4, and 7 and 8. You will arrive on A♭.

5.51

Count up from F
to locate step 8.
↓

Once you have determined that the major scale associated with the F Aeolian mode is A♭ major, apply its key signature to the pitches you placed on the staff in example 5.50. The key signature for A♭ major has four flats. (Refer to the key signatures at the beginning of this chapter if necessary.)

5.52

The F Aeolian mode uses the key signature of A♭ major

Exercise 2

Construct the following modes using Method Two (applying key signatures).

5.53a   A Dorian mode

5.53b   B♭ Phrygian mode

5.53c   C♯ Locrian mode

5.53d   D Mixolydian mode

5.53e   E♭ Lydian mode

CONSTRUCTING MODES, METHOD THREE: RELATING TO MAJOR AND MINOR SCALES

Method Two employed major key signatures to determine the correct pitches of a mode. Since a few of the modes do not have an associated key signature, this method may not be applied to them. For example, the key signature associated with the D♭ Locrian mode would have to be E♭♭ major, and the key signature for the C♯ Lydian mode would have to be G♯ major, neither of which exists.

If you needed to improvise or write music in these modes, you would have to use their associated enharmonic keys. For example, D♭ Locrian would be changed to its enharmonic key of C♯ Locrian and use the D major key signature, and C♯ Lydian would be changed to its enharmonic key of D♭ Lydian and use the key signature of A♭ major. There is, however, an efficient method of computing the correct pitches of any mode that does not require you to compute enharmonically equivalent key signatures.

Another way to think of the modes is that they are permutations of major and pure minor scales.

In Mode Table III, each mode is compared to the major or minor scale that it most closely resembles. The table illustrates how the alteration of one or two pitches of a major or minor scale will quickly produce the correct pitches of any desired mode. Musicians involved with improvisation and the analysis or composition of music will benefit the most from this information because it provides an expanded view of harmonic relationships.

Mode Tables I, II, and III provide three different ways of understanding mode construction; the specific musical situation one is in will determine which table will be the most useful. For example, if you wanted to construct the G Mixolydian mode, it would be quicker to use Mode Table III, because it is more efficient to think of it as a major scale with scale degree 7 lowered one half step (see Mode Table III). If you wanted to construct the C Dorian

Mode Table III

Mode	Associated Scale and Pitch Alteration
Ionian	major scale
Locrian	pure minor scale with lowered steps 2 and 5
Aeolian	pure minor scale
Mixolydian	major scale with lowered step 7
Lydian	major scale with raised step 4
Phrygian	pure minor scale with lowered step 2
Dorian	pure minor scale with raised step 6

mode, it might be quicker to think in terms of Mode Table II, because this indicates that it is constructed on scale degree 2 of a major scale.

In order to understand the information in Mode Table III more fully, let's identify the pitch differences between the C major and C pure minor scales. One way to describe these differences is to say that the pure minor scale is the major scale with scale degrees 3, 6, and 7 lowered one half step. Example 5.54 illustrates this distinction.

5.54   C Major scale   C pure minor scale

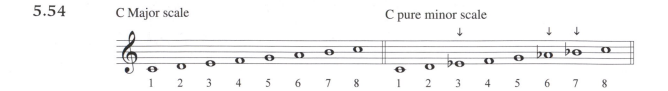

The following examples compare each of the modes to a major or minor scale in the same fashion and illustrate the information in Mode Table III.

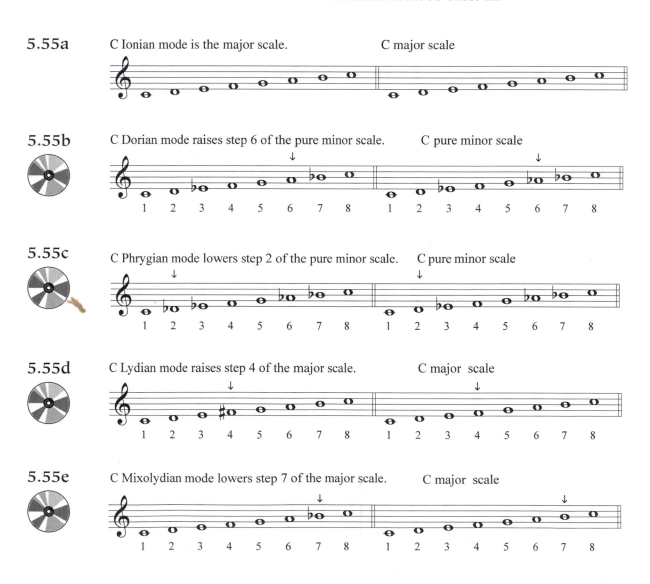

5.55a   C Ionian mode is the major scale.   C major scale

5.55b   C Dorian mode raises step 6 of the pure minor scale.   C pure minor scale

5.55c   C Phrygian mode lowers step 2 of the pure minor scale.   C pure minor scale

5.55d   C Lydian mode raises step 4 of the major scale.   C major scale

5.55e   C Mixolydian mode lowers step 7 of the major scale.   C major scale

5.55f

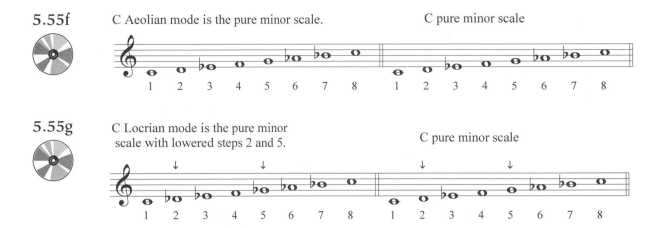

C Aeolian mode is the pure minor scale.

C pure minor scale

1 2 3 4 5 6 7 8   1 2 3 4 5 6 7 8

5.55g

C Locrian mode is the pure minor scale with lowered steps 2 and 5.

C pure minor scale

1 2 3 4 5 6 7 8   1 2 3 4 5 6 7 8

The preceding information will be understood more fully by playing the modes and their associated scales on an instrument and hearing and seeing the different scale patterns. For musicians engaged in any type of musical improvisation, this knowledge is essential to understanding the relationships among chords, **harmonic progression**, and modal playing. Experimentation with these modes in improvisation will reveal their beauty and open the door to new musical vistas.

Now that you understand how to construct modes, let's learn a simple method of singing them, so that you are able to distinguish their aural differences.

SINGING THE MODES

The process of singing scales will develop the ear's capacity to distinguish the differences among the various modes and establish a sense of a tonal center. A musician's best tool is a refined "musical ear," which is among the most important skills a musician must cultivate.

You do not have to be an experienced singer to sing the modes, nor do you need a pleasant singing voice, but you must make an attempt to focus your voice so that you are able to match a pitch. A good beginning exercise for developing a sense of pitch is to sing along with the modes as you play them on the piano. Do not be concerned if you have never played the piano; all you will be required to do is to play the C major scale, which involves only the white keys of the piano keyboard.

The C major scale is selected because the span of the pitches should accommodate most people's singing ranges. When you are asked to sing the modes beginning on higher pitches (F Lydian or G Mixolydian), you should try singing them down one octave, so that you will not strain your voice.

Locate a piano and play the C major scale as indicated by the arrows on the keyboard below.

5.56   C major scale

Practice playing and singing this scale until you feel comfortable with its sound. You might want to ask a music teacher or a friend who is more experienced with music to confirm that you are producing the correct pitches. This is extremely important, especially if you are not an experienced singer!

When you practice singing and playing the scale on the piano, you will need to have a method of identifying each pitch as it relates to the key center of C major. One method, called **solmization**, designates the names of the pitches using conventional syllables. It is called ***solfège*** in French and ***solfeggio*** in Italian. In this system each scale degree is identified by a syllable, as follows.

5.57   C major scale

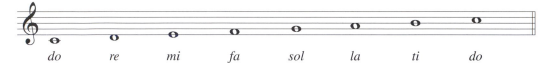

do   re   mi   fa   sol   la   ti   do

The scale degree names are pronounced as follows:

do (dough), *re* (ray), *mi* (me), *fa* (fah), *sol* (soul), *la* (lah), *ti* (tea), *do* (dough)

The benefit of using the *solfège* system is that this method assists musicians in associating all of the pitches within a particular key to a key center, or **tonic.** This acquired musical skill is an important step toward mastering the refined aural ability referred to as **relative pitch**.

Once you are certain that you are correctly singing the C major scale, you are ready for the next step. Mode Table IV illustrates *solfège* syllables for every scale degree of the seven modes.

Mode Table IV

Mode	Major Scale Degree Numbers	Solfège Syllables
Ionian	1 to 8 (1)	*do, re, mi, fa, sol, la, ti, do*
Locrian	7 to 7	*ti, do, re, mi, fa, sol, la, ti*
Aeolian	6 to 6	*la, ti, do, re, mi, fa, sol, la*
Mixolydian	5 to 5	*sol, la, ti, do, re, mi, fa, sol*
Lydian	4 to 4	*fa, sol, la, ti, do, re, mi, fa*
Phrygian	3 to 3	*mi, fa, sol, la, ti, do, re, mi*
Dorian	2 to 2	*re, mi, fa, sol, la, ti, do, re*

Let's learn how to apply the information in Mode Table IV to singing a mode.

Skill Development

Suppose you wanted to sing the D Dorian mode. Mode Table IV indicates that the Dorian mode uses the scale degree numbers 2–2, or the *solfège* syllables *re–re*. You *do not* have to be concerned with key signatures to sing a mode. What is important is that you realize that the Dorian mode begins and ends on *re* of a major scale

Process

Step 1. **Tonicize** *do* (establish the key center) in your mind by singing and playing the C major scale on the piano (the scale that is associated with the D Dorian mode).

5.58

Tonicize *do* by singing the C major scale.

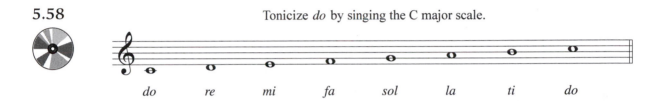

do   re   mi   fa   sol   la   ti   do

Step 2. Sing steps 1, 3, 5, and 8 of the scale using *solfège* syllables *do, mi, sol,* and *do.*

5.59

Sing steps 1, 3, 5, and 8 using *solfège* syllables.

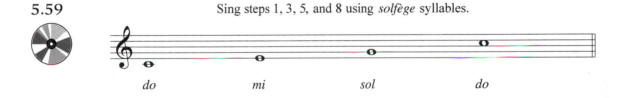

do   mi   sol   do

Step 3. Once *do* is clearly established in your mind, sing the section of the C major scale that begins and ends on *re*. This is the *D Dorian* mode. This will take some practice and you may wish to repeat steps 1 and 2 if this step is difficult.

5.60

D Dorian mode using *re–re* solmization.

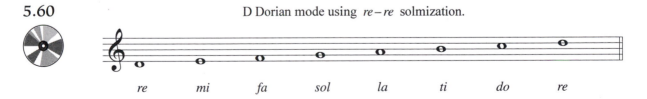

re   mi   fa   sol   la   ti   do   re

Skill Development

Let's apply this same process to singing the E Phrygian mode.

Mode Table IV indicates that the Phrygian mode uses scale degree numbers 3–3, or the *solfège* syllables *mi* to *mi*.

Process

Step 1. Tonicize *do* (establish the key center) in your mind by singing and playing on the piano the C major scale.

5.61

Tonicize *do* by singing the C major scale.

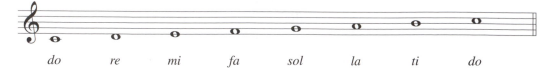

do   re   mi   fa   sol   la   ti   do

Step 2. Sing steps 1, 3, 5, and 8 of the scale by using *solfège* syllables *do, mi, sol,* and *do.*

5.62

do   mi   sol   do

Step 3. Once *do* is clearly established in your mind, sing the section of the C major scale that begins and ends on *mi.* This is the E Phrygian mode. This will take some practice; you may wish to repeat steps 1 and 2 if this step is difficult.

5.63

E Phrygian mode using *mi–mi* solmization

mi   fa   sol   la   ti   do   re   mi

Skill Development

Let's apply this same process to singing the G Mixolydian mode.

Process

Mode Table IV indicates that the Mixolydian mode uses scale degree numbers 5–5, or the *solfège* syllables *sol* to *sol.*

Step 1. Tonicize *do* (establish the key center) in your mind by singing and playing the C major scale on the piano.

5.64

Tonicize *do* by singing the C major scale.

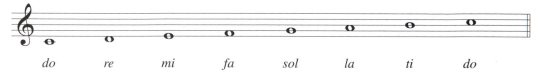

do   re   mi   fa   sol   la   ti   do

Step 2. Sing steps 1, 3, 5, and 8 of the scale using *solfège* syllables *do, mi, sol,* and *do.*

5.65

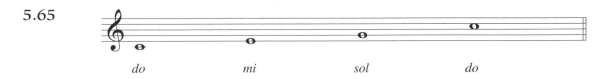

Step 3. Once *do* is clearly established in your mind, sing the section of the C major scale that begins and ends on *sol*. This is the G Mixolydian mode. This will take some practice, and you may wish to repeat steps 1 and 2.

The following example illustrates that if the last pitch in the first measure, G, is too high for you, you may sing the mode beginning one octave lower.

5.66

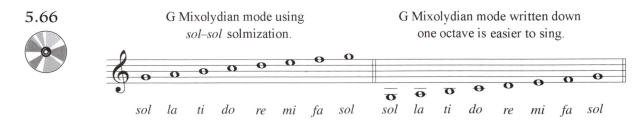

Practice singing the following modes in any octave that is comfortable for your voice. Remember to use the appropriate solmization and, if necessary, refer to Mode Table IV (page 242) to identify the major scale degrees associated with each mode.

1. F Lydian
2. B♭ Dorian
3. G Phrygian
4. C Locrian
5. A Ionian
6. E♭ Aeolian
7. F♯ Mixolydian
8. C♯ Dorian
9. A♭ Phrygian
10. B Lydian

REVIEW OF PRINCIPLES

Principle 1
Modes associated with major scales will have half steps where the numbers 3 and 4, and 7 and 8 (1) are placed. All other distances between adjacent scale degrees will be whole steps.

Principle 2
To determine the actual scale degrees at which half steps occur in a mode, first construct the mode according to Mode Table II and then renumber it in ascending order using the numbers 1 through 8.

Principle 3

To identify the major key signature associated with a mode, establish the scale degree number for the first and last note of the mode, as illustrated in Mode Table II. Next, count up or down to locate scale degrees 1 or 8 of the major scale associated with the mode and apply its key signature to the mode.

ANSWER SHEETS TO CHAPTER 5

Exercise 1

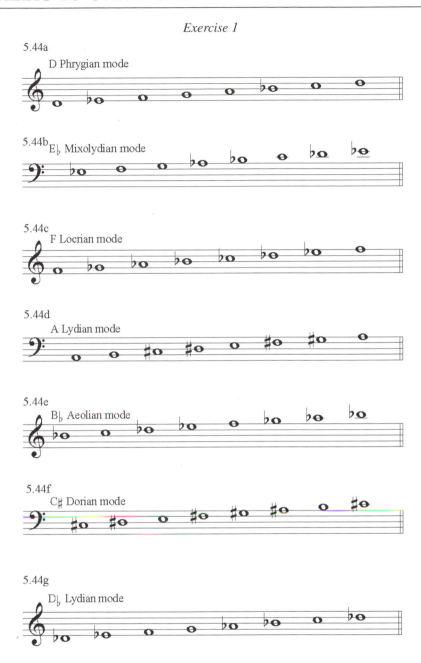

5.44a
D Phrygian mode

5.44b
E♭ Mixolydian mode

5.44c
F Locrian mode

5.44d
A Lydian mode

5.44e
B♭ Aeolian mode

5.44f
C♯ Dorian mode

5.44g
D♭ Lydian mode

Exercise 2

5.53a

A Dorian mode

5.53b

B♭ Phrygian mode

5.53c

C♯ Locrian mode

5.53d

D Mixolydian mode

5.53e

E♭ Lydian mode

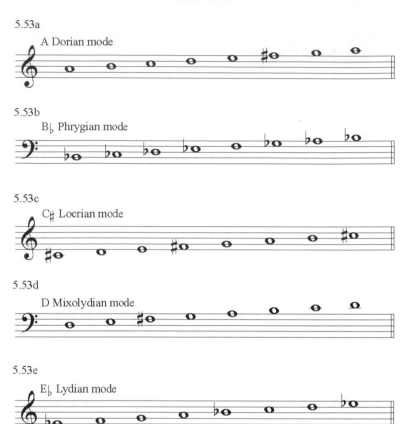

WORKSHEETS FOR CHAPTER 5

Name

Construct the following modes:

1. G Aeolian

2. B Dorian

3. G♭ Lydian

4. D Locrian

5. E♭ Phrygian

6. F♯ Ionian

7. A♭ Mixolydian

8. E♯ Locrian

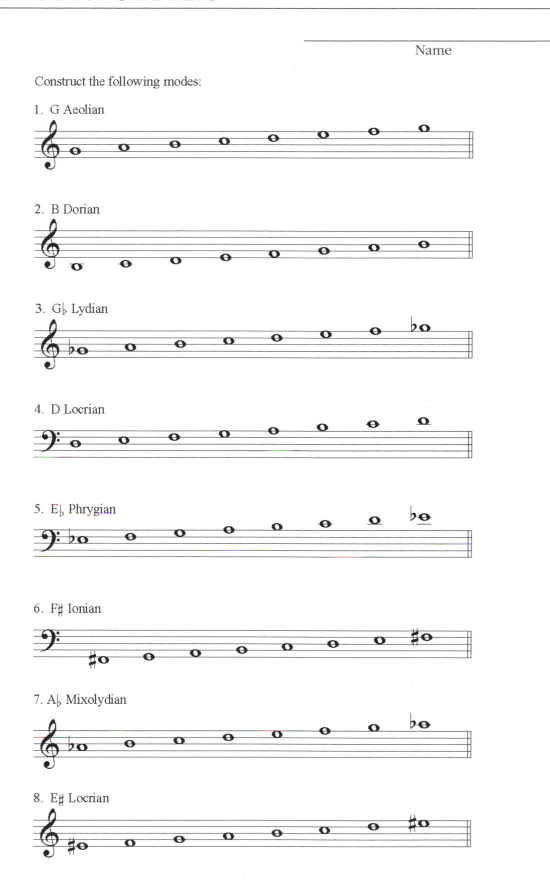

Name

9. F Dorian

10. D Lydian

11. B Phrygian

12. C♯ Mixolydian

13. E♭ Aeolian

14. C♯ Lydian

15. B♭ Locrian

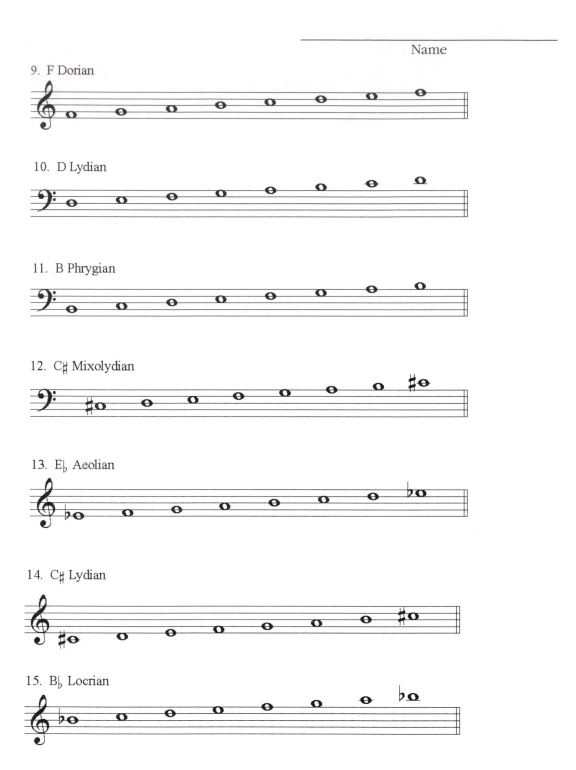

Find additional Skill Development Drills on the accompanying CD-ROM and on the book companion Web site: http://music.wadsworth.com/kinney1e.

Intervals

I have been told that Wagner's music is much better than it sounds.
—MARK TWAIN

An **interval** is the measured distance between two musical pitches. The ability to quickly identify and construct any interval is a skill required of all serious musicians, because it affects nearly every aspect of how they understand and articulate numerous aspects of a musical composition. Although there are a number of approaches available to mastering this proficiency, the method presented in this chapter will focus on applying the major key signatures as an efficient means to understanding the issues related to intervals.

Before beginning the study of intervals, review the major key signatures below. If you have not already done so, commit them to memory.

6.1a

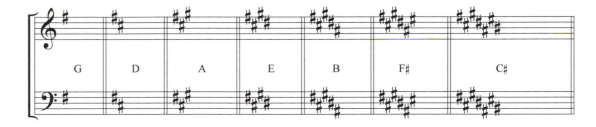

6.1b

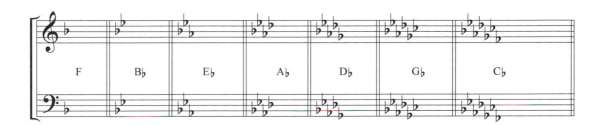

MELODIC AND HARMONIC INTERVALS

Melodic and harmonic intervals are the two basic interval types used in the writing and performing of music. A **melodic interval** is a linear concept related to the distance between any two *consecutive* pitches, while a **harmonic interval,** as its name suggests, is the measured distance between two *simultaneously performed* pitches. When a melody is performed, each pitch produces a melodic interval with the following pitch.

Melodic Intervals

Principle **1**

The distance between two pitches that are written or played consecutively is called a melodic interval.

In the following example, there are four pitches that create three melodic intervals. The distance between the first two pitches, F and A, is called a melodic 3rd, because F is counted as one; the second line, G, is counted as two; and A is counted as three. The distance between A and B is a melodic 2nd, and the distance between B and D is a melodic 6th.

6.2

Harmonic Intervals

A harmonic interval occurs when two pitches are played simultaneously. An example of this would be if you were singing or playing a harmony part (a higher or lower part) to a song. The two parts performed together produce harmonic intervals. The Christmas song "Silent Night" is often performed with a lower harmony part, which produces a harmonic interval with every pitch of the melody.

6.3   *Silent Night*

> ## Principle *2*
>
> The distance between two pitches that are written or played simultaneously is called a harmonic interval.

The distance from the lower pitch to the upper pitch in each of the four intervals in the following example is a harmonic interval.

6.4

SIMPLE AND COMPOUND INTERVALS

The numeric distance in a harmonic interval may be determined by assigning the numeral 1 to the lower pitch, and counting the lines and spaces up to and including the upper pitch. Intervals within one octave (octaves were discussed in Chapter 1; see examples 1.19a and 1.19b) are called simple, and those exceeding the octave are called compound. Below are examples of **simple** and **compound** harmonic **intervals**.

6.5   *Simple Intervals*

(intervals within the span of one octave)

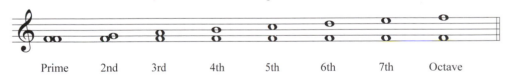

6.6   *Compound Intervals*

(intervals exceeding the span of one octave)

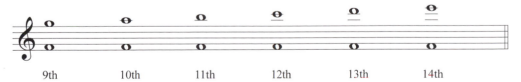

MEASURING INTERVALS

In example 6.7a, there are three harmonic intervals of the 6th. Although the basic numerical distance is the same, they are not equidistant because the number of half steps separating the two pitches for each interval is different.

On the keyboard below, locate the pitch G and determine the number of half steps separating the pitches in each interval by counting all of the black and white keys until you reach the top pitch (count G♯ as the first half step, A as the second, and so forth).

6.7a

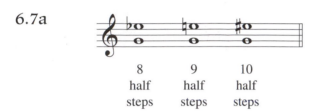

The principles presented in this chapter apply to melodic and harmonic intervals, but will be illustrated using simple harmonic intervals (those that do not exceed the octave). The process of accurately identifying and constructing compound intervals (those greater than the octave) will be addressed later on.

IDENTIFYING MAJOR INTERVALS

The exact distance between any two pitches may be measured and qualified as one of the following five basic interval types: **major**, **minor**, **perfect**, **diminished**, and **augmented**. When measuring intervals, it is possible to count the number of half steps between the lower and upper pitches and assign the total number to a specific interval. For example, we could say that the interval of the major 3rd contains four half steps, the perfect 5th seven half steps, the minor 7th ten half steps, and so on.

6.7b

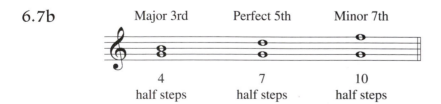

To memorize every interval in this manner would be very time consuming. A simpler and more efficient way to identify intervals is to utilize the key signatures you learned in Chapter 4.

Principle 3

An interval is major when the upper pitch is in the key (major scale) of the lower pitch (except when the interval is a 4th, 5th, prime, or octave).

The following harmonic intervals are *major* because the upper pitch occurs in the key, or major scale, of the lower pitch.

6.8

Maj. 3rd   Maj. 3rd   Maj. 6th   Maj. 7th   Maj. 2nd

In the first interval in example 6.8, the upper pitch, C♯, is *diatonic* (in the scale of) in the key of A, and therefore may be identified as a major 3rd. Please refer to the major key signature for A, and you will see that C is sharped.

In the second example, the upper pitch, D, is diatonic in the key of the pitch below it (B♭), and therefore this interval is also identified as a major 3rd. The major key signature for B♭ comprises two flats and indicates that only B and E are flatted in that key, while all other pitches are natural. If this process at this point is unclear to you, please review Chapter 3, "Scales," and Chapter 4, "Key Signatures."

In the third example, the upper pitch E is in the key of the pitch below it, G (G has only F♯ in its key signature), and the interval is identified as a major 6th. The remaining two intervals are major for the same reason (their upper pitches are in the keys of the lower pitches).

Major intervals never include the 4th, 5th, octave, or prime, because these intervals share a special quality. They are called perfect intervals and will be discussed later on.

Exercise 1

Please identify the following intervals:

6.9a

6.9b

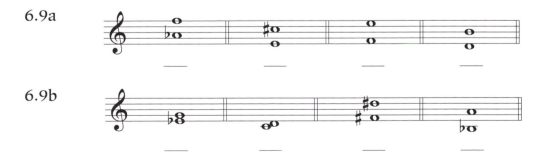

CONSTRUCTING A MAJOR INTERVAL ABOVE A GIVEN PITCH

Skill Development

Intervals may be constructed above or below any pitch. Let's learn the process by constructing a major 6th above E.

Process

Step 1. Place E on the staff and count it as scale degree 1. Ascend to scale degree 6 by counting every space and line. Scale degree 6 is C.

6.10a

Step 2. Place the C on the staff. You have created the interval of the 6th, but you have not yet determined if it is a major 6th.

6.10b

Step 3. Review the definition of a major interval (**Principle 3**) and ask yourself the following question: Is the upper pitch, C, in the key of the lower pitch, E? In order to determine this, you need to know the key signature for E major. The key signature for E major has four sharps. Observe that in the key of E major, C is the second sharp from the left.

6.11

Step 4. Place a sharp before the pitch C. This interval now is a major 6th.

6.12

Complete the following intervals in exactly the same manner and check your answers with those at the end of this chapter.

Exercise 2

Construct major intervals above the following pitches. Remember that the upper pitch must be in the key (scale) of the lower pitch.

6.13a

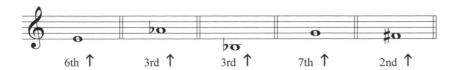

6.13b   Be careful—this example is in the bass clef! ☺

IDENTIFYING MINOR INTERVALS

A minor interval results when the distance between the two pitches of a major interval is reduced by one half step. Minor intervals *do not* include the intervals of the 4th, 5th, prime, or octave. It is only the major intervals of the 2nd, 3rd, 6th, and 7th (and their associated compound intervals) that, when brought closer together by one half step, will become minor.

Principle **4**

Minor intervals are 2nds, 3rds, 6ths, and 7ths (or their compound equivalents) that are one half step smaller than their corresponding major intervals.

When identifying the quality of an interval (major, minor, augmented, or diminished), you must begin by mentally constructing a major interval above the given lower pitch, then checking to see if and how the upper pitch has been altered. If the interval is minor, the major interval will have been made smaller by one half step!

Skill Development

Identify the following interval.

6.14

Process

Step 1. Determine the basic numeric distance of the interval. Is it a 2nd, 3rd, 6th, or 7th? Counting the lower pitch, C, as scale degree 1, count up to E♭, which is scale degree 3. The basic interval is a 3rd, but now you must determine its quality.

Step 2. Construct a major 3rd above the lower pitch by making certain the upper pitch is in its key (scale). The lower pitch is C, and its key signature has no sharps or flats. The upper pitch, E, is in the key of C; the interval C–E therefore must be a major 3rd.

6.15

Major 3rd

Step 3. Look back at the original interval, C–E♭, and determine how the major 3rd illustrated in example 6.15 has been altered. You will see that the upper pitch, E, has been lowered one half step, to E♭.

Step 4. Observe that by lowering the upper pitch of the major interval by one half step, the distance between the two pitches has been made smaller. The interval C–E♭ is now minor and reflects **Principle 4**.

6.16

Minor 3rd

Exercise 3

Identify the numeric distances and qualities (major or minor) of the following intervals.

6.17a

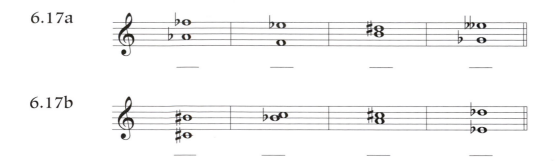

6.17b

CONSTRUCTING A MINOR INTERVAL ABOVE A GIVEN PITCH

Now that you are able to identify minor intervals, constructing them will involve almost the same process.

Skill Development

Let's construct a minor 7th above B♭.

Process

Step 1. Count B♭ as scale degree 1 and ascend to scale degree 7, which is A.

6.18a

Step 2. Place A on the staff. You have created the interval of the 7th, but have not yet determined if it is a minor 7th.

6.18b

Step 3. Now construct the interval of the major 7th by making sure the upper pitch of the interval is in the key of the lower pitch, B♭. The A will not require a sharp or flat, because the key of B♭ major has only B♭ and E♭ in its key signature. In example 6.18b, you have created the interval of the major 7th, which now must be adjusted to create the minor 7th. To accomplish this, you must make the interval one half step smaller, by lowering A to A♭. This interval is now a minor 7th.

6.19

Minor 7th

Skill Development

Construct the interval of a minor 3rd above E♭.

Process

Step 1. Count E♭ as scale degree 1 and count up to scale degree 3, which is G.

Step 2. Place G on the staff. You now have constructed a 3rd, but have not yet determined if it is a minor 3rd.

6.20

Step 3. Now construct the interval of the major 3rd by checking the key signature for E♭ and determining how the pitch, G, occurs in that key. Is it sharped? Is it flatted? The key signature for E♭ major indicates that the pitch G is unaltered in the key of E♭. Because G is diatonic in the key of E♭, the interval in example 6.20 is a major 3rd.

Step 4. The major 3rd you have constructed must be made smaller by one half step in order to make it a minor 3rd. (You must not alter the lower pitch, E♭, because your task is to construct a minor 3rd above it.) To accomplish this, you will need to lower the upper pitch, G, one half step by placing a flat before it. You have now created a minor 3rd above E♭, because the major 3rd has been made smaller by one half step.

6.21

Minor 3rd

Exercise 4

Construct minor intervals above the following pitches using the same process. (Lowercase "m" indicates minor.)

6.22a

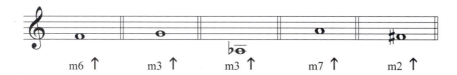

m6 ↑   m3 ↑   m3 ↑   m7 ↑   m2 ↑

6.22b   Be careful—this example is in the bass clef! ☺

m6 ↑   m7 ↑   m2 ↑   m6 ↑   m3 ↑

IDENTIFYING PERFECT INTERVALS

The perfect intervals, which include the 4th, 5th, prime, and octave, are never identified as major or minor. This may seem confusing at first, but these intervals are unique in a number of ways.

Please observe that in all major and minor intervals, only one of the pitches is in the key of the other pitch. In a major interval the upper pitch is in the key of the lower pitch, but the lower pitch is not in the key of the upper pitch.

In example 6.23, the upper pitch E *is in the key* of the lower pitch, C, but C *is not in the key* of the upper pitch, E. The interval is a major 3rd.

6.23

Major 3rd

In a minor interval, the upper pitch *is not in the key* of the lower pitch, but the lower pitch *is in the key* of the upper pitch. In the example below, the upper pitch, E♭, is not in the key of the lower pitch, C, but C is in the key of the upper pitch, E♭. The interval is a minor 3rd.

6.24

Minor 3rd

In example 6.25, the first interval is a perfect 5th because not only does the upper pitch, F♯, occur diatonically in the key of the lower pitch, B, but also the lower pitch, B, is in the key of the upper pitch, F♯. (Please check the key signatures to confirm this.) Although this interval looks major, it will be identified as *perfect*. This unique reciprocity is found only among the perfect intervals. The prime, 4th, 5th, and octave share this unique relationship.

6.25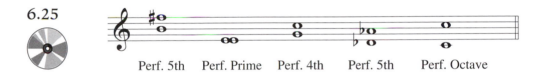

Perf. 5th   Perf. Prime   Perf. 4th   Perf. 5th   Perf. Octave

CONSTRUCTING A PERFECT INTERVAL ABOVE A GIVEN PITCH

In constructing the perfect intervals of the 4th, 5th, and octave *above* a given pitch, apply the same process as for constructing major intervals above a given pitch. When the upper pitch of these intervals is in the key of the lower pitch, they will be called perfect, even though they look major.

Principle 5

When the upper pitch of a 4th, 5th, or octave is in the key of the lower pitch, the interval is called perfect. (This applies to the prime even though there is no actual distance between the two pitches.)

Skill Development

Construct a perfect 5th above A♭.

Process

Step 1. Count A♭ as scale degree 1 and count up to scale degree 5, which is E.

Step 2. Place A♭ and E on the staff. You have created a 5th, but do not know if it is a perfect 5th. In order for it to be perfect, the upper pitch must be in the key of the lower pitch.

6.26

Step 3. Check the key signature for A♭ to see how E occurs in that key. The key signature will indicate that E is flatted in the key of A♭.

Step 4. By placing a flat in front of E and changing it to E♭, you will have constructed a perfect 5th.

6.27

Perf. 5th

Skill Development

Let's try another example. Construct a perfect 4th above B♭.

Process

Step 1. Count up from B♭ to scale degree 4 and place E in the space.

Step 2. You now have created the interval of the 4th, but have not yet determined if it is perfect. Remember, for this interval to be perfect, the upper pitch must be in the key of the lower pitch! Check the key signature for B♭, and determine if E is diatonic in the key of B♭.

6.28

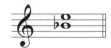

Step 3. The key of B♭ major has two flats, B♭ and E♭. By placing a flat in front of E, you will have constructed a perfect 4th, because E♭ is in the key of B♭.

6.29

Perf. 4th

Exercise 5

Construct the indicated intervals above the following pitches in the same manner.

6.30a   *(P = Perfect) (PP = Perfect Prime)*

P8 ↑   P5 ↑   P4 ↑   P4 ↑   P5 ↑

6.30b   Be careful—this example is in the bass clef! ☺

P5 ↑   P5 ↑   P4 ↑   P4 ↑   PP ↑

IDENTIFYING DIMINISHED INTERVALS

A characteristic of a diminished interval is that both the upper and lower pitches have no diatonic relationship with one another: they do not occur in each other's key. Please recall that in any major or minor interval, one of the two pitches will be in the key of the other pitch, and that both pitches of a perfect interval occur in each other's key.

*Principle **6***

When the pitches of a minor or perfect interval are brought closer together by one half step, the interval is called diminished.

Observe in example 6.31 that the upper pitch, F, is not in the key of the lower pitch B, and that B is not in the key of the upper pitch, F. Please check your key signatures to confirm this. This interval is said to be diminished.

6.31

Notice that it is the minor and perfect intervals that become diminished when brought closer together by one half step. In order for a *major interval* to become diminished, it must first be made minor. The sequence appears as follows:

major ⟶ minor ⟶ diminished

Remember that *perfect intervals are never major or minor!* When *perfect intervals* are brought closer by one half step, they become diminished. The sequence of creating a diminished interval from a minor or perfect interval would appear as follows:

minor ⟶ diminished
perfect ⟶ diminished

The following minor interval has been made diminished by lowering the upper pitch one half step.

6.32

Min. 3rd   Dim. 3rd

The same minor interval also could have been made diminished by raising the lower pitch one half step.

6.33

Min. 3rd   Dim. 3rd

The following perfect 5th may be made diminished either by lowering the upper pitch or by raising the lower pitch one half step.

6.34

Perf. 5th   Dim. 5th   Dim. 5th

Let's study the process of identifying diminished intervals.

Skill Development

Please identify the following interval:

6.35

Process

Step 1. Count up from the lower pitch, A, to E♭, and you will have identified this interval as a 5th. At this point you must determine the quality of the 5th. Is it perfect? Is it diminished?

Step 2. First establish how a perfect 5th above the lower pitch would appear determine if the upper pitch is in the key of the lower pitch. The key signature for A is three sharps (F♯, C♯, and G♯). The upper pitch, E♭, in example 6.35 is the key of A. By mentally removing the flat you will determine that E *is* in the key of A and that the interval A to E therefore is a perfect 5th.

6.36

Perfect 5th

Step 3. The original interval you were asked to identify (in example 6.35) is A–E♭. A perfect interval made smaller by one half step becomes diminished. A to E♭ is a diminished 5th.

6.37

Diminished 5th

Exercise 6

Please circle the diminished intervals.

6.38

CONSTRUCTING DIMINISHED INTERVALS ABOVE A GIVEN PITCH

Constructing diminished intervals above any given pitch follows almost the same method as identifying intervals. Remember that perfect and minor intervals become diminished when brought closer together by one half step; major intervals become minor when brought together by one half step and diminished when brought together by two half steps.

Skill Development

Construct a diminished 7th above B.

Process

Step 1. Count B as scale degree 1 and count up to scale degree 7, which is A.

Step 2. Place A on the staff. You now have created the interval of the 7th, but you have not determined if it is a diminished 7th.

6.39

Step 3. Next, construct the interval of the major 7th above B. Determine how the upper pitch, A, would occur in the key of B. Check the key signature for the key of B, and you will determine that A is sharped. By changing A to A♯, you will have constructed a major 7th above B.

6.40

Maj. 7th

Step 4. The major 7th you have constructed needs to be made minor before it can become diminished. Remember, you cannot alter the original pitch, B, because your task is to construct a diminished 7th above it! By removing the sharp in front of the pitch A, you will have brought the interval closer together by one half step and constructed a minor 7th. Please recall that any major interval brought closer together by one half step becomes minor.

6.41

Min. 7th

Step 5. The minor 7th you have created now must be brought closer together once again by lowering the upper pitch, A. By placing a flat before the pitch, you will have brought the interval closer together by one half step, resulting in a diminished 7th!

6.42

Dim. 7th

Skill Development

Let's construct a diminished 5th above D♭.

Process

Step 1. Place D♭ on the staff and count up to scale degree 5, which is A.

Step 2. Place A on the staff. You now have constructed a 5th, but have not yet determined if it is diminished.

6.43

Step 3. Now create the perfect 5th above D♭ by making sure the upper pitch is in the key of D♭. After checking the key signature for D♭, you will need to

place a flat in front of the pitch A, because it is flatted in that key. By changing A to A♭, you will have created a perfect 5th. Remember that the intervals of the prime, 4th, 5th, and octave will never be identified as major. They might look major, but will be called perfect!

6.44

Perf. 5th

Step 4. In order to make the perfect 5th a diminished 5th, you now must bring it closer together by one half step. Please recall that perfect intervals brought closer together by one half step will never be called minor! In order to achieve this, you must alter the upper pitch. You *cannot* alter the lower pitch because you have been asked to construct a diminished 5th above it! Lower the upper pitch A♭ one half step by changing it to A♭♭. You have now created a diminished 5th above D♭.

6.45

Dim. 5th

The process of creating diminished intervals is relatively simple when you remember that major intervals first become minor and then diminished as the distance between the pitches decreases in half steps. Perfect and minor intervals immediately become diminished when brought closer together by one half step. Once again, the perfect intervals, which include the prime, 4th, 5th, and octave, are never called major or minor! When the upper pitch in any one of these intervals (including the prime, although both pitches are the same) is in the key of the lower pitch, it will be called perfect.

Exercise 7

Construct diminished intervals above the following pitches.

6.46a

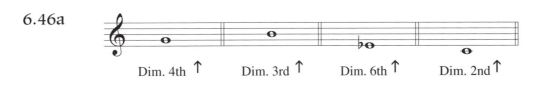

Dim. 4th ↑   Dim. 3rd ↑   Dim. 6th ↑   Dim. 2nd ↑

6.46b Be careful—this example is in the bass clef! ☺

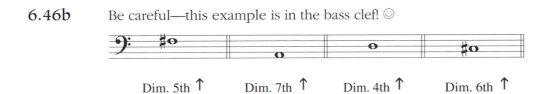

Dim. 5th ↑   Dim. 7th ↑   Dim. 4th ↑   Dim. 6th ↑

IDENTIFYING AUGMENTED INTERVALS ABOVE A GIVEN PITCH

An augmented interval is produced when the distance between a major or perfect interval is made *larger* by one half step. This may be achieved either by raising the upper pitch or by lowering the bottom pitch. In practical terms, the augmented interval generally is formed by raising the upper pitch.

Principle 7

When the distance between the two pitches of a major or perfect interval is increased by one half step, the interval is called augmented.

When identifying any interval, you must first determine how the interval would look if it were major or perfect, and then if and how it has been altered.

Skill Development

Identify the quality (major, minor, diminished, or augmented) of the following interval.

6.47

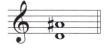

Process

Step 1. Determine the basic distance between the two pitches, D and A♯. The distance is a 5th, but you do not know its quality.

Step 2. Construct a perfect 5th above the lower pitch, D. A perfect 5th above D is A, because A is in the key of D. (If you need to review this, refer to **Principle 5**.)

6.48

Perf. 5th

Step 3. You will notice in example 6.47 that A is sharped. The distance between the perfect 5th (D to A) has been increased by one half step, resulting in an augmented 5th.

6.49

Aug. 5th

Skill Development

Identify the following interval.

6.50

Process

Step 1. Determine the numeric distance between B♭ and E. The basic distance is a 4th.

Step 2. Now mentally construct what a perfect 4th would look like above B♭. By checking the key signature for B♭ (B and E are flatted in the key signature), you will determine that E needs to be E♭ in order for the interval to be perfect.

6.51

Perf. 4th

Step 3. By removing the flat from E♭ and changing it to E natural, the perfect 4th (B♭ to E♭) has been made one half step larger and therefore is augmented.

6.52

Aug. 4th

Exercise 8

Circle the augmented intervals.

6.53

CONSTRUCTING AUGMENTED INTERVALS

The process for constructing augmented intervals is almost the same as for identifying them. Carefully follow the steps below, and remember that any major or perfect interval made larger by one half step will become augmented.

Skill Development

Construct an augmented 6th above G.

Process

Step 1. Place G on the staff and count up six scale degrees to the pitch E. By placing E on the staff, you have created the interval of the 6th.

6.54

Step 2. You now must determine what a major 6th would look like above G. Is E in the key of G? By checking the key signature, you will determine that F♯ is the only altered pitch in the key of G, and that E is diatonic in the key of G. The pitch E therefore is a major 6th above G.

Step 3. You must augment this interval by making it larger by one half step. Remember that you must not alter the lower pitch, because your task is to create an augmented 6th above it. To make this interval augmented, you must raise the upper pitch E to E♯.

6.55

Aug. 6th

Skill Development

Construct an augmented 5th above F♯.

Process

Step 1. Count up five steps from F♯ and place the pitch C on the staff. You have created the interval of a 5th, but have not yet determined if it is augmented.

6.56

Step 2. Construct a perfect 5th above F♯. The key signature for F♯ indicates that C is sharped in the key of F♯, so you must place a sharp before the pitch. You now know what a perfect 5th above F♯ looks like.

6.57

Perf. 5th

Step 3. In order to construct an augmented 5th, you now must increase the distance between the two pitches by one half step. This will be accomplished by sharping C♯ and changing it to C𝄪. The interval F♯–C𝄪 is an augmented 5th.

6.58

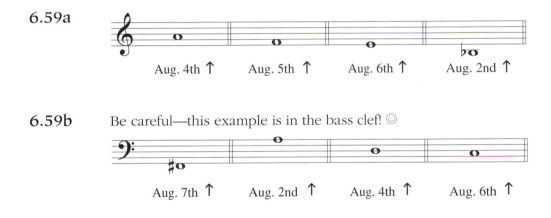

Aug. 5th

The process of creating augmented intervals is simple when you remember that any major or perfect interval made larger by one half step is augmented.

Exercise 9

Construct augmented intervals above the following pitches.

6.59a

Aug. 4th ↑   Aug. 5th ↑   Aug. 6th ↑   Aug. 2nd ↑

6.59b   Be careful—this example is in the bass clef! ☺

Aug. 7th ↑   Aug. 2nd ↑   Aug. 4th ↑   Aug. 6th ↑

DOUBLY AUGMENTED AND DOUBLY DIMINISHED INTERVALS

Occasionally it is necessary to write doubly augmented and doubly diminished intervals.

Principle 8

An augmented interval made larger by one half step is called doubly augmented.

Principle 9

A diminished interval made smaller by one half step is called doubly diminished.

Although the doubly augmented interval is written in tonal music, the doubly diminished interval is more a theoretical construct than a practical notion. When these intervals do occur, they assist the performer (and the composer) in visualizing the ways altered pitches resolve to their musical conclusions within the framework of the commonly accepted practices of tonal music.

The use of chromatically altered pitches (those pitches that are not diatonic to the key in which a piece of music is written) is very common to tonal music and great care must be taken to ensure that they resolve in the direction of their inflection. (Within a given key, raised pitches resolve upward and lowered pitches downward.)

It is not uncommon to find an interval such as the perfect 5th, A♭–E♭, rewritten as A♭–D♯ (doubly augmented 4th). In this instance, the D♯ will resolve upward by a half step to E♮, and the A♭ will resolve downward by a half step to G, as illustrated in the following example.

6.60a   The interval of the perfect 5th is rewritten as a doubly augmented 4th.
The D♯ will resolve to E, and the A♭ to G.

Perfect 5th   Doubly augmented 4th   Maj. 6th

Because of the fairly complex harmonic implications of these intervals, it is not necessary, at this point, to study them in depth. A few examples of these intervals are illustrated below.

6.60b   (DA=Doubly Augmented)   (DD=Doubly Diminished)

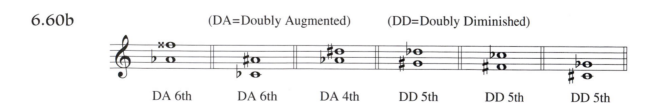

DA 6th   DA 6th   DA 4th   DD 5th   DD 5th   DD 5th

COMPOUND INTERVALS

A compound interval is one in which the distance between two pitches exceeds the octave.

Principle 10

Compound intervals are intervals that are greater than the octave. They are identified and constructed in the same manner as simple intervals.

Intervals such as the 9th, 10th, 11th, 12th, 13th, and 14th are called compound intervals.

6.61

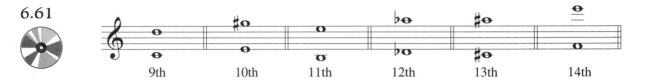

9th   10th   11th   12th   13th   14th

In example 6.61, each of the upper pitches occurs diatonically in the key of the lower pitch. The first compound interval, C–D, is a major 9th because D, which is the 2nd scale degree of the C major scale, has been written up one octave. The second interval, E–G♯, is a major 10th, because G♯, the 3rd scale degree of the E major scale, has been written up one octave. The remaining intervals also share a diatonic relationship.

Please notice in example 6.62 that in the first interval, the upper pitch, D (9th), when written down one octave, produces the interval of the major 2nd. In the next interval (E to G♯), when the upper pitch, G♯ (10th) is taken down one octave, the interval produced is a major 3rd. In the third interval (B to E), when the upper pitch, E (11th), is taken down one octave, it will produce the interval of the perfect 4th. Please recall that the 4th, 5th, prime, and octave are never called major or minor.

6.62

Maj. 9th   Maj. 2nd   Maj. 10th   Maj. 3rd   Perf. 11th   Perf. 4th

Although the distance between two pitches may exceed the 14th, compound intervals, when occurring within **chords**, will generally comprise those intervals up to the 13th.

When constructing a compound interval, it helps to know the simple interval with which it is associated. For example, a perfect 4th will expand to a perfect 11th when either the upper or lower pitch of the interval is moved one octave.

6.63

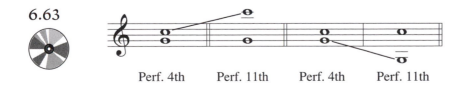

Perf. 4th   Perf. 11th   Perf. 4th   Perf. 11th

A major 6th will expand to a major 13th, and a perfect 5th will expand to a perfect 12th.

6.64a

Maj. 6th   Maj. 13th   Maj. 13th   Perf. 5th   Perf. 12th   Perf. 12th

Notice in the first measure of example 6.64a that the simple interval of the major 6th expands to the compound interval of the major 13th either by moving the upper pitch (D) up one octave or by moving the lower pitch (F) down one octave. In the second measure, the perfect 5th expands to a perfect 12th in the same manner. Simple intervals expand to their respective compound intervals as follows:

2nd⟶9th   3rd⟶10th   4th⟶11th   5th⟶12th   6th⟶13th

The simple interval of the 7th would expand to a 14th, but this is not a common practice in tonal music and has been omitted from the list.

The ability to quickly compute and construct compound intervals is important to musicians primarily within the context of how they occur in chords. Even though you have not yet studied chord construction, you may observe in example 6.64b how the compound interval of the major 13th would appear within a 13th chord.

6.64b

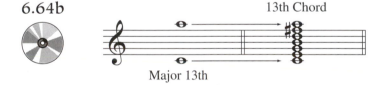

13th Chord

Major 13th

It is not unusual in certain styles of music for a vocalist to sing the interval of a 9th above a given pitch. Also, instrumentalists may be asked to play pitches that are located a 13th or ♯11 ("sharp eleven"—the 11th raised one half step) above a given pitch. Because compound intervals contain pitches that are separated by distances greater than the octave, it is not efficient to construct or identify them using the process you learned earlier in this chapter, because it would necessitate counting numerous lines and spaces. If you were asked to construct the correct pitches located a major 13th, ♯11, or a 9th above C, it would require an inordinate amount of time to compute them, and you might run the risk of making a mistake in counting all of the lines and spaces between pitches.

Please observe in example 6.65 how far apart the pitches of these intervals appear.

6.65

13th   ♯11th   9th

Principle *11*

A compound interval may be reduced to its simple interval by subtracting the number 7.

One effective way of simplifying the process of identifying and constructing a compound interval is to reduce it to its associated simple interval by subtracting the number 7. For example, the compound interval of the 13th would reduce to the 6th, the ♯11 to the ♯4, and the 9th to the 2nd. This technique applies to *all* compound intervals written within two octaves, regardless of their quality (major, minor, diminished, or augmented) and provides musicians an efficient means of quickly identifying these distant pitches.

Let's look at a few examples that will illustrate the benefits of using this process.

Skill Development

Suppose you are asked to sing or play the ♯11 (augmented 11th) above D. How would you quickly determine the pitch?

Process

Step 1. The pitch located at ♯11 is more than an octave above D. By subtracting 7 from ♯11, you will bring the pitch down one octave and quickly determine that it is the same as ♯4 above D (or an augmented fourth above D). It is much quicker to figure out what ♯4 is than to count up to ♯11! Before you are able to determine what the ♯4 above D actually is, you must first construct a perfect 4th above D and then raise it one half step.

Step 2. Count up a 4th from D (do not forget to count D as scale degree 1) and you will arrive on the pitch G.

Step 3. Check the key signature for D and make certain that G is diatonic in this key. The key signature for D has two sharps (F♯ and C♯), and G is in this key. The interval between D and G is therefore a perfect 4th.

6.66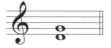

Perf. 4th above D

Step 4. The G will require a sharp, because you have been asked to construct a ♯11 above D. By changing G to G♯, you will have created the ♯4 that is the ♯11 down one octave.

6.67

Aug. 4th

Step 5. Now place the G♯ up one octave and you will have constructed the ♯11 above D.

6.68a

♯11 above D

The practice of calling an augmented 11th a ♯11 (sharp 11), or, for that matter, calling a minor 9th a ♭9 (flat nine), is very common.

You might be wondering why the interval of the ♯11 (sharp eleven) is not called an augmented 11th. It is, in fact, just that: an augmented 11th above the lower pitch! Chromatically altered compound intervals of the 9th, 11th and 13th are often identified by their accidentals rather than by their respective interval qualities; particularly in **commercial music** or **jazz**, as they occur within the context of an **extended chord**.

Sometimes it is more practical for musicians to identify how a compound interval appears within a chord rather than to determine its exact quality (major, minor, etc.). Chords will be discussed in the next chapter, and this issue will become clearer to you.

Example 6.68b illustrates not only how it is possible to identify the exact distance of an interval, but also how it is possible to indicate only the numerical distance and the chromatic alteration (sharp or flat) of the pitch when it is placed within a chord.

6.68b

The interval of the augmented 11th	F♯ is called the ♯11	The interval of the Minor 9th	D♭ is called the ♭9.

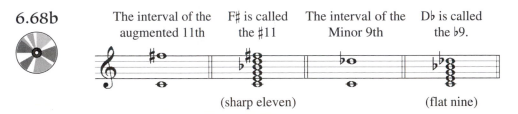

(sharp eleven) (flat nine)

Imagine that you have been asked to sing or play the 13th of an E chord. This means you quickly need to identify the interval of the major 13th above E. You will have to count a long way up from E to determine the correct pitch, and you might make a mistake in computing the exact distance. Let's apply the method you are learning and see how simple it is to quickly compute the correct pitch of a compound interval.

Skill Development

Identify the pitch that is located a 13th (this implies a major 13th) above E.

Process

Step 1. The interval of the 13th is a compound interval (because it exceeds the octave). In order to determine the upper pitch, you must subtract 7 from 13. By doing so, you now know that the pitch that will be located a 13th above E is the same pitch located a 6th above it, but written up one octave.

Step 2. Count up six scale degrees from E to C.

6.69

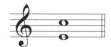

Step 3. Now you must make this interval major, because the interval of the 13th is an implied major interval. Check the key signature for E, and you will see that C needs to be sharped.

Step 4. Place a sharp in front of C. You have constructed a major 6th.

6.70

Maj. 6th

Step 5. Now, write C♯ up one octave and you will have created the 13th above E.

6.71

Maj. 13th

Exercise 10

Construct the following compound intervals above the given pitches. In each instance, first subtract 7 to arrive at the simple interval associated with each compound interval. Then create the appropriate interval above the given pitch and write it up one octave.

6.72

9th ↑   ♯11 ↑   ♯11 ↑   9th ↑   13th ↑   13th ↑

IDENTIFYING INTERVALS WHEN THE LOWER PITCH HAS NO ASSOCIATED KEY SIGNATURE

Until now, the identification and construction of intervals have been accomplished by determining the diatonic key relationship between the upper and lower pitches. The method you have been studying has provided you with intervals in which there are key signatures associated with the lower pitches. In many instances, there will *not* be an associated key signature for the lower pitch, and you will need to modify the method you have learned.

In example 6.73 you will observe an interval in which the lower pitch is G♯

and the upper pitch is E♯. This interval is a 6th, but what is its quality? Is it major, minor, augmented, or diminished? The method you have learned up to this point requires you to first construct a major 6th above the lower pitch. In order to accomplish this, you must determine if the upper pitch, E♯, is in the key of G♯. If E♯ is in the key of G♯, then the interval will be major.

Skill Development

What is the key signature for G♯? *There is no key signature for G♯!* In this situation, the method you have studied needs to be slightly adjusted, because key signatures do not exist for every pitch of the chromatic scale!

 6.73

In order to identify the interval in example 6.73, you will need to add a few steps to the method you have learned. Let's carefully examine the technique for identifying an interval of this type.

Process

Step 1. First determine the basic numerical distance of the interval and then remove all accidentals (sharps and flats) associated with the pitches. The basic interval is a 6th.

6.74

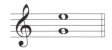

Step 2. Identify this interval as you would any interval. (If you need to review this process, return to the beginning of this chapter.) Since E is in the key of the lower pitch, G, this interval is a major 6th.

Step 3. Next, apply the sharps to both pitches, and you will have raised them one half step but not altered the distance between them. The interval between G♯ and E♯ is still a major 6th.

6.75

Maj. 6th

Remember, if G–E is a major 6th, and both pitches are altered in the same manner, the distance between them remains the same. Therefore, G♯ to E♯ must be a major 6th. In fact, for the same reason, G♭–E♭ is also a major 6th!

 6.76

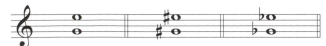

These intervals are Major 6ths.

The method of first removing accidentals from both pitches of an interval, when the lower does not have an associated key signature, will facilitate identification or construction of any interval.

Skill Development

Identify the following interval.

6.77a

Process

Step 1. Identify the numerical distance of the interval. It is a 3rd.

Step 2. Observe that there is no key signature for the lower pitch, F♭. Remove the flats from both pitches. You now have the pitches F and A.

6.77b

Step 3. Determine the quality of this interval. Since the upper pitch, A, is in the key of the lower pitch, F, this interval is a major 3rd.

6.78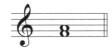

Maj. 3rd

Step 4. Now place flats before both pitches, and change them to F♭ and A♭. You still will have a major 3rd, because the distance between the two pitches has not changed.

6.79

Maj. 3rd

Step 5. Lower the A♭ again one half step by flatting it and changing it to A♭♭. You now have brought the major 3rd of F♭–A♭ together one half step. The interval may now be identified as a minor 3rd.

6.80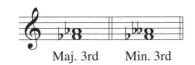

Maj. 3rd   Min. 3rd

Exercise 11

Identify the following intervals using the same process.

6.81a

6.81b

CONSTRUCTING INTERVALS ABOVE PITCHES HAVING NO ASSOCIATED KEY SIGNATURE

Constructing intervals above pitches in which there is no associated key signature for the lower pitch will require you to use almost the same method as for identifying intervals. When constructing or identifying intervals of this type, you must always first remove the accidental from the lower pitch, construct the desired interval over the new pitch, and then adjust the interval as needed.

Skill Development

Construct a diminished 4th above B♯.

Process

Step 1. Because there is no key signature for the pitch B♯, remove the sharp and place B and the pitch that is located a 4th above it (E) on the staff.

6.82

Step 2. Now construct a *perfect 4th* above B. The perfect 4th above B is E, because E is in the key of B.

6.83

Perf. 4th

Step 3. Because your task is to construct a diminished 4th above B♯, first construct the pitch that is located a diminished 4th above B. This pitch is E♭, because a perfect interval made smaller by one half step becomes diminished (**Principle 6**).

6.84

Dim. 4th

Step 4. Now apply a sharp to both pitches: E♭ will be raised to E♮, and B will be raised to B♯. By doing this, you will have changed the pitch names, but not altered the distance between them. You will have constructed a diminished 4th above B♯.

6.85

Dim. 4th

Skill Development

Construct a minor 7th above D♯.

Process

Step 1. Because there is no key signature for the lower pitch D♯, remove the sharp and place D and the pitch that is located a 7th above it (C) on the staff.

6.86

Step 2. Now construct a minor 7th above D. To do this, first construct a major 7th above D. This pitch is C♯ because it is sharped in the key of D.

6.87

Maj. 7th

Step 3. Now remove the sharp from C♯ and you will have constructed the interval of a minor 7th above D. (A major interval brought closer together by one half step becomes minor.)

6.88

Min. 7th

Step 4. Now place a sharp in front of each pitch. Although the pitches have changed, the distance between them has not! The interval remains a minor 7th.

6.89

Min. 7th

Exercise 12

Construct the indicated intervals above the following pitches using the same method.

6.90a

Perf. 5th ↑   Aug. 4th ↑   Maj. 6th ↑   Min. 7th ↑

6.90b

Maj. 6th ↑   Aug. 5th ↑   Perf. 4th ↑   Maj. 7th ↑

INVERSIONS OF SIMPLE INTERVALS

The **inversion** of a simple interval occurs when the two pitches have exchanged their original positions, so that the pitch that was originally on the bottom now is on the top, and the pitch that was originally on the top now is on the bottom!

Confused? Think of the pitches as having been flip-flopped. The flipping of the pitches may occur in one of two ways: (1) the lower pitch of an interval may be written up one octave, or (2) the upper pitch of an interval may be written down one octave.

6.91

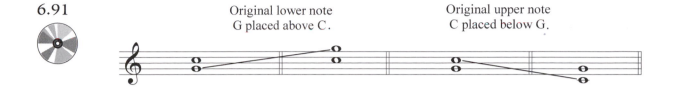

When an interval is inverted, regardless of its quality (major, minor, diminished, or perfect), it produces another interval that, when numerically summed with the original interval, will add up to the number 9. The prime will invert to the octave: the 2nd will invert to the 7th; the 3rd to the 6th; the 4th to the 5th; the 5th to the 4th; the 6th to the 3rd; the 7th to the 2nd; and the octave to the prime. Please observe in the first and third measures of example 6.91 that the interval of the perfect 4th (G–C), which inverts to a perfect 5th (measures 2 and 4), adds up to a sum of 9.

Principle *12*

An interval and its inversion will add up to the number 9.

In every measure of example 6.92, the lower pitch of the first interval has been moved up one octave, resulting in inversions that add up to the number 9. *The same interval would have resulted if the upper pitch had been moved down one octave.*

6.92

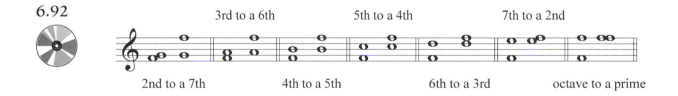

Principle *13*

Every simple interval shares a reciprocity with its inversion. A major interval inverts to a minor; a minor inverts to a major; an augmented inverts to a diminished; and a diminished inverts to an augmented. The perfect intervals invert to perfect intervals.

Principle 13 is illustrated in the following table:

Interval Inversion Reciprocity Table

Major ⟷ *Minor*

Major 2nd ⟷ Minor 7th

Major 3rd ⟷ Minor 6th

Perfect ⟷ *Perfect*

Perfect Octave ⟷ Perfect Prime

Perfect 4th ⟷ Perfect 5th

Augmented ⟷ *Diminished*

Augmented Prime ⟷ Diminished Octave

Augmented 2nd ⟷ Diminished 7th

Augmented 3rd ⟷ Diminished 6th

Augmented 4th ⟷ Diminished 5th

Augmented 5th ⟷ Diminished 4th

Augmented 6th ⟷ Diminished 3rd

Augmented 7th ⟷ Diminished 2nd

In each example illustrated in the Interval Inversion Reciprocity Table, the original interval plus its inversion add up to the number 9!

From now on, interval qualities will be identified with the following abbreviations:

M = Major   **m** = Minor   **P** = Perfect   **A** = Augmented   **D** = Diminished
DA = Doubly Augmented   **DD** = Doubly Diminished

Here are some examples of interval inversion reciprocity.

6.93

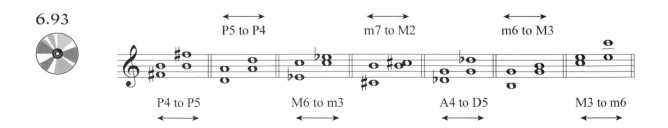

P5 to P4   m7 to M2   m6 to M3

P4 to P5   M6 to m3   A4 to D5   M3 to m6

Constructing Simple Intervals below a Given Pitch

Up to this point, you have learned how to identify and construct intervals *above a given pitch.* In this section, you will learn how to construct simple intervals *below a given pitch.*

There are two common methods of constructing intervals below a given pitch. You may use the one that makes more logical sense to you. Ultimately, both methods are important to know, because in certain musical situations one method may be more efficient than the other.

The two methods of constructing an interval below a given pitch are:

1. Construct the inversion of an interval above a given pitch, then write the upper pitch down one octave.
2. Place a pitch below a given pitch at the required numeric distance, identify the interval, then adjust the lower pitch as necessary to construct the desired interval.

Method One: Using the inversion process to construct an interval below a given pitch.

Principle 14

To construct an interval below a given pitch, determine the inversion of the interval above the given pitch, then write the upper pitch down one octave.

Skill Development

Let's apply **Principle 14** and construct a diminished 4th below B♭.

Process

Step 1. **Principle 14** states that before constructing an interval below a pitch, you first need to construct its inversion above the given pitch. Therefore, construct the inversion of a diminished 4th, which is an augmented 5th, above B♭. (If this inversion relationship is unclear to you, review examples 6.91 and 6.92 and the Interval Inversion Reciprocity Table on page 284.) Place B♭ on the staff, count up five scale degrees (count B♭ as scale degree 1), and place F on the staff. You have now constructed a 5th, but you need to determine what an augmented 5th should look like.

6.94

Step 2. In order to identify the interval you have created in example 6.94, you first must determine what a perfect 5th above B♭ would be. Check the key signature for B♭, and determine how F occurs in that key. The key signature for B♭ is two flats (B♭ and E♭). The pitch F is in the key (scale) of B♭, and therefore is a perfect 5th above B♭.

6.95

P5

Step 3. You need to construct the interval of the augmented 5th above B♭. By sharping the pitch F, you will increase the distance between the pitches of the perfect 5th by one half step, thereby making the interval augmented.

6.96

A5

Step 4. Now write the upper pitch, F♯, down one octave, and place it below B♭. You have successfully constructed a diminished 4th below B♭. Observe that the augmented 5th above B♭ has inverted to a diminished 4th below B♭.

6.97

The F♯ above B♭ has been moved down one octave to create a diminished 4th below B♭

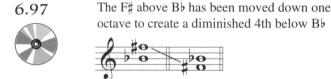

A5   D4

Skill Development

Construct a major 7th below G.

Process

Step 1. In order to construct a major 7th below G, you first will have to construct its inversion, a minor 2nd, above G. Begin by writing G on the first space above the staff and then placing the pitch A above it. This interval is a 2nd.

6.98

Step 2. You have constructed a 2nd, but have not determined the quality of the interval. Is it major, minor, augmented, or diminished? Because you need to construct a minor 2nd above G, first determine the pitch that would be a major 2nd above it. Check the key signature for G (G has an F♯ in the key signature). You will determine that the pitch A is diatonic in the key of G and therefore is a major 2nd above G.

6.99

M2

Step 3. Make the major 2nd a minor interval by bringing the pitches closer together one half step. Remember, you cannot alter the pitch G, because your task is to construct a major 7th below it! Decrease the size of the major interval G to A by one half step by changing the A to A♭. The interval now is a minor 2nd.

6.100

m2

Step 4. Now move the A♭ down one octave below G, and you will have constructed the major 7th below G. Do you see how the minor 2nd above G has inverted to a major 7th below G?

6.101

M7

Exercise 13

Construct intervals *below* the given pitches using Method One.

6.102a

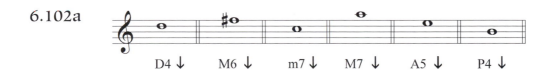

D4 ↓   M6 ↓   m7 ↓   M7 ↓   A5 ↓   P4 ↓

6.102b   Be careful—this example is in the bass clef! ☺

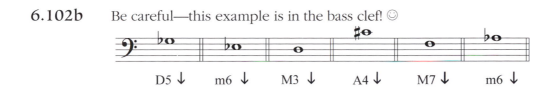

D5 ↓   m6 ↓   M3 ↓   A4 ↓   M7 ↓   m6 ↓

METHOD TWO: Construct an interval below a given pitch without using the inversion process. Place a pitch at the required numerical distance below the given pitch, identify the interval, and then adjust the lower pitch as necessary to construct the desired interval.

Sometimes it is quicker and more efficient to not use inversions when constructing intervals below a given pitch. In Method Two, you will immediately place the pitch of the interval you are trying to create below the given pitch, analyze what you have constructed, and then adjust it as necessary. Having a good command of the key signatures will facilitate this process and make constructing intervals below a given pitch quick and easy!

Principle **15**

To construct an interval below a given pitch, place a pitch at the correct numerical distance below the given pitch, analyze the quality of the interval, then adjust the lower pitch as necessary.

Skill Development

Construct a major 6th below C, using Method Two.

Process

Step 1. Count down a 6th from C, and you will arrive on the first line, E. Check the key signature for the key of E major, and you will observe that the interval of E–C♯ is a major 6th, because C♯ is in the key of E major. E–C therefore must be a minor 6th. If you need to review major and minor intervals, please refer to **Principles 3** and **4**.

6.103   By placing E under C you
have created a minor 6th.

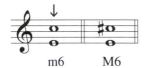

Step 2. Because your goal is to construct a major 6th below C, the minor 6th (E–C) must be made larger by one half step. Recall that a minor interval *is* a major interval, brought closer together by one half step (**Principle 4**), so you must reverse the process and make this minor interval major by making it one half step *larger.* By lowering the pitch E to E♭, you have created a major 6th below C.

6.104

Skill Development

Let's try another example using Method Two. Construct a diminished 5th below D.

Process

Step 1. Place D on the staff and count down a fifth to G. Identify the interval you have constructed by determining if the upper pitch, D, is in the key of G. The key signature for G is one sharp (F♯), and D is diatonic in the key of G. The interval you have constructed is a perfect 5th.

6.105

P5

Step 2. You have been asked to construct a diminished 5th below D. Now you must bring the perfect 5th closer together one half step by *raising the lower pitch G to G♯.* You must not alter the upper pitch D, because you were asked to construct a diminished 5th below it. You now have constructed a diminished 5th below D. Recall that a perfect interval is never major or minor, and that when the distance between the two pitches of this interval is decreased by one half step, it becomes diminished! Review **Principle 6** if needed.

6.106

D5

Exercise 14

Construct the following intervals *below* the given pitches using Method Two.

6.107a

A4 ↓   m6 ↓   M7 ↓   D7 ↓   A5 ↓   P4 ↓

6.107b   Be careful—this example is in the bass clef! ☺

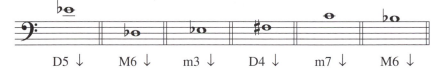

D5 ↓   M6 ↓   m3 ↓   D4 ↓   m7 ↓   M6 ↓

Deciding which method to use in constructing an interval below a given pitch will be your choice. After you are comfortable with both methods, you will know which one is more appropriate and efficient in a given situation.

THE TRITONE: "THE DEVIL IN MUSIC"

Because of its unique **dissonance** (musical tension), the **tritone**, known in the Middle Ages as the "The Devil in Music" (*Diabolus in Musica*), was forbidden in the music for the Roman Catholic Church. Although its harmonic and melodic implications will not be addressed in this textbook, it merits attention regarding its identification and construction.

Principle 16

The tritone is an interval comprising three whole steps, that produces the augmented 4th or the diminished 5th.

The interval below is an augmented 4th and may be referred to as a tritone.

6.108

A4   Three whole steps above C is a tritone.

When the interval is inverted, it retains its three whole steps but produces a diminished 5th. (Refer to the Interval Inversion Reciprocity Table on page 284).

6.109

D5

The interval of the tritone, regardless of how it is spelled (as an augmented 4th or diminished 5th), results in a musical tension between two pitches that is identified as a **dissonance**. When the pitches of the tritone are correctly resolved, they will produce a **consonance** (a lack of tension). If it is possible to play the augmented 4th and its inversion, the diminished 5th, on the piano or a guitar, you will clearly hear this dissonance, and also the direction in which each pitch has to move in order to resolve to a consonance.

When the tritone occurs in music, either as an augmented 4th or diminished 5th, the dissonance created by the interval is generally handled very carefully (and often creatively) by composers and arrangers, and results in beauty and harmonic interest for the listener.

Exercise 15

Construct the tritone as an augmented 4th above the following pitches. (If you need to review augmented intervals, refer to **Principle 7**.)

6.110a

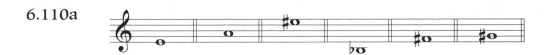

6.110b   Be careful—this example is in the bass clef! ☺

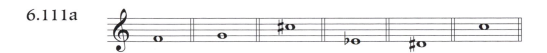

Now construct the tritone as a diminished 5th over the following pitches. (Refer to **Principle 6** if you need to review diminished intervals.)

6.111a

6.111b

Principle *17*

Both pitches of the tritone, when written as an augmented 4th, will resolve outward by one diatonic half step. Both pitches of the tritone, when written as a diminished 5th, will resolve inward by one diatonic half step.

In the following example, observe that each pitch of the tritone has resolved outward one diatonic half step to create the interval of the 6th. The upper pitch, B, has resolved upward to C, and the lower pitch, F, has resolved downward to E. The *outward diatonic half step movement of both pitches* is the correct resolution of the tritone when it is written as an augmented 4th.

6.112   The augmented 4th resolving outward

A4

Observe in example 6.113 that when the pitches of the tritone are written as a diminished 5th, it is necessary to resolve them *inward by one diatonic half step.*

6.113   The diminished 5th resolving inward

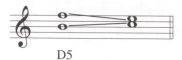

D5

Exercise 16

Resolve the following augmented 4ths to their appropriate consonances.

6.114

Resolve the following diminished 5ths to their appropriate consonances.

6.115

CONSONANCE AND DISSONANCE

The terms consonance and dissonance are used to describe the general qualities of resolution (stability) and tension (instability) occurring among two or more sounds in music. In some cases the perceived differences between these terms are subtle, but in general, music in which there is a calming effect with a lack of discordant sounds is said to be consonant. Consonance is achieved when the ear perceives a type of musical stasis.

The harmonic intervals that produce a consonant effect include the **perfect consonances**: perfect prime, perfect 4th (depending on specific musical contexts), perfect 5th, perfect octave; and the **imperfect consonances**: all major and minor 3rds and 6ths. All other intervals, such as the perfect 4th (occurring over a bass pitch), and all types of 2nds, 7ths, and augmented and diminished intervals are identified as dissonances because they create harmonic tension. Harsh-sounding chords and various combinations of instruments playing discordant sounds also are said to be dissonant.

Historically, composers and arrangers have created imaginative ways of preparing and resolving dissonances. Master composers such as Josquin Desprez (c. 1440–1521), Giovanni Palestrina (c. 1525–1594), Johann Sebastian Bach (1685–1750), Wolfgang Mozart (1756–1791), Ludwig van Beethoven (1770–1827), Giacomo Puccini (1858–1924), Aaron Copland (1900–1990), and big band composer Duke Ellington (1899–1974), to name but a few, have provided memorable examples of how music can be enriched by the careful balance between consonant and dissonant elements in musical compositions. Taking the time to listen to any of their compositions and focusing on this aspect of the music will be a rewarding experience.

Many composers, throughout the history of music, have disregarded the resolution of dissonances and exploited their inherent tensions to produce new and exciting musical expressions. A substantial amount of music from the late nineteenth and early twentieth centuries contains unresolved dissonances that defined the stylistic harmonic practices of that time. Composers such as Claude Debussy (1862–1918), Maurice Ravel (1875–1937), Igor Stravinsky (1882–1971), and Arnold Schoenberg (1874–1951) took bold steps in exploring, and, in the case of Schoenberg, exploiting, the use of dissonance in their music.

Modern composers and songwriters have employed and embraced dissonance to varying degrees in virtually all musical genres. Unresolved harmonic and melodic dissonances in the chord structures and melodies of jazz and popular music are accepted as stylistic idioms. Jazz composers frequently use the 7th, 9th, and ♯11ths of chords (dissonant intervals occurring over the **root** of a chord) to construct beautiful and memorable melodies resulting in a style of music very different from the more traditional styles of musical composition.

Example 6.116 illustrates a type of 9th chord that contains a dissonant 7th (F♯) and 9th (A) above the lowest pitch, G. These dissonant intervals are considered consonances in jazz.

6.116   9th Chord

When performing the "blues," singers and instrumentalists nearly always exploit the ♭3, ♭5, and ♭7 of a chord (lowered steps 3, 5, and 7 of a major scale, called "blue notes") and do not resolve the dissonances produced by performing these pitches against chords containing ♮3 and ♮5 (pitches on scale degree steps 3 and 5 without a sharp or flat). This dissonance is a fundamental and very effective component of the blues style. Chords will be addressed in the next chapter and this concept will become much clearer to you.

6.117

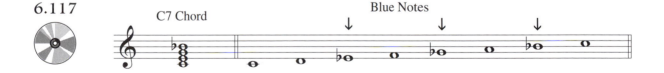

The history of Western music (music from Europe) clearly indicates that a great deal of what used to be considered dissonance in music has been, since the early twentieth century, accepted as consonant! This acceptance of musical dissonance also is reflected in society's mores and cultural expressions. Many of the social taboos (dissonances) of a century ago, such as avoiding vulgar language in everyday conversation, are considered old-fashioned, because in today's world nearly everything seems acceptable (consonant). Music has not escaped this trend, but rather has become a harbinger, in accelerating it through much of the popular music of young adults. What used to be thought of as dissonant, in language and music, has very naturally, along with society's changing culture, evolved to being accepted as normal (consonant).

Many older individuals living in the middle of the twentieth century regarded the rock-and-roll of the early 1950s as "dissonant music." Compared to the rock music of the late twentieth and early twenty-first centuries, the rock music of the 1950s seems relatively tame (consonant). Likewise, the big swing bands in the 1930s and 1940s were slow to gain acceptance with the older generation. The music of Stan Kenton and Duke Ellington (particularly Billy Strayhorn's compositions) was clearly more dissonant than the "sweet" and "swing" sounds of the Glenn Miller and Tommy Dorsey bands, but eventually people learned to enjoy and embrace both styles. In order to fully appreciate these differences, you can seek out a few recordings and compare the approaches to using consonance and dissonance.

The history of music clearly indicates a sustained pattern of change, growth, and development, and we should expect nothing less of the future. Tonal music has survived the twentieth century's preoccupation with **atonality** (music without a defined key center or clear form), and the basic precepts of consonance and dissonance are still intact in the twenty-first century.

REVIEW OF PRINCIPLES

Principle 1
The distance between two pitches that are written or played consecutively is called a melodic interval.

Principle 2
The distance between two pitches that are written or played simultaneously is called a harmonic interval.

Principle 3
An interval is major when the upper pitch is in the key (major scale) of the lower pitch (except when the interval is a 4th, 5th, prime, or octave).

Principle 4
Minor intervals are 2nds, 3rds, 6ths, and 7ths (or their compound equivalents) that are one half step smaller than their corresponding major intervals.

Principle 5
When the upper pitch of a 4th, 5th, or octave is in the key of the lower pitch, the interval is called perfect. (This applies to the prime even though there is no actual distance between the two pitches.)

Principle 6
When the pitches of a minor or perfect interval are brought closer together by one half step, the interval is called diminished.

Principle 7
When the distance between the two pitches of a major or perfect interval is increased by one half step, the interval is called augmented.

Principle 8
An augmented interval made larger by one half step is called doubly augmented.

Principle 9
A diminished interval made smaller by one half step is called doubly diminished.

Principle 10
Compound intervals are intervals that are greater than the octave. They are identified and constructed in the same manner as simple intervals.

Principle 11
A compound interval may be reduced to its simple interval by subtracting the number 7.

Principle 12
An interval and its inversion will add up to the number 9.

Principle 13
Every simple interval shares a reciprocity with its inversion. A major interval inverts to a minor; a minor inverts to a major; an augmented inverts to a diminished; and a diminished inverts to an augmented. The perfect intervals invert to perfect intervals.

Principle 14
To construct an interval below a given pitch, determine the inversion of the interval above the given pitch, then write the upper pitch down one octave.

Principle 15
To construct an interval below a given pitch, place a pitch at the correct numerical distance below the given pitch, analyze the quality of the interval, then adjust the lower pitch as necessary.

Principle 16
The tritone is an interval comprising three whole steps, that produces the augmented 4th or the diminished 5th.

Principle 17
Both pitches of the tritone, when written as an augmented 4th, will resolve outward by one diatonic half step. Both pitches of the tritone, when written as a diminished 5th, will resolve inward by one diatonic half step.

ANSWER SHEETS TO CHAPTER 6

Exercise 5

6.30a

6.30b

Exercise 6

6.38

Exercise 7

6.46a

6.46b

Exercise 8

6.53

Exercise 9

6.59a

6.59b

Exercise 10

6.72

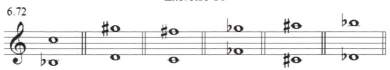

Exercise 11

6.81a

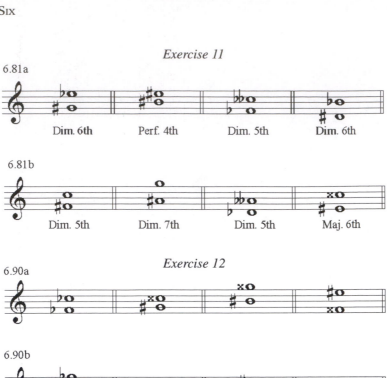

Dim. 6th   Perf. 4th   Dim. 5th   Dim. 6th

6.81b

Dim. 5th   Dim. 7th   Dim. 5th   Maj. 6th

Exercise 12

6.90a

6.90b

Exercise 13

6.102a

6.102b

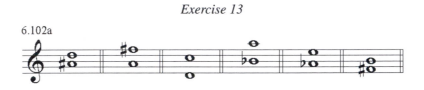

Exercise 14

6.107a

6.107b

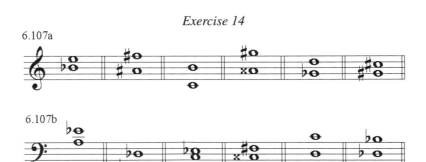

Exercise 15

6.110a

6.110b

6.111a

6.111b

Exercise 16

6.114

6.115

WORKSHEETS FOR CHAPTER 6

Name _____

1. Identify the following intervals.

_____ _____ _____ _____ _____ _____

_____ _____ _____ _____ _____ _____

2. Construct the following intervals above the given pitches.

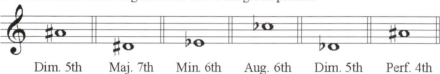

Dim. 5th   Maj. 7th   Min. 6th   Aug. 6th   Dim. 5th   Perf. 4th

Aug. 5th   Min. 7th   Min. 2nd   Perf. 4th   Dim. 6th   Maj. 3rd

3. Construct the following intervals below the given pitches.

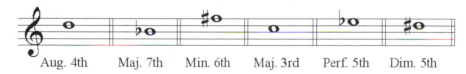

Aug. 4th   Maj. 7th   Min. 6th   Maj. 3rd   Perf. 5th   Dim. 5th

Min. 7th   Maj. 3rd   Min. 6th   Dim. 5th   Perf. 5th   Dim. 4th

Name _____

4. Identify the following compound intervals.

5. Construct **compound** intervals above the following pitches.

Maj. 9th   Aug. 11th   Maj. 13th   Min. 10th   Min. 9th   Maj. 13th

Aug. 12th   Min. 13th   Maj. 9th   Min. 10th   Perf. 11th   Maj. 10th

6. Circle the **intervals** that are tritones.

7. Construct **the indicated tritone** above the following pitches.

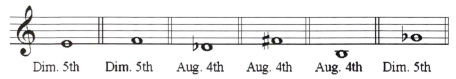

Dim. 5th   Dim. 5th   Aug. 4th   Aug. 4th   Aug. 4th   Dim. 5th

8. Correctly resolve the tritone written as a diminished 5th.

9. Correctly resolve the tritone written as an augmented 4th.

Find additional Skill Development Drills on the
accompanying CD-ROM and on the book companion
Web site: http://music.wadsworth.com/kinney1e.

7

Triads

Never look at the trombones, it only encourages them! —Richard Strauss

The trombones are too sacred for frequent use. —Felix Mendelssohn

A **triad** is a three-note chord consisting of a root, 3rd, and 5th, and is constructed using the basic interval of the 3rd. Most of the music heard through the media (movies, radio, television, etc.) utilizes triads to (1) provide harmonic support to a melody, (2) establish a sense of tonality (major or minor) and key center, and (3) furnish a sense of harmonic progression.

The harmonic practice of constructing triads in 3rds, known as **tertian harmony**, has helped define our concept of tonal music for at least four hundred years. Triads continue to be an indispensable component of nearly all the music we hear on a daily basis, even though many twentieth- and twenty-first-century composers have explored alternatives to traditional music composition such as **chord clusters**, **microtonality**, **atonality**, and **polytonality**, to name a few.

Since the late nineteenth century, traditional and nontraditional composers also have written tonal music based on the basic interval of the 4th. This **quartal harmonic** concept produces very interesting sonorities in numerous genres of music, and is easily identifiable in jazz. When quartal and tertian approaches are combined, the resulting harmony produces a hybrid sound that is distinctive and expressive. If possible, try playing the following examples on the piano and you will immediately hear the differences among the sonorities.

7.1

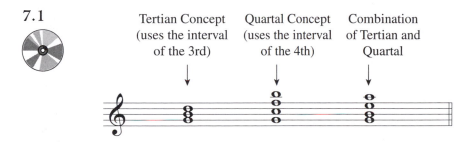

Although there are a number of possible approaches to developing an understanding of triads, this chapter will use the major key signatures as the basic tool for their identification and construction. Employing the key signatures is

very efficient, accurate, and fast, and the process will be familiar to you because it is basically the same approach used to identify and construct the intervals presented in Chapter 6. The major key signatures are listed below, but you must continually review them until you can easily recall them from memory.

7.2

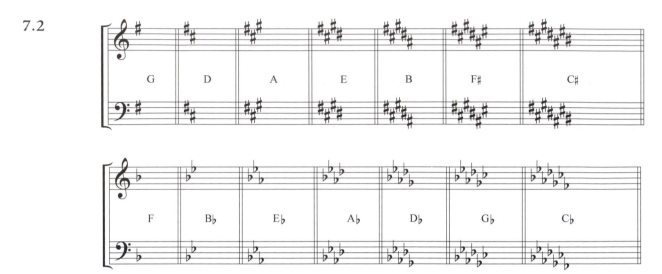

TRIAD TYPES

There are four basic triad types: **major**, **minor**, **diminished**, and **augmented**. Each of these triad types is comprised of a root, 3rd and 5th that are "stacked up" in thirds with the root as the lowest pitch. When the root is located on a line, the 3rd and 5th will also be located on a line. When the root is located on a space, the 3rd and 5th also occur on spaces. Please observe this in the following example.

7.3

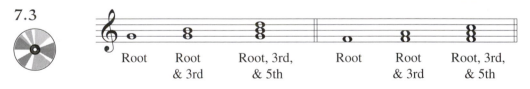

In the following example, observe how the root, 3rd, and 5th illustrated in the triads in example 7.3 are the same pitches that are located on the degrees of the scale associated with the root (step 1 of a scale):

7.4

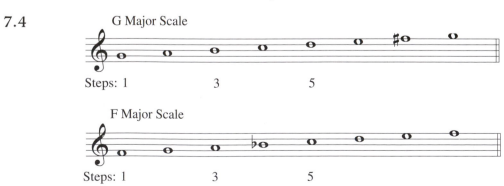

QUALITIES OF TRIADS

In the following example, the root of the triad is C. The 3rd and 5th have been added by placing a pitch on each of the next two staff lines above C.

7.5

Observe that E is a major 3rd above C, and that G is a minor 3rd above E. Triads with this configuration (a major 3rd and a minor 3rd "stacked" above the root) are called *major*.

7.6

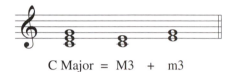

C Major = M3 + m3

Although this observation of the 3rds is important, it also is true that the pitch E is a major 3rd above C, and G is a perfect 5th above C. The pitches E and G are diatonic to the key of C major (they occur in the C scale).

7.7

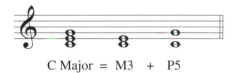

C Major = M3 + P5

In most instances, it is much quicker to identify triads by determining if the 3rd and 5th are diatonic to the root (in which case the triad is major) than it is to identify the types of 3rds constructed above the root.

Principle 1

A triad is major when the 3rd and 5th are in the major key of the root.

Recall that the musical alphabet consists of the pitch names A through G. The key signature of a piece of music indicates which of these pitches (if any) must be altered by a sharp or flat in order to establish the sense of a tonic (key center). For example, the key of G major, which requires an F♯, contains all of the pitches of the musical alphabet, A–G, *except F,* which must be replaced by F♯. Although the pitch F is not at all associated with the key of G, F♯ is vital to establishing G as a tonal center. All of the remaining pitches of the musical alphabet are in the key of G and are said to be diatonic.

IDENTIFYING MAJOR TRIADS

Skill Development

Let's apply **Principle 1** and identify the quality (major, minor, diminished, and augmented) of the following triad.

7.8

Process

Step 1. First, identify the root of the triad. The root is G because the triad "stacks up" in 3rds above this pitch.

Step 2. Next, establish if the 3rd (B) and the 5th (D) are in the key of G. To determine this, refer to the key signature for G major. You will see that only F is sharped in the key of G. This means that the 3rd (B) and the 5th (D) are unaltered in the key of G and are said to be diatonic.

7.9   Key of G

Step 3. **Principle 1** states that when the 3rd and 5th of a triad are in the major key of the root, the triad is major. The triad in example 7.8 is G major.

Skill Development

Identify the following triad.

7.10

Process

Step 1. Identify the root of the triad. The root is A♭ because the triad "stacks up" in 3rds above this pitch.

Step 2. Determine if the 3rd (C) and the 5th (E♭) are in the key of the root (A♭).

Step 3. Check the key signature of A♭, and you will see that it has four flats.

7.11

Step 4. Observe that the 3rd (C) and the 5th (E♭) in example 7.10 *are* in the key of A♭. (Remember that key signatures indicate the pitches of the musical alphabet that need to be altered in a particular key.) Because C and E♭ *are* diatonic in the key of A♭, the triad is A♭ major!

Exercise 1

Circle the major triads in the following example. Remember, in order for the triad to be major, both the 3rd and 5th must be in the key of the root.

7.12

CONSTRUCTING MAJOR TRIADS

In the previous section you learned how to identify major triads by determining if the 3rd and 5th were in the key of the root. In actuality, you were mentally constructing major triads above the root in order to identify them. The following information will seem more like a review rather than a new method for constructing triads, but this is a very important part of the process of learning to quickly identify and construct triads. In this section, you will once again be applying **Principle 1**: A triad is major when the 3rd and 5th are in the major key of the root.

Skill Development

Let's construct a major triad above E.

Process

Step 1. Place the root E on the staff and write in the 3rd (G) and 5th (B) above it.

7.13

Step 2. You have constructed a triad stacked in 3rds, but have not yet determined its quality. In order for this triad to be major, the 3rd and 5th must be in the key of the root (E)! Check the key signature for E, and you will see that G is sharped and that B is diatonic. Remember, a pitch is said to be diatonic when it occurs in the scale (key) that you are in. G♯ and B are in the scale of E major and are identified as diatonic pitches.

7.14   Key of E

Step 3. You now must place a sharp in front of G and change it to G♯.

7.15   E Major

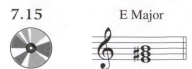

Principle 1 states that when the 3rd and 5th are in the major key of the root, the triad is major. The above triad is E major because the 3rd (G♯) and the 5th (B) are diatonic in the key of E.

Skill Development

Construct a major triad above D♭.

Process

Step 1. Place D♭ on the staff and write in the 3rd (F) and 5th (A) above it.

7.16

Step 2. Determine the key signature for D♭ and check to see if F and A are diatonic in this key. The key signature for D♭ is five flats.

7.17

Step 3. The 3rd (F) is diatonic in the key of D♭, but the 5th (A) is not. It needs to be adjusted to A♭ because A is flatted in the key signature for D♭.

7.18

Step 4. The 3rd (F) and the 5th (A♭) are diatonic in the key of D♭, and therefore the triad is major!

Exercise 2

Construct major triads above the following pitches.

7.19a

7.19b

IDENTIFYING MINOR TRIADS

Minor triads are major triads with the third lowered one half step. Identifying minor triads is a relatively simple task because it is very similar to identifying major triads.

Principle 2

A triad is minor when the 3rd of a major triad has been lowered one half step.

Skill Development

Identify the following triad.

7.20

Process

Step 1. The root of the triad in example 7.20 is F♯. Before you are able to determine the quality of this triad, you must construct an F♯ major triad. Determine the key signature for F♯, and you will see that all pitches of the musical alphabet (A through G) are sharped except for B.

7.21 Key of F♯

Step 2. In order for the triad in example 7.20 to be major, the 3rd and 5th must be in the key of F♯. This means that you will need to change A to A♯ and C to C♯, because this is how they occur in the key of F♯. You now have constructed an F♯ major triad.

7.22 F♯ Major

Step 3. Major triads become minor when the third is lowered one half step (**Principle 2**). In order to change F♯ major into a minor triad, you will need to lower the 3rd (A♯) one half step to A♮. Removing the sharp will lower the pitch one half step. The triad is now minor.

7.23   F♯ Minor

Skill Development

Identify the following triad.

7.24

Process

Step 1. The root of the above triad is B. Before you are able to determine the quality of this triad, you must construct a B major triad. Checking the key signature for B major, you will determine that D and F are sharped.

7.25   Key of B

Step 2. The triad below is B major, because the 3rd and 5th are diatonic pitches in the key of B major.

7.26   B Major

In example 7.24, the triad you are trying to identify *does not* have a sharp in front of the 3rd (D). D♯ has been lowered by one half step. This triad therefore must be minor.

7.27   B Minor

Observe in example 7.28 that the B minor triad is constructed with a minor 3rd between the root and the 3rd, and a major 3rd between the 3rd and the 5th.

7.28

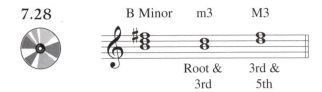

This relationship is opposite to that in major triads, in which the interval between the root and 3rd is major and that between the 3rd and 5th is minor. Please observe this relationship illustrated below in the C major and C minor triads.

7.29

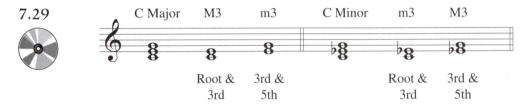

Although this observation provides an interesting comparison between major and minor triads, it is not as essential as understanding **Principle 2**: A minor triad is a major triad with the 3rd lowered one half step.

Exercise 3

Circle the minor triads in the following examples.

7.30a

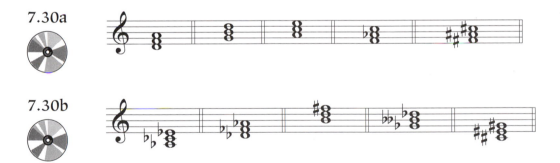

7.30b

IDENTIFYING DIMINISHED TRIADS

In the previous section, you learned that, in major triads, the distance between the root and the 3rd is a major interval, and that between the 3rd and the 5th is a minor interval. In minor triads the distance between the root and the 3rd is a minor interval, and the distance between the 3rd and the 5th is a major interval. Please refer to example 7.29 for review.

Diminished triads consist of two minor 3rds constructed above the root, so that the distance between the root and the 3rd is the same as it is between the 3rd and the 5th. This distance is a minor 3rd.

7.31

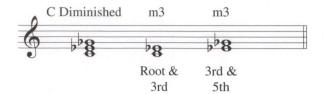

C Diminished   m3   m3

Root &   3rd &
3rd   5th

The knowledge that a diminished triad is constructed of minor 3rds is fundamental to understanding its basic structure and quality. However, to quickly identify a diminished triad, simply think of it as a major triad with the 3rd and 5th lowered one half step.

Principle 3

A triad is diminished when the 3rd and 5th of a major triad have been lowered one half step.

Skill Development

Identify the following triad.

7.32

Process

Step 1. In the above example, the root of the triad is G. In order to determine the triad type (major, minor, diminished, or augmented), you must first construct a major triad on G.

Step 2. A triad is said to be major when its 3rd and 5th are in the key of the root (**Principle 1**). The key signature for the key of G has one sharp (F♯) and its major scale therefore contains both B and D. The G major triad is illustrated in the following example:

7.33   Key of G

G Major

Step 3. Now that you know what the G major triad looks like, compare it to the triad in example 7.32. You will see that the 3rd (B) and 5th (D) have been lowered one half step by placing a flat before each pitch. Any major triad with the 3rd and 5th lowered one half step is said to be diminished (**Principle 3**).

7.34   G Diminished

Skill Development

Let's try another example. Identify the following triad.

7.35

Process

Step 1. In the above example, the root of the triad is D. In order to determine the triad type, you must first construct a D major triad. The D major triad must contain a 3rd and 5th above the root that are diatonic in the key of D. The key signature for D major indicates that both F and C are sharped.

7.36   Key of D

Step 2. The D major triad is shown below.

7.37   D Major

Step 3. Now that you know how a D major triad should appear, compare it to the triad in example 7.35. Notice that the 3rd and 5th have been lowered one half step. The 3rd (F♯) has been lowered to F♮, and the 5th (A) has been lowered to A♭. **Principle 3** states that when the 3rd and 5th of a major triad have been lowered one half step, the triad is diminished.

7.38   D Diminished

Exercise 4

Circle the diminished triads in the example below.

7.39

IDENTIFYING AUGMENTED TRIADS

Augmented triads consist of two major intervals constructed above the root in which the distance between both the root and the 3rd and between the 3rd and the 5th is a major 3rd.

7.40

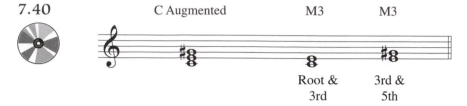

C Augmented   M3   M3

                              Root &   3rd &
                              3rd   5th

When identifying augmented triads it can be somewhat cumbersome to calculate the two major 3rds above the root. It is more efficient to think of this as a major triad with the 5th raised one half step.

Principle 4

A triad is augmented when the 5th of a major triad is raised one half step.

Skill Development

Identify the following triad.

7.41

Process

Step 1. In the above example, the root of the triad is F. In order to determine its quality, construct an F major triad. Check the key signature for F major and determine the correct pitches for the 3rd and 5th. The key of F has one flat (B♭).

7.42   F Major

Step 2. An F major triad consists of an A and C placed above the root because these pitches are diatonic in the key of F.

7.43   F Major

Step 3. Now that you know the correct 3rd and 5th of an F major triad, observe in example 7.44 that the fifth (C) has been raised one half step to C♯. By applying **Principle 4** you will determine that this is an F augmented triad.

7.44   F Augmented

Skill Development

Identify the following triad.

7.45

Process

Step 1. The root of the triad is A♭. Your next step is to determine how an A♭ major triad should look. In order for the above triad to be major, the 3rd and 5th must be in the key of A♭. The key signature for A♭ has four flats.

7.46   Key of A♭

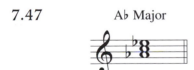

Step 2. An A♭ major triad would therefore have the pitches C and E♭ above the root. These pitches are diatonic in the key of A♭.

7.47   A♭ Major

Step 3. Now that you know what A♭ major looks like, notice that in example 7.45 the 5th (E♭) has been raised one half step to E♮. The triad therefore must be A♭ augmented.

7.48   A♭ Augmented

Exercise 5

Circle the augmented triads in the example below.

7.49

CONSTRUCTING MINOR, DIMINISHED, AND AUGMENTED TRIADS

In this chapter you have learned to identify the four triad types and construct major triads. In this section, you will be asked to construct the remaining triad types. Before you continue, please review the four principles you have studied up to this point: **Principle 1**: A triad is major when the 3rd and 5th are in the major key of the root; **Principle 2**: A triad is minor when the 3rd of a major triad has been lowered by one half step; **Principle 3**: A triad is diminished when the 3rd and 5th of a major triad have been lowered one half step; **Principle 4**: A triad is augmented when the 5th of a major triad is raised one half step. The following example illustrates the four principles you have been studying:

7.50

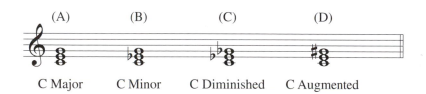

In the previous section, as you progressed through the process of identifying triads, your first task was to visualize major triads. In effect, you first had to construct major triads by determining the diatonic 3rd and 5th located above the root of each triad. In example 7.50, the triad at letter (A) is C major and it illustrates **Principle 1** because the 3rd and 5th are in the major key of the root. Example (B) illustrates **Principle 2** because the 3rd of the C major triad has been lowered one half step. Example (C) illustrates **Principle 3** because the original C major triad now has the 3rd and 5th lowered one half step, which results in a diminished triad. **Principle 4** is illustrated in example (D) because the 5th has been raised one half step to produce an augmented triad.

When constructing any of the four triad types, first construct the major triad and then adjust the 3rd and 5th as necessary.

Skill Development

Construct a minor triad above B♭.

Process

Step 1. Place B♭ on the staff and write the 3rd (D) and the 5th (F) above it.

7.51

Step 2. Before you determine the pitches of a B♭ minor triad, construct the B♭ major triad. To do this, check the key signature for B♭ and determine if the 3rd (D) and the 5th (F) are diatonic in the key of B♭. The key signature for B♭ has two flats (B♭ and E♭).

7.52a   Key of B♭

The pitches D and F are diatonic in the key of B♭; therefore the triad you have constructed in example 7.51 is major.

7.52b   B♭ Major

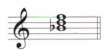

Step 3. Lower the 3rd (D) of the B♭ major triad one half step to D♭. The triad is now minor.

7.53   B♭ Minor

Skill Development

Let's try constructing a diminished triad above C♯.

Process

Step 1. Place C♯ on the staff and above it write in the 3rd (E) and 5th (G).

7.54

Step 2. Construct a major triad above C♯ by adjusting the 3rd and 5th as necessary (**Principle 1**). Recall that in the key of C♯ major, every pitch of the scale is sharped! Place sharps before E and G to construct a C♯ major triad.

7.55   C♯ Major

Step 3. Your task is to construct a diminished triad above C♯, so you will need to lower the 3rd (E♯) and the 5th (G♯) of this C♯ major triad one half step, changing them to E♮ and G♮ (**Principle 3**). You now have constructed a C♯ diminished triad.

7.56   C♯ Diminished

Skill Development

Construct an augmented triad above F♯.

Process

Step 1. Place F♯ on the staff and above it write in the 3rd (A) and 5th (C).

7.57

Step 2. Now construct the F♯ major triad by checking the key signature to determine if A and C are altered in this key.

7.58   Key of F♯

Step 3. The key signature for F♯ indicates that both A and C are sharped in this key. Recall that in the key of F♯ major, every pitch is sharped except B. By sharping both A and C, you will have created the F♯ major triad.

7.59   F♯ Major

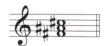

Step 4. Now raise the 5th (C♯) one half step to C𝄪 (**Principle 4**). Remember that the double sharp is required because you are raising an already sharped pitch. You have now constructed the F♯ augmented triad.

7.60   F♯ Augmented

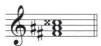

Exercise 6

Construct the indicated triads above the given pitches.

7.61a

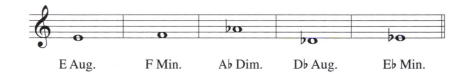

E Aug.   F Min.   A♭ Dim.   D♭ Aug.   E♭ Min.

7.61b   Be careful—this example is in the bass clef! ☺

A Maj.   B♭ Aug.   C♯ Maj.   B Aug.   G♭ Min.

7.61c

F♯ Maj.   C Min.   D Aug.   A Aug.   A♭ Min.

7.61d   Be careful—this example is in the bass clef! ☺

B♭ Min.   B Maj.   A Dim.   C♭ Min.   D♭ Dim.

CONSTRUCTING AND IDENTIFYING TRIADS IN WHICH THE ROOT DOES NOT HAVE AN ASSOCIATED KEY SIGNATURE

The method you are studying for the identification and construction of major, minor, diminished, and augmented triads requires you first to construct major triads above the root and then adjust the 3rd and 5th as necessary. This adjustment process is reflected in the four principles and provides an extremely accurate, efficient, and fast method for triad identification and construction.

As with intervals, there are numerous instances in which you will be required to construct and identify triads in which *there are no associated key signatures with the roots.* When encountering these situations, you will be able to apply the method you are learning with a slight modification to the first step.

If you were asked to construct a D♯ minor triad, normally your first step would be to construct a D♯ major triad and then lower the 3rd one half step (**Principle 2**). In this situation, this process will not work because there is no major key signature for the key of D♯! Please review the next principle very carefully.

Principle 5

When constructing or identifying triads in which there is no key signature for the root: (1) remove the accidental (sharp or flat) from the root; (2) construct a major triad over the new root; (3) reapply the original removed accidental from the root to all members of the triad (this will produce a major triad); and (4) adjust the 3rd or 5th as necessary to achieve the type of triad you wish to construct or identify.

Although this process may seem confusing at first, it is actually simple, and with practice you will appreciate its benefits.

Skill Development

Construct the D♯ minor triad.

Process

Step 1. Because there is no key signature for D♯ major, you will need to remove the sharp and construct the D major triad. Place D on the first space below the staff, and above it write the correct 3rd and 5th that will produce a major triad. The key signature for D major has two sharps (F♯ and C♯), and therefore you will have to sharp the 3rd, changing it to F♯. (If this process is unclear to you, please review **Principle 1** before proceeding.)

7.62   D Major

Step 2. You were asked to construct the D♯ minor triad, so now reapply the removed sharp from the original root (D♯) to all members of the triad and you will have constructed a D♯ major triad (**Principle 5**). Although the pitches will have changed from how they appeared in example 7.62, the distances between the 3rds remain unaltered. Because you raised every pitch of the D major triad one half step, the triad in the following example must be D♯ major!

7.63

D Major   D♯ Major

Step 3. Your task is to construct a D♯ minor triad. Major triads become minor when the 3rd is lowered one half step (**Principle 2**), so you must lower the F𝗑 one half step to F♯. You now have constructed the D♯ minor triad.

7.64

D♯ Minor

Skill Development

Construct the F♭ minor triad.

Process

Step 1. Because there is no key signature for F♭ major, you will need to remove the flat from the root and construct the F major triad. The key signature for F is one flat (B♭), so place the 3rd (A) and the 5th (C) on the staff and you will have constructed an F major triad. (If this process is unclear to you, please review **Principle 1**.)

7.65

F Major

Step 2. Now reapply the removed flat from the original root (F♭) to all members of the triad and you will have constructed an F♭ major triad (**Principle 5**). Please recall that, although the pitches will be completely different from what you constructed in example 7.65, the distances between the 3rds remain unchanged!

7.66

F Major   F♭ Major

Step 3. Your task is to create an F♭ minor triad. Major triads become minor when the 3rd is lowered one half step (**Principle 2**), so you must lower the A♭ to A♭♭. Example 7.67 illustrates the F♭ minor triad:

7.67

F♭ Minor

Exercise 7

Construct triads above the given pitches, even though a few of them do not occur diatonically in any major or minor key. They will be interesting and fun to create because the process remains the same.

7.68a

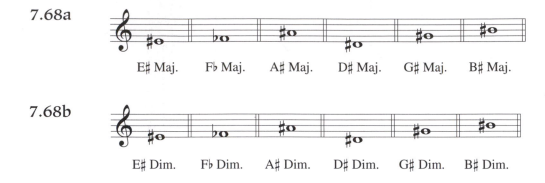

E♯ Maj. F♭ Maj. A♯ Maj. D♯ Maj. G♯ Maj. B♯ Maj.

7.68b

E♯ Dim. F♭ Dim. A♯ Dim. D♯ Dim. G♯ Dim. B♯ Dim.

CONSTRUCTING TRIADS WHEN THE GIVEN PITCH IS NOT THE ROOT

A valuable skill for composers, arrangers and songwriters is the ability to visualize the possibilities of how a given pitch would appear in any triad or larger chord. For example, the pitch G could be the root of one of the four triad types (major, minor, diminished, or augmented), but it could also be the third of an E♭ major triad, or the fifth of the C major or C minor triads. (There are also other extended chord possibilities.)

7.69a   *Possible Triads Spelled Using G*

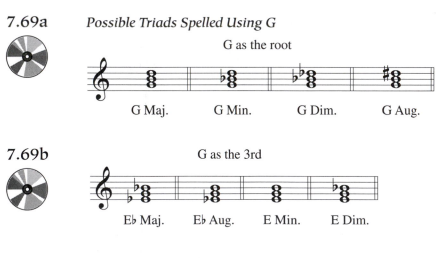

G as the root

G Maj. G Min. G Dim. G Aug.

7.69b

G as the 3rd

E♭ Maj. E♭ Aug. E Min. E Dim.

7.69c

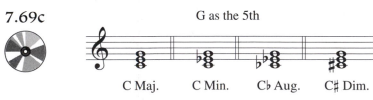

G as the 5th

C Maj. C Min. C♭ Aug. C♯ Dim.

The previous examples are not exhaustive. As you progress in your study of music theory, you will learn the various functions that pitches have in the more complex chromatic and **extended chords**, as well as their functions as **nonharmonic tones**.

Let's review a few observations regarding the construction and identification of triads. Notice that in any major triad, the distance between the root and the 3rd is a major interval, and between the root and the 5th, a perfect interval.

In a minor triad the distance between the root and the 3rd is a minor interval, and between the root and the 5th, a perfect interval.

In a diminished triad, the distance between the root and the 3rd is a minor interval, and between the root and 5th, a diminished interval.

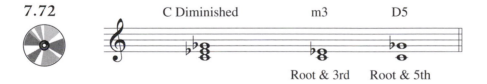

In an augmented triad, the distance between the root and the 3rd is a major interval, and between the root and 5th, an augmented interval.

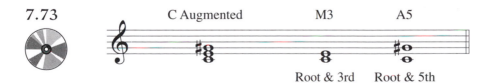

To quickly construct any triad when the pitch you are given is not the root, your first step must be to identify the root. Carefully study the Triad Table on page 326.

Triad Table

Identifying the Root of a Triad from a Given Third or Fifth

Major Triads

To identify the root of a major triad from a given 3rd, descend a major 3rd.

To identify the root of a major triad from a given 5th, descend a perfect 5th.

Minor Triads

To identify the root of a minor triad from a given 3rd, descend a minor 3rd.

To identify the root of a minor triad from a given 5th, descend a perfect 5th.

Diminished Triads

To identify the root of a diminished triad from a given 3rd, descend a minor 3rd.

To identify the root of a diminished triad from a given 5th, descend a diminished 5th.

Augmented Triads

To identify the root of an augmented triad from a given 3rd, descend a major 3rd.

To identify the root of an augmented triad from a given 5th, descend an augmented 5th.

The Triad Table may at first seem like a great deal of information. In fact, you do not need to memorize it at all if you relate it to something you already know: the construction of triads.

If you visualize a C major triad in its four types, you will easily see the distances that the 3rd and 5th are from the root. This visualization technique is an important skill to develop because it will provide you with an efficient means to addressing many future theoretical issues.

The relationships you observe when working in the key of C apply to all keys. As a rule of thumb, *what is true for the key of C is true for all keys*. Therefore, if you can visualize the triad types in the key of C, you can apply this knowledge to triads constructed on any pitch.

The key of C has no sharps or flats in its key signature, so it is easy to identify how the 3rd and/or 5th need to be adjusted to construct the four triad types. Below is a synopsis of examples 7.70–7.73 that will help you determine the distance of the 3rd and 5th from the root among the various triad types.

THE INTERVALS CONTAINED IN THE FOUR C TRIAD TYPES

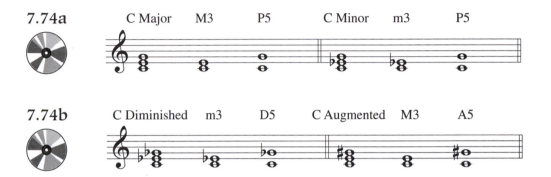

7.74a   C Major   M3   P5   C Minor   m3   P5

7.74b   C Diminished   m3   D5   C Augmented   M3   A5

Please learn the following principle.

> ### Principle 6
>
> When constructing a major, minor, diminished, or augmented triad from a given 3rd or 5th, descend the appropriate interval to identify the root, then determine the remaining triad member by applying the process of triad construction addressed in Principles 1 through 4.

Skill Development

Construct the appropriate minor triad when the given pitch, B♭, is the 3rd.

Process

Step 1. Place B♭ on the staff and identify it as the 3rd of a minor triad.

7.75

Step 2. Locate the root of the chord by descending a minor 3rd. You need to descend this distance because the interval between the root and the 3rd of a

minor triad is a minor 3rd. (Refer to the Triad Table and example 7.74a if you need to review this concept. (If you have trouble constructing an interval below a given pitch, please review Chapter 6.) The minor 3rd below B♭ is G, the root of the chord.

7.76

Step 3. Now that you know G is the root of the minor triad you are trying to construct, place on the staff the pitch that is a 5th above G. (The basic pitch is D, but it might need to be altered.) The method you are learning asks you to first compute how the 3rd and the 5th will occur within the major key of the root. The root, G, has one sharp (F♯) in its major key signature. D and B occur as a diatonic perfect 5th (D) and a major 3rd (B) above it. The triad G–B♭–D is minor because it is a G major triad with the 3rd lowered one half step.

7.77   G Major   G Minor

If you wish to verify that you have constructed a G minor triad, review **Principle 2**.

Skill Development

Construct the appropriate augmented triad when the given pitch, E♯, is the fifth.

Process

Step 1. Place E♯ on the staff and locate the root by descending an augmented 5th. As indicated in the Triad Table, the root of an augmented triad is located an augmented 5th below the given 5th. An augmented 5th below E♯ is A. (If the process of constructing intervals below a given pitch is unclear to you, examine the section in Chapter 6 that addresses "Constructing Intervals Below a Given Pitch.")

7.78

A5

Step 2. The root of the augmented triad you are trying to construct is A. You already know that the 5th of the triad is (E♯), so now you must add the 3rd above the root, which must be diatonic in the key of A (**Principle 6**). Recall that an augmented triad is a major triad with the 5th raised one half step!

Check the key signature for the key of A, and observe that the diatonic third above it is C♯. Place C♯ on the staff, and you will have created the A augmented triad.

7.79

Skill Development

Construct a diminished triad when the given pitch, A♭, is the 5th.

Process

Step 1. Place A♭ on the staff and locate the root of the triad by descending a diminished 5th. (If you find it difficult to descend a diminished 5th, you will need to review Chapter 6.) A diminished 5th below A♭ is D.

7.80

Step 2. Now identify the 3rd of the D diminished triad. You may recall from example 7.31 that diminished triads consist of two minor 3rds constructed above the root, so that the distance between the root and the 3rd is the same as that between the 3rd and the 5th (a minor 3rd). The *quickest way* to determine the 3rd of this triad is to *ascend* a minor 3rd from the root (three diatonic half steps), or *descend* a minor 3rd from the fifth (A♭). Either way, you will arrive on F because diminished triads are constructed in minor 3rds. (If the process of constructing a minor 3rd is unclear to you, review Chapter 6.)

7.81

In example 7.81, once the root was established, it would have been possible to determine the 3rd of the diminished triad by first constructing the D major triad, then lowering the 3rd and the 5th one half step. This process would have yielded the same result, but it is inefficient in this case because you already know that the root is D and the fifth is A♭! However, if it makes more sense to you to compute the lowered 3rd of this triad by first constructing a major triad, then lowering the 3rd one half step, please do it in this manner.

Perhaps the best way to fully understand the construction of triads is to play them on the piano. You do not have to be an accomplished pianist to play triads, and you will derive numerous benefits from hearing them and observing how they are constructed on the piano keyboard. Not only will you be able to actually *see* a 3rd and or 5th being altered from a major triad in order to produce a minor, diminished, or augmented triad, but you will be able to hear and compare the unique sonorities of the triads you play. The ability to aurally discriminate the differences among the various triad qualities is an important skill for all musicians. If you have never tried playing the piano, this is an excellent time to begin!

Exercise 8

Construct the following **major triads** when the given pitch is the **3rd**.

7.82a

7.82b   Be careful—this example is in the bass clef! ☺

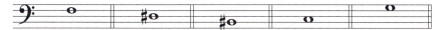

Construct the following **minor triads** when the given pitch is the **3rd**.

7.83a

7.83b   Be careful—this example is in the bass clef! ☺

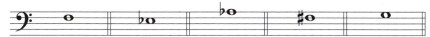

Construct the following **augmented triads** when the given pitch is the **3rd**.

7.84a

7.84b   Be careful—this example is in the bass clef! ☺

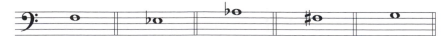

Construct the following **diminished triads** when the given pitch is the **3rd**.

7.85a

7.85b   Be careful—this example is in the bass clef! ☺

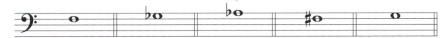

Construct the following **major triads** when the given pitch is the **5th**.

7.86a

7.86b   Be careful—this example is in the bass clef! ☺

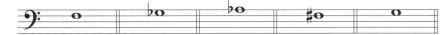

Construct the following **minor triads** when the given pitch is the **5th**.

7.87a

7.87b   Be careful—this example is in the bass clef! ☺

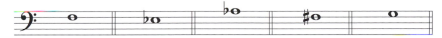

Construct the following **augmented triads** when the given pitch is the **5th**.

7.88a

7.88b   Be careful—this example is in the bass clef! ☺

Construct the following **diminished triads** when the given pitch is the **5th**.

7.89a

7.89b   Be careful—this example is in the bass clef! ☺

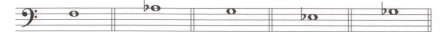

INVERSIONS OF TRIADS

Triads (and other chords) are not always written with the root in the lowest position (bass). Often, the 3rd or 5th may occur as the bass pitch, in which case the triad is said to be in an **inversion**.

Play the following C major triads on the piano and try to identify the subtle differences among them. The most easily distinguishable difference will be what you hear as the lowest pitch (the bass) and the uppermost pitch (the soprano).

7.90

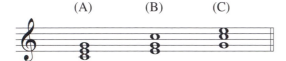

In example 7.90, the C major triad at (A) is said to be in **root position** because the root of the triad, C, is in the lowest voice (the bass). In example (B) the same C major triad is written with the 3rd in the bass and is said to be in **first inversion**. In example (C), the same C major triad now has the 5th in the bass, and it is said to be in **second inversion**.

Principle 7

A triad with the root in the bass (lowest pitch) is said to be in root position. A triad with the 3rd in the bass is said to be in first inversion. A triad with the 5th in the bass is said to be in second inversion.

Principle 7 is illustrated below:

7.91a

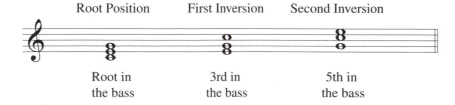

Each of the four triad types (major, minor, diminished, and augmented) may be inverted; however, composers are very careful in their usage and treatment. There are numerous considerations that cannot be ignored when writing inverted triads, but they are for future study and beyond the parameters of this textbook.

Notice in example 7.91b that in each of the illustrated triads, the root, 3rd, and 5th are written (or **voiced**) together as closely as possible. It is impossible to write the pitches C, E, and G any closer!

In first inversion, the lower two pitches (E and G) are voiced so that the uppermost pitch (C) cannot be moved any closer to G. In second inversion, the two upper pitches cannot be placed any closer to the bass pitch G.

7.91b

Root Position   First Inversion   Second Inversion

CLOSE AND OPEN POSITION

When triads are constructed so that the pitches are placed together as closely as possible, they are said to be in **close position**. When a triad is written in any other way, so that the pitches are not placed together as closely as possible, it is said to be in **open position**.

Principle *8*

When a triad is constructed so that the root, 3rd, and 5th are voiced as closely together as possible, it is said to be in close position.

Principle *9*

When a triad is constructed so that the root, 3rd, and 5th are not voiced as closely together as possible, it is said to be in open position.

Close and open positions are illustrated in the following example.

7.92a

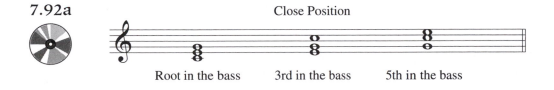

Close Position

Root in the bass   3rd in the bass   5th in the bass

7.92b

Some Examples of Open Position

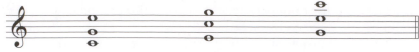

Root in the bass   3rd in the bass   5th in the bass

IDENTIFYING TRIAD VOICINGS AND THEIR INVERSIONS

Now that you know how inverted triads look and how their voicings may differ, let's learn how to identify them.

Skill Development

Identify the following triad and indicate its root, quality, inversion, and voicing (open or close position).

7.93

Process

Step 1. Before you can determine the quality and inversion of the above triad, you first must identify the *root*. To accomplish this, remember that triads must stack up in 3rds (tertian concept).

The pitches in the triad in example 7.93 are D♭, B♭, and F. If the *root* of this triad were D♭, the pitches *above* the root (regardless of the quality of the triad) would have to include some type of F and A (natural, sharp, or flat) because this is how the 3rds would stack up.

7.94   3rds stacked above D♭

D♭ *cannot* be the root of the triad in example 7.93, because the pitches above the bass pitch (D♭) are B♭ and F. If the highest pitch, F, were the root, the pitches in this triad would have to include A and C.

7.95   3rds stacked above F

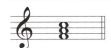

F *cannot* be the root of the triad in example 7.93, because the 3rds stacked above the bass pitch (D♭) are B♭ and F.

The triad in example 7.93 only stacks up in 3rds one way, and that is when B♭ is treated as the root.

7.96   3rds stacked above B♭

Step 2. Now that the root of example 7.93 has been identified as B♭, determine the quality of the triad (major, minor, diminished, or augmented). First, construct the B♭ major triad and then compare it to example 7.93 to see if any pitches of the major triad have been altered. (If you have difficulty constructing major triads, review the beginning of this chapter.) The B♭ major triad looks as follows.

7.97   B♭ Major

In example 7.93, observe that the 3rd of the triad is not D, but D♭. The triad in example 7.93 is therefore B♭ minor (**Principle 2**).

7.98   B♭ Minor

Step 3. Now that you know the quality of the triad in example 7.93, check to see if it is inverted. Observe that the lowest pitch of the triad (the bass) is a D♭. Since this pitch is the 3rd of the triad, the triad is in first inversion (**Principle 7**).

7.99a   B♭ Minor in First Inversion

Step 4. You were also asked to identify the voicing (open or close position) of the triad in 7.93. Check to see if any of the triad tones (B♭, D♭, and F) may be inserted between any two adjacent pitches. If this is the case, and it is, the triad is in open position! Observe in example 7.99a that between the bass (D♭) and the B♭ above it there is room to write an F! Also, between the upper pitches B♭ and F, there is room to write the D♭. This triad therefore is in open position and demonstrates **Principle 9**.

7.99b   B♭ Minor in first inversion
in open position

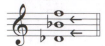

The arrows indicate where it is
possible to insert triad tones.

Skill Development

Identify the root, quality, inversion, and voicing (open or close position) of the following triad.

7.100

Process

Step 1. In the above example there are three pitches: E, C♯, and A. Begin by establishing which one of theses pitches is the root. To do so, identify the pitch upon which it is possible to "stack up" 3rds to produce the pitches of this triad. If the lowest pitch, E, is the root, the 3rds above it would be some type of G and B (regardless of any sharps or flats).

7.101

The pitch E *cannot* be the root of the triad in example 7.100, because it has generated pitches in 3rds (G and B) that are not in the triad you are analyzing. If C♯ is the root, the 3rds stacked above it would produce the pitches E and G (regardless of the quality of the triad).

7.102

The pitch C♯ *cannot* be the root of the triad in example 7.100 because it has generated the pitches E and G, and G is not in the triad you are analyzing. You must locate the root that will generate, and include, the pitches E, C♯, and A.

The remaining pitch in example 7.100 is A. If this is the root, it must generate the pitches C and E in 3rds. (Remember, any sharps or flats are unimportant in determining the root of the triad.) The pitch A is the root of this triad because it has generated C and E in 3rds.

7.103

You have determined that the root of the triad is A.

7.104

Step 2. Now you must identify its quality. (If this procedure is unclear to you, review **Principles 1–4**.) Because the 3rd (C♯) and 5th (E) of this triad are diatonic in the key of A, the triad is major.

7.105   A Major

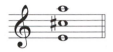

Step 3. Now let's determine the inversion. Notice that the triad in example 7.105 *is not* in root position, because the root, A, is not in the bass (the lowest pitch). The bass pitch is E, which is the 5th of the triad. **Principle 7** states that when the 5th of a triad is in the bass it is said to be in second inversion. The A major triad is in second inversion.

7.106

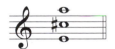

Step 4. Your final task is to determine the voicing of this triad. Is it in open or close position? At this point, determine if it is possible to insert a root, 3rd, or 5th between any two adjacent pitches. You will observe that it is possible to place the root (A) between the lowest pitch, E, and the C♯ directly above it. It also is possible to insert the 5th (E) between the two upper pitches, C♯ and A. This triad therefore is said to be in open position and illustrates **Principle 9**.

7.107   A Major in second inversion
             in open position

Exercise 9

Review the following triads and identify the root, quality, inversion (or root position), and voicing (close or open position), and place your answers on the grid.

7.108a

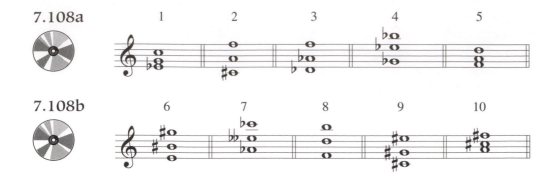

7.108b

Answer Grid for Example 7.108

Root of the Triad	Quality (maj./min./dim./aug.)	Inversion (or root position)	Voicing (open or close position)
1.			
2.			
3.			
4.			
5.			
6.			
7.			
8.			
9.			
10.			

REVIEW OF PRINCIPLES

Principle 1
A triad is major when the 3rd and 5th are in the major key of the root.

Principle 2
A triad is minor when the 3rd of a major triad has been lowered one half step.

Principle 3
A triad is diminished when the 3rd and 5th of a major triad have been lowered one half step.

Principle 4
A triad is augmented when the 5th of a major triad is raised one half step.

Principle 5
When constructing or identifying triads in which there is no key signature for the root: (1) remove the accidental (sharp or flat) from the root, (2) construct

a major triad over the new root, (3) reapply the original removed accidental from the root to all members of the triad (this will produce a major triad), and (4) adjust the 3rd or 5th as necessary to achieve the type of triad you wish to construct or identify.

Principle 6
When constructing a major, minor, diminished, or augmented triad from a given 3rd or 5th, descend the appropriate interval to identify the root, then determine the remaining triad member by applying the process of triad construction addressed in Principles 1 through 4.

Principle 7
A triad with the root in the bass (lowest pitch) is said to be in root position. A triad with the 3rd in the bass is said to be in first inversion. A triad with the 5th in the bass is said to be in second inversion.

Principle 8
When a triad is constructed so that the root, 3rd, and 5th are voiced as closely together as possible, it is said to be in close position.

Principle 9
When a triad is constructed so that the root, 3rd, and 5th are not voiced as closely together as possible, it is said to be in open position.

ANSWER SHEETS TO CHAPTER 7

Exercise 1

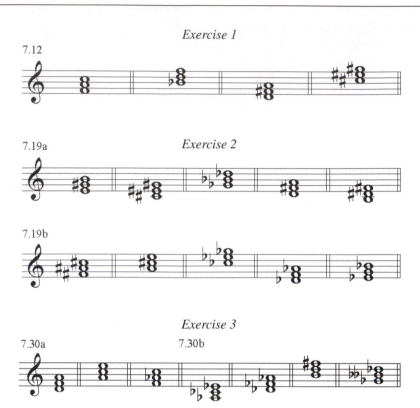

Exercise 2

Exercise 3

Exercise 4

Exercise 5

7.49

Exercise 6

7.61a

7.61b

7.61c

7.61d

Exercise 7

7.68a

7.68b

Exercise 8

Exercise 8 Continued

Answer Grid for Example 7.108

Root of the Triad		Quality (maj./min./dim./aug.)	Inversion (or root position)	Voicing (open or close position)
1.	C	Minor	First Inversion	Close
2.	F	Augmented	Second Inversion	Open
3.	D♭	Major	Root Position	Open
4.	E♭	Minor	First Inversion	Open
5.	D	Minor	First Inversion	Close
6.	E	Augmented	Root Position	Open
7.	A♭	Diminished	Root Position	Open
8.	B	Diminished	Second Inversion	Open
9.	C♯	Major	Root Position	Open
10.	F♯	Minor	First Inversion	Close

WORKSHEETS FOR CHAPTER 7

Name

1. Identify the following triads.

2. Construct the following triads in close position.

Ab Min.   E Aug.   B Maj.   F♯ Dim.   C♯ Aug.

A Maj.   Db Dim.   B Min.   Gb Dim.   D♯ Maj.

3. Identify the inversions of the following triads.

Name _____

4. Identify the root, triad type, inversion, and open or close position for each of the following triads.

_____ _____ _____

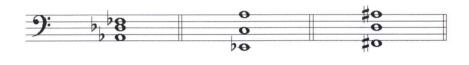

_____ _____ _____

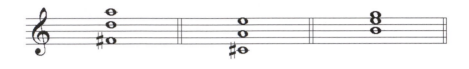

_____ _____ _____

5. Write the following triads in open position and in first inversion.

D Maj.   F♯ Min.   C♯ Aug.   E Dim.   G♭ Min.

A♭ Maj.   B Aug.   C Dim.   E♭ Min.   G Aug.

6. Write the following triads in close position and in second inversion.

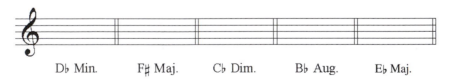

D♭ Min.   F♯ Maj.   C♭ Dim.   B♭ Aug.   E♭ Maj.

A Dim.   B Maj.   C♯ Min.   G♯ Min.   D♯ Min.

Find additional Skill Development Drills on the accompanyng CD-ROM and on the book companion Web site: http://music.wadsworth.com/kinney1e.

8

Harmonic Functions of Triads

Bach is a colossus of Rhodes, beneath whom all musicians pass and will continue to pass. Mozart is the most beautiful, Rossini the most brilliant, but Bach is the most comprehensive; he has said all there is to say.

—Charles Gounod

Historically, numerous composers and songwriters have used triads as a basic tool in helping design and shape the musical forms of their compositions. Songwriters, in particular, continue to rely on triads to provide harmonic support for melodies and establish moods that reflect their particular texts. Nearly all composers of large-scale works, such as operas, concertos, symphonies, jazz compositions, movie and television scores, and a few forms of rock and roll, have employed triads in a more expanded, complex, and intricate fashion, and, regardless of the style with which a musician is associated, triads are fundamental components in most forms of musical expressions.

In this chapter you will study how **diatonic triads** function and contribute to establishing a tonal center in major and minor keys. In order to understand the principles presented in this chapter, you must be able to easily recall the major and minor key signatures presented in Chapter 4. You may wish to take a moment to review the principles and exercises in that chapter.

DIATONIC TRIADS IN MAJOR KEYS

In the following example, the diatonic triads for the key of C major have been constructed by stacking two pitches, a 3rd apart, above each note of the C major scale.

8.1a

The triads in example 8.1a help define the key of C major and may be used to harmonize a melody in this key. For example, if you are singing or playing the pitch G in the key of C major, there are three diatonic triads that could provide it with harmonic support.

8.1b

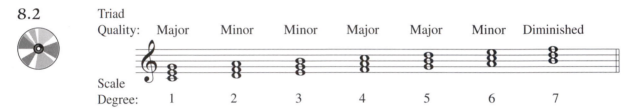

Although the quality (major, minor, diminished, and augmented) of the triad constructed on the first scale degree in a major key is major, the qualities of the remaining triads are not all the same. The triads constructed on scale degrees 1, 4, and 5 in a major key are major; the triads constructed on scale degrees 2, 3, and 6 are minor, and the triad constructed on scale degree 7 is diminished. (The triad constructed on scale degree 8 is the same as that on scale degree 1 and will be omitted from any of the following examples.)

In example 8.2, observe the quality types of the diatonic triads located on the scale degrees of the C major scale.

8.2

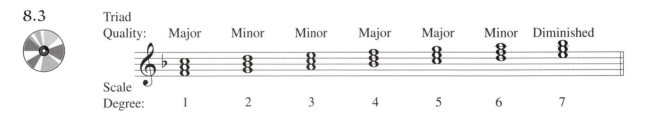

The ordering of the diatonic triad quality types for the key of C major *is the same for all major keys.* If you were performing or composing music in the key of F major, the *qualities* of the diatonic triads at each scale degree would be the same as they are in C major. Observe that, although the triads in example 8.3 differ from those in 8.2, the qualities listed above each one are exactly the same.

8.3

Observe in examples 8.2 and 8.3 that the same triad quality type occurs on each scale degree as follows:

Scale Degree 1: major triad
Scale Degree 2: minor triad
Scale Degree 3: minor triad

Scale Degree 4: major triad
Scale Degree 5: major triad
Scale Degree 6: minor triad
Scale Degree 7: diminished triad

Upper- and lowercase roman numerals are used to distinguish the different tonal qualities among the diatonic triads located on specific scale degrees. In major keys, uppercase roman numerals indicate that major triads occur on scale degrees 1, 4, and 5 and are expressed as I, IV, and V. Lowercase roman numerals indicate that minor triads occur on scale degrees 2, 3, and 6, and are expressed as ii, iii, and vi. The lowercase roman numeral with a degree sign (vii°) indicates a diminished triad on scale degree 7, and an uppercase roman numeral with a plus sign (III+), which may occur diatonically in a minor key, indicates an augmented triad on scale degree 3.

Observe in example 8.4 how the qualities of the diatonic triads located on each scale degree in the key of F major are expressed by using roman numerals:

8.4

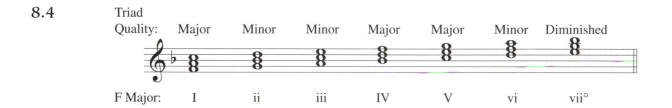

Triad
Quality: Major   Minor   Minor   Major   Major   Minor   Diminished

F Major: I   ii   iii   IV   V   vi   vii°

The diatonic triads that occur in the key of F major are: F major (I), G minor (ii), A minor (iii), B♭ major (IV), C major (V), D minor (vi), and E diminished (vii°). If you were writing a piece of music in the key of F major, these triads would be used to **harmonize** the melody!

By knowing the exact pitch of a particular scale degree, you can quickly determine its associated diatonic triad. This information is very helpful to musicians in a variety of ways, because it places music within a context of a theoretical model that organizes sound and provides a framework for musical composition, analysis, and performance.

Let's suppose you are a songwriter who has an idea for a melody or a catchy rhythmic phrase that needs the addition of various triads to make it more beautiful and interesting. How would you go about selecting the triads that would assist you in expressing your musical ideas? Perhaps you have not yet established a clear introduction to your song and wish to introduce the melody by playing a few triads that will create a specific mood. How would you go about selecting them? These are very common questions for anyone attempting to write music. A first step in solving these musical problems is to determine the diatonic triads for the key in which you are working.

Let's assume that you want to write a piece of music in the key of A♭ major. Your first step in establishing the diatonic triads for this key would be to know every note of the A♭ major scale as determined by its key signature. The key signature for A♭ is four flats.

8.5

The A♭ major scale is as follows.

8.6   A♭ Major Scale

The diatonic triads in the key of A♭ major are as follows.

8.7

I   ii   iii   IV   V   vi   vii°

Skill Development

What are the diatonic triads for the key of G major?

Process

Step 1. Determine the key signature for G major. It has one sharp.

8.8   G Major

Step 2. Construct the diatonic triads for G major above each step of the scale, and place the appropriate roman numeral and triad name under each triad.

8.9   Diatonic triads for G major

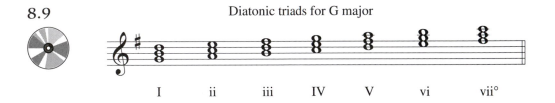

I   ii   iii   IV   V   vi   vii°

The diatonic triads for the key of G major are: G major (I), A minor (ii), B minor (iii), C major (IV), D major (V), E minor (vi), and F♯ diminished (vii°).

Exercise 1

In the following examples, place the correct key signature on the staff and write the diatonic triads for each of the indicated major keys. Under each triad provide the correct roman numeral (as illustrated in examples 8.7 and

8.9) and, on the lines provided, write the name of the triad and its quality (major, minor, diminished, or augmented).

8.10a   Eb Major

Triads: (I) _____, (ii) _____, (iii) _____,

(IV) _____, (V) _____, (vi) _____,

(vii°)_____.

8.10b   A Major

Triads: (I) _____, (ii) _____, (iii) _____,

(IV) _____, (V) _____, (vi) _____,

(vii°) _____.

8.10c   Bb Major

Triads: (I) _____, (ii) _____, (iii) _____,

(IV) _____, (V) _____, (vi) _____,

(vii°) _____.

8.10d   E Major

Triads: (I) _____, (ii) _____, (iii) _____,

(IV) _____, (V) _____, (vi) _____,

(vii°) _____.

DIATONIC TRIADS IN MINOR KEYS

You will recall from Chapter 3 that there are three forms of the minor scale: (1) pure minor (natural), (2) harmonic minor, and (3) melodic minor. Because each form generates its own set of triads (some of which are duplicates in the other forms), a minor key has nearly twice as many available triads as a major key! While major keys have only seven diatonic triads, there are thirteen diatonic triads from which to choose when harmonizing a melody in a minor key.

Observe the triads associated with the pure form of A minor and the associated roman numerals identifying their quality.

8.11

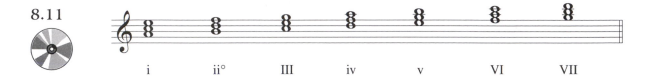

i   ii°   III   iv   v   VI   VII

The diatonic triads resulting from the use of the pure form of the A minor scale are: A minor (I), B diminished (ii°), C major (III), D minor (iv), E minor (v), F major (VI), and G major (VII). Recall that the triad located on scale degree 7 of the pure minor form is major (VII) and is called the **subtonic** (see Chapter 3). These triad quality types will occur in all minor keys when applying the pure minor form.

DIATONIC TRIADS IN THE HARMONIC MINOR FORM

In general, the harmonic minor form is the most frequently used because the tonic of the scale (scale degree 8 or 1) is approached by one half step from below (scale degree 7). Establishing the tonic in this manner helps the ear identify a clear tonal center toward which all of the pitches within that key will gravitate. Recall that the melodic form should be used sparingly and that it is a "correction" for the harmonic minor (Chapter 3).

When constructing the harmonic minor form of the scale, it is necessary to raise the pitch on scale degree 7 of the pure minor form one half step. This process will create the leading tone to the minor key that you are in.

In the key of A minor, the harmonic form of the scale (with the raised 7th scale degree) will establish the leading tone, G♯, and *will affect three diatonic triads* in the following manner: the triad on the 3rd scale degree (III), which was a major triad in the pure form, is now augmented (III+); (v), which was a minor triad, is now major (V); and the subtonic (VII), which was a major triad, is now diminished (vii°) and is identified as the leading tone triad.

Leading tone triads always are located one half step below the tonic in both major and minor keys!

Example 8.12 illustrates the triads in the harmonic form of the A minor scale.

8.12

The diatonic triads for the key of A minor that result from using the harmonic form of the scale are: A minor (i), B diminished (ii°), C augmented (III+), D minor (iv), E major (V), F major (VI), and G♯ diminished (vii°).

DIATONIC TRIADS IN THE ASCENDING MELODIC MINOR FORM

The ascending melodic minor scale raises scale degrees 6 and 7 of the pure minor scale one half step. The impact of the raised 7th scale degree has been discussed, so let's focus on the triads that will be affected by raising the 6th scale degree.

When the pitch located on the 6th scale degree in the key of A minor is raised one half step (F to F♯—melodic form), it will affect three diatonic triads that existed in the pure form: the triad on scale degree 2 (ii°), which was a diminished triad, is now minor (ii); the triad on scale degree 4 (iv), which was a minor triad, is now major (IV); and the triad on scale degree 6 (VI), which was a major triad, is now diminished (vi°).

The diatonic triads for the key of A minor that result from using the melodic form of the scale are A minor (i), B minor (ii), C augmented (III+), D major (IV), E major (V), F♯ diminished (vi°), and G♯ diminished (vii°), and are illustrated in example 8.13a.

8.13a

 Diatonic triads in the A Melodic Minor scale (ascending only)

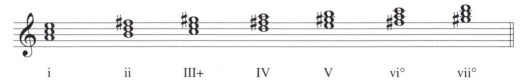

When writing in a minor key, it is possible to use any of the diatonic triads in each of the three forms of the minor. Example 8.13b illustrates the available diatonic triads in A major and those in A minor.

8.13b

 Possible diatonic triads for the key of A major

Possible diatonic triads for the key of A minor (all forms)

A min.   B min.   C aug.   D maj.   E maj.   F# dim.   G# dim.
    B dim.   C maj.   D min.   E min.   F maj.   G maj.

Skill Development

Construct the diatonic triads for each of the three forms of D minor.

Process

Step 1. Determine the key signature for D minor. The key signature is B♭. (If you need to review minor key signatures, review Chapter 4.) Place B♭ on the staff and construct the diatonic triads of the pure minor form above each scale degree beginning on D.

8.14

Step 2. Place the correct roman numerals and triad symbols for the pure minor form under each scale degree.

8.15

Diatonic triads for D minor using the pure form

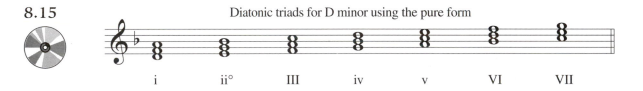

i   ii°   III   iv   v   VI   VII

The diatonic triads in D minor resulting from the pure form are: D minor (i), E diminished (ii°), F major (III), G minor (iv), A minor (v), B♭ major (VI), and C major (VII).

Step 3. Now raise scale degree 7 of the pure form one half step (C–C♯) and construct the triads for D harmonic minor. Remember, the raising of scale degree 7 will impact three triads!

8.16

Diatonic triads for D minor using the harmonic form
(The arrows indicate the triads affected by using the harmonic form.)

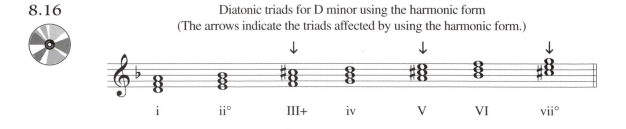

i   ii°   III+   iv   V   VI   vii°

The diatonic triads in D minor resulting from the harmonic form are: D minor (i), E diminished (ii°), F augmented (III+), G minor (iv), A major (V), B♭ major (VI), and C♯ diminished (vii°).

Step 4. Now, establish the triads in the melodic minor form by raising scale degree 6 of the pure minor scale (you already raised scale degree 7 in the previous step) and construct the triads for D melodic minor. Scale degree 6 of the pure form of the D minor scale is B♭, which must be raised to B natural. An additional three triads will be impacted by this alteration. Compare example 8.17 to 8.16.

8.17

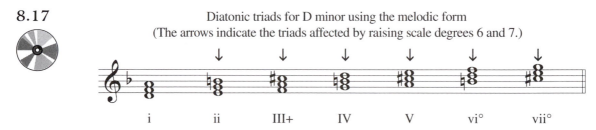

Diatonic triads for D minor using the melodic form
(The arrows indicate the triads affected by raising scale degrees 6 and 7.)

i   ii   III+   IV   V   vi°   vii°

The diatonic triads in D minor resulting from the melodic form are: D minor (i), E minor (ii), F augmented (III+), G major (IV), A major (V), B diminished (vi°), and C♯ diminished (vii°).

Exercise 2

Construct the diatonic triads for the three forms of B minor and place the correct roman numeral under each one.

8.18   Pure form   Diatonic triads for B minor

Harmonic form   Diatonic triads for B minor

Melodic form   Diatonic triads for B minor

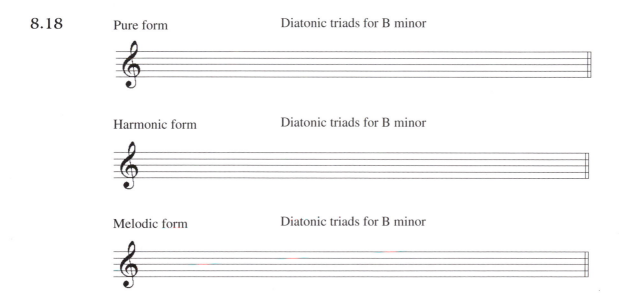

Construct the diatonic triads for each of the three forms of F♯ minor.

8.19a   Pure form   Diatonic triads for F♯ minor

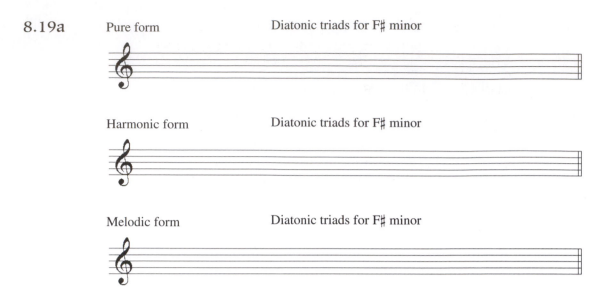

Harmonic form   Diatonic triads for F♯ minor

Melodic form   Diatonic triads for F♯ minor

TRIADS AND THEIR FUNCTIONS

A triad's *function* refers to its role in defining a tonal center and providing a sense of harmonic progression within a composition. To understand and clearly appreciate the function of a triad, you must be able to hear its relationship to the tonic and its overall contribution to the linear harmonic aspects of a composition unfolding over time. This important skill may be cultivated by developing a more in-depth approach to your listening habits. You will learn how to appreciate music at a much deeper level by perceiving not only the melody of a musical composition (and text when applicable), but also how music is supported by other tones within the harmonic context.

In order to develop an aural awareness of the subtle qualitative differences among the triads, it is highly recommended that you play on a piano keyboard or guitar the diatonic triads that occur in both major and minor keys (the harmonic form is preferred). You soon will discover that the tonic and dominant triads are the most important to establishing a sense of key, and initially will be the easiest to identify. With moderate practice you will be able to hear the differences and similarities among the triads occurring on various scale degrees and correctly identify their harmonic functions. You do not have to be an accomplished musician to do this and it should be an enjoyable experience!

Play the following triads on a guitar or a piano. Begin by playing them in the order in which they appear on the staff and then later on in a random fashion to see if you are able to identify the tonic, dominant, and subdominant triads.

8.19b   Diatonic triads for C major

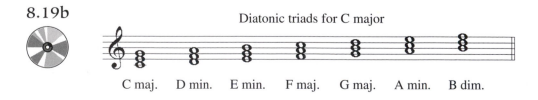

C maj.   D min.   E min.   F maj.   G maj.   A min.   B dim.

Diatonic triads for C minor (harmonic form)

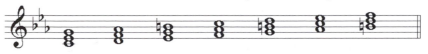

C min.　D dim.　E♭ aug.　F min.　G maj.　A♭ maj.　B dim.

The roman numerals employed in identifying a triad's scale degree, position, and quality are equally important in distinguishing a triad's diatonic function. The following example indicates the established names assigned to triads for each scale degree in both major and minor keys.

8.20

Major Keys	**Minor Keys (harmonic form)**
I Tonic	i Tonic
ii Supertonic	ii° Supertonic
iii Mediant	III+ Mediant
IV Subdominant	iv Subdominant
V Dominant	V Dominant
vi Submediant	VI Submediant
vii° Leading tone	vii° Leading tone

The diatonic triads in the key of D major are identified as follows.

8.21

Diatonic triads and their functions in D major

Tonic　　　　Mediant　　　　Dominant　　　Leading tone
　　Supertonic　　　Subdominant　　　Submediant

Please take a moment and practice writing the names of the function associated with each scale degree as illustrated in example 8.20 (the minor scale degree functions are exactly the same except for scale degree 7 in pure minor, which is identified as the subtonic):

Scale Degree 1 _____

Scale Degree 2 _____

Scale Degree 3 _____

Scale Degree 4 _____

Scale Degree 5 _____

Scale Degree 6 _____

Scale Degree 7 _____

Scale Degree 7 (pure minor form) _____

THE FUNCTIONS OF THE DIATONIC TRIADS IN THE HARMONIC MINOR FORM

The functions of the diatonic triads in the key of D (*harmonic form*) are listed below. This form is the most functional and is listed first because it illustrates the creation of the leading tone resulting from raising the 7th scale degree of the pure form. The leading tone is extremely important in helping to establish the tonic in any major or minor key. A leading tone and an unambiguous set of triads are needed to clearly define a key center. In a minor key, the harmonic minor provides an effective way to achieve this.

8.22

Diatonic triads and their functions in D harmonic minor

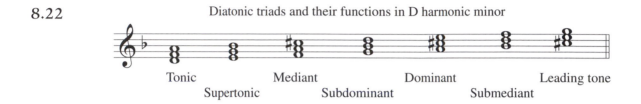

Tonic   Mediant   Dominant   Leading tone

Supertonic   Subdominant   Submediant

THE FUNCTIONS OF THE DIATONIC TRIADS IN THE PURE MINOR FORM

The *pure form* of the minor provides many of the same triads as the harmonic form with three exceptions: the mediant, which was augmented (III+), now is a major triad (III); the dominant (V), which was major, now is minor and may be identified as a **nonfunctioning dominant** (v), because it no longer contains the leading tone; and the subtonic (VII), which replaces the leading tone triad is a major triad constructed one full step below the tonic.

8.23a

Diatonic triads and their functions in D minor—pure form

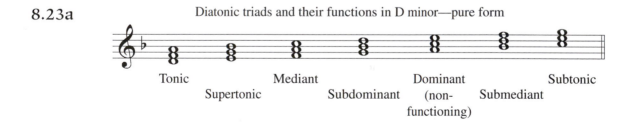

Tonic   Mediant   Dominant   Subtonic

Supertonic   Subdominant   (non-   Submediant

functioning)

Before we review the functions of the diatonic triads in the melodic minor form, let's take a closer look at the nonfunctioning dominant and the subtonic.

THE NONFUNCTIONING DOMINANT TRIAD

In example 8.23a (the pure form of the minor) observe that the triad constructed on the 5th scale degree (A) is a *minor triad* and is labeled as a nonfunctioning dominant triad. It does *not* contain the leading tone of the key within which it occurs (the leading tone in D minor is C♯, which would occur as the 3rd of the dominant triad). The aural effect of the minor dominant triad is that the listener will not easily be able to perceive this sonority as having a true dominant function. A functioning dominant triad, in both the major and minor modes, *must* contain the leading tone of the key in which it occurs. Because the dominant triad in example 8.23a *does not* contain the leading tone of D minor (C♯), it is labeled as a nonfunctioning dominant.

THE SUBTONIC

Notice in example 8.23b that the quality of the triad built on scale degree 7 in the key of D minor is major, and is called the subtonic triad. This triad, which is constructed one full step below the tonic in the *pure form* of the minor, provides a useful tonal color when writing music. However, because it *does not contain* the leading tone (C♯) of the key of D minor, it is not useful in helping to establish D as a tonal center. The diminished triad in the second measure, however, *is* constructed on the leading tone in D minor and is very important to establishing its key center.

8.23b

The subtonic triad occurs in the pure minor form.   The leading-tone triad occurs in the harmonic minor form.

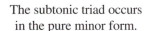

VII   vii°

Composers of modal music frequently use the subtonic to create a sense of exoticism or mystery. While this triad certainly may be employed when writing music in minor (and often in major), it does not assist in clearly defining the tonic of the key, and therefore is secondary in importance to the leading-tone triad (resulting from the harmonic form).

Examples of the subtonic (VII) triad may be found in nearly all styles of music. When the subtonic (VII) replaces the leading-tone triad (vii°) *in a major key* the music reflects the sound of the Mixolydian mode.

8.23c

If, in C Major, the subtonic (VII) replaces the leading tone (vii°), the scale sounds like the C Mixolydian mode!   C Mixolydian mode

VII vii°   VII

In a minor key, if the subtonic (VII) replaces the leading-tone triad (vii°), the music sounds like the Aeolian mode (pure minor).

8.23d

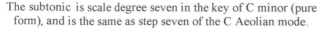

The subtonic is scale degree seven in the key of C minor (pure form), and is the same as step seven of the C Aeolian mode.

In the harmonic form, the raised seventh scale degree produces the leading-tone triad.

The subtonic triad may be used to harmonize melodies in major and minor keys, but it is not a substitute for the powerful leading-tone triad that clearly directs the "ear" toward a tonal center. If you prefer listening to or composing music in modes, you will enjoy the subtonic a great deal!

THE FUNCTIONS OF THE DIATONIC TRIADS IN THE ASCENDING MELODIC MINOR FORM

The leading tone, in both major and minor keys, is located one half step below the tonic and will always be the 3rd of the dominant triad (V) and the root of the leading-tone triad (vii°). In a minor key, the leading tone is the product of the harmonic minor scale, which raises scale degree 7 of the pure minor form.

In the melodic form of the minor, scale degree 6 is raised one half step (in addition to the raised 7th scale degree resulting from the harmonic form) and will impact three triads from the pure minor. Recall that the melodic form of the minor scale is an adjustment to the harmonic minor form where the establishment of a leading tone produced the musically awkward interval of the augmented second between scale degrees 6 and 7.

8.24a

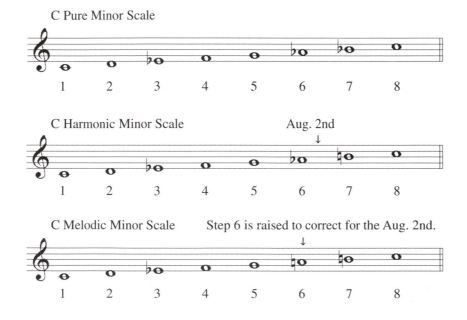

C Pure Minor Scale

1 2 3 4 5 6 7 8

C Harmonic Minor Scale   Aug. 2nd

1 2 3 4 5 6 7 8

C Melodic Minor Scale   Step 6 is raised to correct for the Aug. 2nd.

1 2 3 4 5 6 7 8

The melodic minor is a smoother form of the ascending minor scale, which, if left as is, sounds too much like a major scale. (For review, see Chapter 3, "Scales.") This is why the scale restores the pure minor form when it descends! Of the three forms of minor, the melodic form is used the least.

Example 8.24b illustrates the functions of the diatonic triads that occur in the melodic form of the minor scale

8.24b

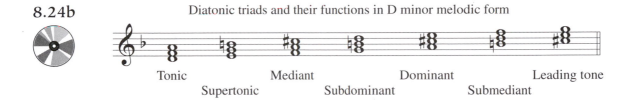

Diatonic triads and their functions in D minor melodic form

Tonic   Mediant   Dominant   Leading tone
Supertonic   Subdominant   Submediant

TRIADS IN PERSPECTIVE

The entire history of musical thought has been the result of composers and songwriters offering their own unique musical voices by constantly experimenting with melodies and harmonies. There are no "right" or "wrong" triads, and whatever is acceptable to the listener ultimately is "musically correct." The musical question related to this issue is: What is the most effective and efficient way to achieve musical expression?

The study of music theory provides an ordered method of discussing and understanding the compositional and harmonic practices of composers, as well as systematizing compositional procedures. The "common practice" approach to writing tonal music, which has evolved over many centuries, continues to be challenged by new ideas and techniques.

Continual experimentation with the unusual harmonization of melodies has been an important and exciting part of the development of musical thought and certainly will continue throughout the twenty-first century.

CONSTRUCTING DIATONIC TRIADS IN MAJOR KEYS

Skill Development

It is important to be able to construct any of the diatonic triads occurring in all of the major and minor keys.

How would you go about determining the correct pitches of the mediant (iii) triad in D major?

Process

Step 1. Determine the key signature for the key of D major. There are two sharps in the key of D.

8.25   D Major

Step 2. Locate the pitch on scale degree 3 of the D major scale and construct the triad above it.

8.26

D: iii

If the key signature were not indicated on the staff, the triad would have to reflect the accidentals and would appear as follows.

8.27

D: iii

Observe that the lowercase roman numeral indicates that the mediant triad is minor. It is a good idea to continually check and make sure that the triads you create reflect the quality types indicated by the roman numerals.

Skill Development

Let's try another! Construct the subdominant (IV) triad in E♭ major.

Process

Step 1. Determine the key signature for E♭ major. There are three flats in this key.

8.28   E♭ Major

Step 2. Determine the pitch on scale degree 4 of this key. The pitch is A♭. Place A♭ on the staff and construct the 3rd and 5th above it.

8.29a

E♭: IV

If the key signature were not indicated on the staff, the triad would look as follows.

8.29b

Eb: IV

Construct the following diatonic triads without placing key signatures on the staff.

Exercise 3

8.30a

G: iii   E: IV   Eb: vii°   A: iii

8.30b

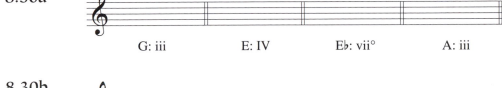

Bb: ii   D: V   Ab: vi   F: vii°

8.30c   Be careful—this example is in the bass clef! ☺

C#: V   Eb: iii   Db: V   F#: IV

CONSTRUCTING DIATONIC TRIADS IN MINOR KEYS

Now let's learn how to construct the diatonic triads that function in minor keys. Remember that there are three forms of the minor, each with its own set of triads, of which the harmonic and melodic forms will reflect raised scale degrees.

Skill Development

Construct the dominant (V) triad in the key of F# minor (remember that the V results from the harmonic form of the scale—see example 8.12).

Process

Step 1. Determine the key signature for F# minor. There are three sharps in this key. (If you have any difficulty with this step, review Chapter 4.)

8.31   F♯ Minor

Step 2. Locate the pitch on scale degree 5 and construct the 3rd and 5th above it.

8.32

Step 3. Now sharp the 3rd (E). Remember that the 3rd of the dominant triad (V) *is* the leading tone that results from the harmonic form of the minor scale.

8.33

f♯: V

If the key signature were not indicated on the staff, the triad would appear as follows.

8.34

f♯: V

Observe in example 8.34 that the key of F♯ minor is indicated with the lower-case letter (f♯) while in example 8.29b, E♭ major was indicated with the uppercase letter (E♭). The writing of the key signature followed by a colon and a roman numeral indicating the harmonic function of a triad is a convention that will be used throughout this chapter. Key signatures written in uppercase indicate major keys; key signatures written in lowercase indicate minor keys.

Skill Development

Construct the vii° (leading-tone triad) in the key of E minor.

Process

Step 1. Determine the key signature for E minor. There is one sharp in this key.

8.35   E Minor

Step 2. Determine the pitch located on scale degree 7 of the pure minor and place the 3rd and 5th above it. Now raise the root of this triad one half step, because the vii° results from using the harmonic form of the minor. Scale degree 7 in the E pure minor form is D, which must be raised to D♯. If you fail to do this, you will have created the subtonic triad.

8.36

If the key signature for E minor were not placed on the staff, the triad would have to reflect the accidentals, and would appear as follows.

8.37

Skill Development

Construct the III+ (mediant) in B♭ minor.

Process

Step 1. Determine the key signature for B♭ minor. There are five flats in the key signature.

8.38

B♭ Minor

Step 2. Locate the pitch on scale degree 3 of the scale and place the 3rd and 5th above it.

8.39

Step 3. Now raise scale degree 7 of the scale (A♭) one half step to A♮. This is what will generate the augmented triad (III+) of the harmonic or melodic minor. If you do not apply the natural, the mediant triad will be major.

8.40

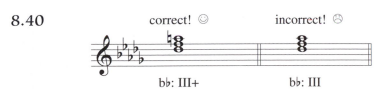

Notice in example 8.40 that the III+ is an augmented triad resulting from the harmonic form of the scale and that the major triad in the second measure (the incorrect example) results from the pure form of the minor scale.

If the key signature for B♭ minor were not on the staff, the mediant triad (III+) would look as follows.

8.41
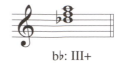

b♭: III+

Exercise 4

Construct the following diatonic triads without placing the key signatures on the staff. Insert the appropriate accidentals.

8.41a

A: vi   D: iii   B: IV   E♭: ii   G♭: V

8.41b

g: VI   d: III+   f♯: VI   c: ii°   a♯: iv

8.41c   Be careful—this example is in the bass clef! ☺

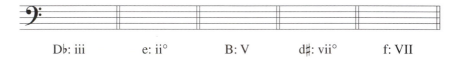

Db: iii   e: ii°   B: V   d♯: vii°   f: VII

MULTIPLE FUNCTIONS
OF DIATONIC TRIADS

Now that you know how triads function in a given major or minor key, we will study how triads function in multiple keys. Observe in example 8.42 that the G major triad functions as the I (tonic) in G major; III (mediant) in E pure minor; IV (subdominant) in D major; V (dominant) in both C major and C minor; VI (submediant) in B minor; and VII (subtonic) in A pure minor.

8.42   G major triad in its various functions

(Subtonic)

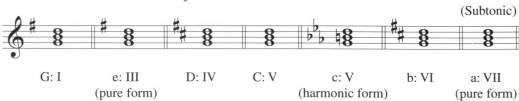

G: I   e: III   D: IV   C: V   c: V   b: VI   a: VII
             (pure form)   (harmonic form)   (pure form)

Example 8.42 is not an exhaustive illustration of the functions of the G major triad. There are other ways this triad may function within a more complex chromatic and harmonic setting, but these are issues for more advanced study.

Skill Development

Now we will study the method of determining the various major and minor keys in which a triad will function. Let's begin by identifying the *major keys* in which the G minor triad occurs.

Process

Step 1. Study the following Table of Harmonic Functions and establish a mental image of the possible diatonic functions of minor triads in major and minor keys (all forms). This may seem to be a considerable task, but later on you will be presented with a simple method of memorizing all of this information. Please recall that the lowercase roman numerals indicate minor triads!

Table of Harmonic Functions

Major Keys		Minor Keys (pure form)	
I	Tonic	i	Tonic
ii	Supertonic	ii°	Supertonic
iii	Mediant	III	Mediant
IV	Subdominant	iv	Subdominant
V	Dominant	v	Dominant (nonfunctioning)
vi	Submediant	VI	Submediant
vii°	Leading tone	VII	Subtonic

Minor Keys (harmonic form)		Minor Keys (melodic form)	
i	Tonic	i	Tonic
ii°	Supertonic	ii	Supertonic
III+	Mediant	III+	Mediant
iv	Subdominant	IV	Subdominant
V	Dominant	V	Dominant
VI	Submediant	vi°	Submediant
vii°	Leading tone	vii°	Leading tone

Step 2. List the functions of minor triads in both major and minor keys in the following fashion.

MINOR TRIAD FUNCTIONS IN MAJOR KEYS	MINOR TRIAD FUNCTIONS IN MINOR KEYS (ALL FORMS)
ii	i
iii	ii (melodic form)
vi	iv
	v (pure form)

The illustration in step 2 indicates that in major keys, minor triads will occur diatonically as ii, iii, and vi. This means that a specified minor triad may be constructed on scale degrees 2, 3, and 6 of three different major keys. The illustration also indicates that a specific minor triad will occur diatonically in minor keys (all forms) as i, ii, iv, and v when constructed on scale degrees 1, 2, 4, and 5 in four different minor keys. Now that you know how a minor triad functions, you need to determine the keys in which G minor occurs.

Principle *1*

To identify the keys in which a diatonic triad will occur, ascertain the quality of the triad, then compare it to the diatonic triad qualities of the scale degrees in both major and minor keys.

In the next step, refer to the Table of Harmonic Functions and establish the major keys in which G minor will function as a diatonic triad.

Step 3. Since minor diatonic triads occur in major keys as ii, iii, and vi, you must determine the keys in which the pitch G (the root of the G minor triad) is scale degree 2, 3, or 6. Place G on the staff and assign it each scale degree number (2, 3, and 6), then count downward or upward (whichever is closer) to scale degree 1 or 8. Remember, you are in a major scale, so when you encounter scale degrees 3 and 4, and 7 and 8, there must be a half step between them!

8.43

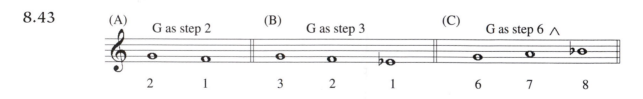

Step 4. At (A) in example 8.43, observe that G occurs on the second scale degree of the F major scale. At (B) and (C), G occurs as scale degree 3 in E♭ major and scale degree 6 in B♭ major, respectively. The example at (C) illus-

trates the arrival at scale degree 1 (or 8) by counting upward from G, beginning with scale degree 6.

Step 5. Now, add the 3rd (B♭) and 5th (D) above G in each measure of example 8.44. You will have constructed the G minor diatonic triad as it occurs in each of the three major keys. Observe that the G minor triad has a different function in each of the three keys.

8.44

The functions of the G minor triad may be illustrated as follows.

DIATONIC FUNCTIONS OF THE G MINOR TRIAD IN MAJOR KEYS

F: ii
E♭: iii
B♭: vi

Skill Development

Now, using the same method, let's identify the *minor keys* in which the G minor triad functions.

Process

Step 1. Apply **Principle 1** and review the Table of Harmonic Functions (on page 367) to determine the diatonic functions of minor triads in minor keys (all forms). Notice that a minor triad will function in the following ways:

MINOR TRIAD FUNCTIONS IN MINOR KEYS (ALL FORMS)

i (all forms)
ii (melodic form)
iv (pure and harmonic form)
v (pure form)

Step 2. You now know that a minor triad will function in a minor key as the i (tonic), which is constructed on scale degree 1; as the ii (supertonic), which is constructed on scale degree 2 in the melodic minor form; as the iv (subdominant), which is constructed on scale degree 4 in the pure and the harmonic forms; and as the v (nonfunctioning dominant), which is constructed on scale degree 5 in the pure minor form.

Place G on the staff and label it as scale degrees 1, 2, 4, and 5, then count downward or upward (whichever is closer) to scale degree 1. Use the pure form of the minor scale and remember that half steps occur between scale degrees 2 and 3, and 5 and 6.

Table of Harmonic Functions

Major Keys

I	Tonic
ii	Supertonic
iii	Mediant
IV	Subdominant
V	Dominant
vi	Submediant
vii°	Leading tone

Minor Keys (pure form)

i	Tonic
ii°	Supertonic
III	Mediant
iv	Subdominant
v	Dominant (nonfunctioning)
VI	Submediant
VII	Subtonic

Minor Keys (harmonic form)

i	Tonic
ii°	Supertonic
III+	Mediant
iv	Subdominant
V	Dominant
VI	Submediant
vii°	Leading tone

Minor Keys (melodic form)

i	Tonic
ii	Supertonic
III+	Mediant
IV	Subdominant
V	Dominant
vi°	Submediant
vii°	Leading tone

8.45

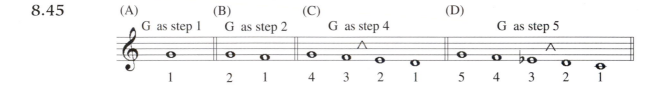

Step 3. Add the 3rd and 5th above the root of the G minor triad and indicate its function in the various keys:

8.46

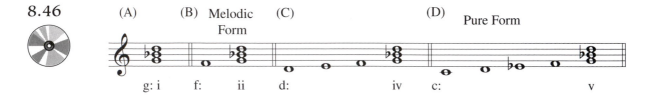

Example 8.46 illustrates that the G minor triad will function as the tonic (i) in G minor; the supertonic (ii) in F minor (melodic form); the subdominant (iv) in D minor; and as a nonfunctioning dominant (v) in C minor (pure form).

Notice that in example 8.46 section (B), the supertonic triad, G minor, functions as a diatonic triad (ii) in the melodic form of the key of F minor. The supertonic triad in the pure and harmonic forms of a minor key is diminished, but it occurs as a minor triad in F melodic minor because scale degree 6, D♭, is raised to D natural.

Recall that the triad constructed on scale degree 5 in the pure minor (nonfunctioning dominant) cannot function as an actual dominant (V), because it does not contain the leading tone of the key in which it occurs. In example 8.46 section (D), the triad constructed on scale degree 5 in the pure form of C minor is G minor. Because it lacks the leading tone for the key of C minor (the note B), it is labeled as a nonfunctioning dominant triad (v).

In every measure of example 8.46, the G minor triad has a flat placed before the 3rd (B♭) because the key signatures for the keys in which this triad functions have not been written on the staff. The respective keys are, however, indicated with a lowercase letter below the staff. If you were looking at an actual piece of music, the triads would appear within the context of their keys signatures as illustrated in example 8.47.

8.47

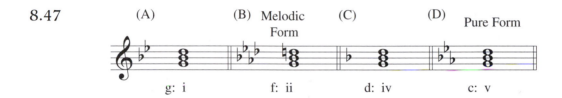

(A)	(B) Melodic Form	(C)	(D) Pure Form
g: i	f: ii	d: iv	c: v

The functions of the G minor triad in minor keys may be illustrated as follows:

DIATONIC FUNCTIONS OF THE G MINOR TRIAD IN MINOR KEYS

g: i   (all forms)
f: ii   (melodic form)
d: iv   (pure and harmonic form)
c: v   (pure form)

Skill Development

Determine the harmonic functions, in both major and minor keys, of the following triad:

8.48

Process

Step 1. First, you need to identify the quality of this triad. The triad is F♯ diminished. (See Chapter 7 if you need to review.)

Step 2. Now review the Table of Harmonic Functions on page 370 to determine the diatonic functions of diminished triads in major and minor keys (all forms).

The table indicates that a diminished triad functions in the following manner:

**Diminished Triad Functions
in Major Keys**

vii°

**Diminished Triad Functions
in Minor Keys (all forms)**

ii° (pure and harmonic forms)
vi° (melodic form)
vii° (harmonic and melodic forms)

Step 3. Diminished triads occur as diatonic leading-tone triads (vii°) constructed on the scale degree 7 in both major and minor (harmonic and melodic forms) keys. Locate the tonic of the major and minor keys by counting up one half step from F♯ to G. The F♯ diminished triad functions as the vii° (leading-tone) triad in G major and G harmonic and melodic minor.

8.49

Step 4. Refer to the Table of Harmonic Functions and notice that in minor keys, diminished triads also will function as ii° and vi°.

Step 5. To determine the key in which F♯ diminished functions as the ii°, count down one step and identify scale degree 1 of a minor scale. F♯ is scale degree 2 of the E minor scale and therefore functions as the ii° (supertonic) in E minor.

8.50

Now let's identify the minor key in which F♯ diminished functions as a vi°.

The Table of Harmonic Functions illustrates that the diminished submediant triad (vi°) is diatonic in the melodic form of the minor scale. This means that it is constructed on the *raised 6th scale degree* of the pure minor. There are numerous methods for determining the tonic of the key in which the vi° occurs, and the following is but one of many.

Step 6. Remove the accidental from the root of the F♯ diminished triad. (In this case it is a sharp.) The pitch with which you now are working, F, will be considered scale degree 6 of a pure minor scale. (Recall that F♯ diminished is the submediant triad built on the *raised 6th scale degree* in the melodic minor (vi°) and that by removing the sharp you have restored scale degree 6 of the pure minor form.)

8.51   F♯ as the raised step 6 in the melodic minor

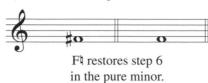

F♮ restores step 6
in the pure minor.

Step 7. Now that you know F is scale degree 6 of a pure minor scale, count up to scale degree 8 (1) and identify the tonic. Remember that you are in the pure form of the minor and must ascend in whole steps to reach scale degree 8. Counting upward from F (scale degree 6) will place you on A. F is the 6th scale degree in A pure minor.

8.52

6   7   8

Step 8. Now raise F to F♯ and add the 3rd and 5th above it. The triad produced is diatonic to the melodic form of the A minor scale and is the diminished submediant triad (vi°).

8.53   F♯ diminished functions as the
submediant (vi°) in A melodic minor.

vi°   vii°   i

Exercise 5

Determine the diatonic functions of the A major triad in both major and minor keys (all forms).

8.53a   A Major

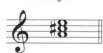

The Possible Diatonic Functions of the A Major Triad

MAJOR KEYS AND FUNCTIONS   MINOR KEYS AND FUNCTIONS

_____   _____

_____   _____

_____   _____

                              _____

                              _____

Determine the diatonic functions of the E minor triad in both major and minor (all forms) keys.

8.53b   E Minor

The Possible Diatonic Functions of the E Minor Triad

MAJOR KEYS AND FUNCTIONS   MINOR KEYS AND FUNCTIONS

_____   _____

_____   _____

_____   _____

                          _____

A TECHNIQUE FOR REMEMBERING THE POSSIBLE FUNCTIONS OF DIATONIC TRIADS IN DIFFERENT KEYS

It may seem daunting to remember all of the numerous possible diatonic functions of triads in major and minor keys, as listed in the Table of Harmonic Functions, but actually, it is a relatively simple task. The following method is one way to organize the information so that it may easily be recalled.

Principle 2

What is true for the key of C major and its relative minor is true for all keys.

This principle may seem simplistic, but it holds a great deal of musical truth! It is meant to suggest that the *fundamental relationships* that are demonstrated in the key of C major and its relative minor, with respect to constructing major and minor scales and intervals and diatonic triads, are the same in all other keys. Therefore, if you can master all of the information presented up to this point regarding the harmonic functions of triads and frame it within the context of the keys of C major and A minor, you may apply this information to all other keys.

You might be wondering why **Principle 2** refers to the key of C major and A minor and not the other keys. Because these keys require no sharps or flats in their key signatures, it is extremely easy to identify the qualities of, and compute, the diatonic triads occurring on various scale degrees. Additionally, these keys are the white notes on the piano keyboard, and this makes visualizing and playing the various triads and scales an uncomplicated task.

In your mind, visualize the pitches of the C major scale and its relative minor, A, in its pure form.

8.54

Because the pitches in these scales are identical, the diatonic triads are the same for both keys.

8.55

Notice that, although the triads are identical, they function differently in their respective keys.

8.56

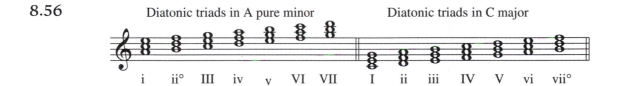

Observe that: (1) the diatonic triads in A pure minor are the same triads that occur diatonically in C major beginning on scale degree 6, and (2) the triads on scale degrees 6 and 7 of the C major scale occur as diatonic triads on scale degrees 1 and 2 in the A minor scale. Therefore: the tonic (i) in A minor is the same triad as the submediant (vi) in C major; the supertonic (ii°) in A minor is the same triad as the leading tone (vii°) in C major; the mediant (III) in A minor is the same triad as the tonic (I) in C major; the subdominant (iv) in A minor is the same as the supertonic (ii) in C major; and so on. These relationships are illustrated in example 8.57.

8.57

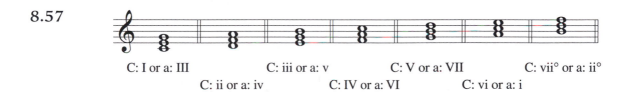

Because the diatonic triads of a major key are identical to the triads of its relative minor, it is unnecessary to compute their qualities (major, minor, diminished, and augmented) when they occur in the pure minor form. As long as you can visualize that the diatonic triads in C major *are the same* as the diatonic triads in A minor, you will have no difficulty in remembering their tonal qualities.

To illustrate this point, please observe in example 8.57 that the F major triad in the fourth measure, which functions as the IV (subdominant) in C major, *is* the same triad that functions as the VI (submediant) in A minor. Since you know that this triad is major in both keys, you may transfer this knowledge to all other keys. This means that the subdominant (IV) in, let's say, the key of D major (G major), will be the same triad as VI in its relative minor key, B minor!

TIP #1   When determining the possible functions of a triad, you must be able to determine the major and the minor keys (all forms of the minor) in which it will be diatonic. If you begin by visualizing how the triads in C major function as diatonic triads in the key of A minor (remember, these are the same as C major beginning on scale degree 6), you always will know the qualities of the diatonic triads as they appear in any major or minor (pure form) key. The qualities of these diatonic triads will never change.

Observe in the Table of Harmonic Functions (p. 370) that a triad's quality and function for the major and the pure form of the minor reflects example 8.56. This information does not need to be memorized, so long as you can establish that the diatonic triads of the pure minor form are the same as the triads in a major key beginning on scale degree 6.

TIP #2   To determine the possible functions of a triad in the harmonic and melodic forms of the minor, compute the qualities of the diatonic triads in *only the melodic form of the minor,* because this form reflects the altered 6th and 7th scale degree of the pure minor.

DIATONIC TRIADS RESULTING FROM THE MELODIC FORM OF THE MINOR SCALE

Let us now explore a method for determining all of the triads that are impacted by the raised 6th and 7th scale degrees in the melodic minor. It is not necessary to determine the triads that will be affected in the harmonic minor form, because they will be included in the melodic form. Recall that because the melodic scale raises scale degrees 6 and 7 when ascending, any triad altered in the harmonic form will appear as a diatonic triad in the melodic form.

Let's determine which diatonic triads of the pure form of the minor will be altered when the melodic form is used. Be aware that the raising of scale degrees 6 and 7 will impact six triads!

In the example below, the pitch F, which is located on scale degree 6 of the A minor scale, occurs in three triads in the pure form (ii°, iv, and VI).

8.58a

$$\text{i} \qquad \text{ii}° \qquad \text{III} \qquad \text{iv} \qquad \text{v} \qquad \text{VI} \qquad \text{VII}$$

It is important to realize that the raised 6th and 7th scale degrees will function as either the root, 3rd, or 5th of a triad.

Observe in example 8.58b that by raising scale degree 6 of the pure minor, F, to F♯, three triads in the pure form now have different qualities: the supertonic (B diminished) now is B minor (F♯ is the 5th of the triad); the subdominant (D minor) now is D major (F♯ is the 3rd), and the submediant (F major) now is F♯ diminished (F♯ is the root). The three triads in the following example reflect the raised 6th scale degree of A melodic minor.

8.58b

In the key of A minor, three triads of the pure form are affected by the raising of scale degree 7 (G to G♯): the mediant (C major) now is C augmented (G♯ is the 5th); the nonfunctioning dominant, E minor, now is E major and functions as a dominant triad (G♯ is the 3rd); and the subtonic, G major, now is G♯ diminished (G♯ is the root) and functions as a leading-tone triad. The three triads below reflect the raised 7th scale degree of the melodic minor.

8.58c

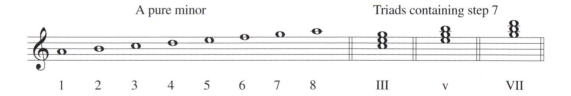

All of the triad qualities expressed in examples 8.58a, 8.58b, and 8.58c are illustrated in the Table of Harmonic Functions.

To quickly recall the qualities of the triads in both the pure and melodic forms, first visualize the diatonic triads in the pure form. It will help a great deal if you are able to play these triads on the piano.

Try playing the triads in the key of A minor in the pure form. (Do not forget that these are the same triads that occur in the relative major, but with different functions.) Observe which triads are impacted by the raising of the 6th and 7th scale degrees. With minimal practice, your mind's eye will visualize the piano keyboard and easily identify those triads in A minor that are altered by the raising of the 6th and 7th scale degrees. The following example organizes and illustrates this concept:

8.58d

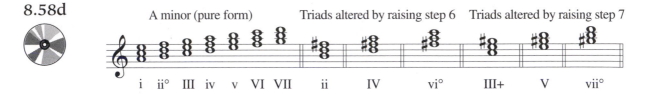

You will never need to memorize these alterations if you can visualize the piano keyboard and the effects of the altered 6th and 7th scale degrees. When you are able to identify the quality of the triads in both C major and all forms of A minor, you may apply this information to all other keys (**Principle 2**).

Skill Development

Let's determine the possible harmonic functions for the B minor triad.

Process

Step 1. Since the triad with which you are working is minor, mentally identify where minor triads function in the key of C major. You will recall that minor triads will function in a major key as: ii, iii, and vi.

8.59a   Minor triads occuring diatonically in C Major

Step 2. Now visualize the same minor triads in the key of A minor (pure form) and you will notice that they function as: iv, v, and i.

8.59b   Minor triads occuring diatonically in A pure minor

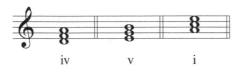

Step 3. Now let's determine the scale degrees at which minor chords occur in the melodic form of the minor. Raise scale degrees 6 (F to F♯) and 7 (G to G♯) of the A minor scale and *observe which triads from the pure form have been modified to a minor quality.* The only triad affected in this manner is the *supertonic*; its diminished quality in the pure form (ii°) is minor in the melodic form (ii).

8.59c

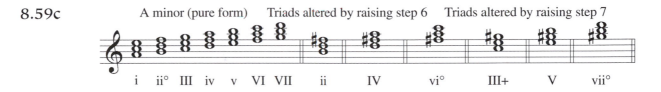

A minor (pure form)   Triads altered by raising step 6   Triads altered by raising step 7

i   ii°   III   iv   v   VI   VII   ii   IV   vi°   III+   V   vii°

The process you have completed in steps 1 through 3 has allowed you to construct the information regarding the functions of minor triads for the keys of C and A minor.

8.60

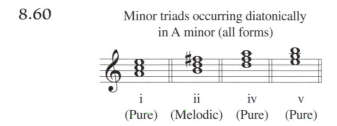

Minor triads occurring diatonically
in A minor (all forms)

i   ii   iv   v
(Pure) (Melodic) (Pure) (Pure)

Principle 2 states that what is true for the key of C and its relative minor is true for all keys. Minor triads, therefore, will occur in both major and minor keys (all forms) in the following ways.

THE POSSIBLE DIATONIC FUNCTIONS OF A MINOR TRIAD IN
MAJOR AND MINOR KEYS

Major Keys	*Minor Keys*
ii	i (pure form)
iii	ii (melodic form)
vi	iv (pure form)
	v (pure form)

Now that you have identified the possible diatonic functions of minor triads in both major and minor keys, apply **Principle 2** to determine the keys in which the B minor triad will function.

Step 4. First let's determine how B minor will function diatonically in major keys. Place the B minor triad on the staff and consider it as being constructed on scale degrees 2, 3, or 6 of a major scale. Why? Because minor triads occur diatonically in major keys on these scale degrees as ii, iii, and vi! Count up or down (whichever is closer) from each number, and locate scale degree 1 or 8 (remember that half steps in major scales occur between scale degrees 3 and 4, and 7 and 8.) When you locate scale degree 1 (or 8), you will have identified the *major keys* in which B minor functions as a diatonic triad.

Example 8.61a illustrates the possible diatonic functions of the B minor triad in a major key.

8.61a   B minor occurring as a diatonic triad on various scales in major keys

The B minor triad therefore functions in three *major keys:* as the supertonic (ii) in the key of A; as the mediant (iii) in the key of G; and as the submediant (vi) in the key of D.

8.61b   B minor occurring as a diatonic triad in various major keys

Now determine where the B minor triad occurs diatonically in *minor keys*. Review example 8.60 and observe that minor triads will occur as i, ii (in the melodic form), iv, or v.

Step 5. Place the B minor triad on the staff and label it with the appropriate scale degree numbers: 1, 2, 4, and 5. (Minor triads occur diatonically on these scale degrees.) Locate scale degree 1 or 8 (whichever is closer). Do not forget that half steps will occur between scale degrees 2 and 3, and 5 and 6.

8.62a

The B minor triad functions in four minor keys: as the tonic (i) in the key of B minor; as the supertonic (ii) in the key of A minor (melodic form); as the subdominant (iv) in the key of F♯ minor; and as a nonfunctioning dominant (v) in the key of E minor (pure form).

8.62b

Exercise 6

Determine the possible harmonic functions of the following triads in both major and minor keys.

8.63   D Minor

THE POSSIBLE DIATONIC FUNCTIONS
OF THE D MINOR TRIAD

MAJOR KEYS AND FUNCTIONS   **MINOR KEYS AND FUNCTIONS**

_____   _____

_____   _____

_____   _____

                                   _____

                                   _____

8.64   E Major

THE POSSIBLE DIATONIC FUNCTIONS
OF THE E MAJOR TRIAD

MAJOR KEYS AND FUNCTIONS   **MINOR KEYS AND FUNCTIONS**

_____   _____

_____   _____

_____   _____

                                   _____

                                   _____

SONGWRITING TIPS

At this point, you may be wondering about two questions: (1) Is music referred to as being in the key of, for example, G pure minor, G harmonic, or G melodic minor? and (2) How will I know which form of the minor to use when writing music?

The answer to the first question is No. Regardless of the particular form of the minor you are using when writing music, your key signature will never reflect the minor form(s) you use. The various forms of the minor scale are employed for musical variety and, when necessary, to assist in establishing a clear sense of the minor mode and an unambiguous tonal center for the listener.

The well-known Christmas melody "What Child Is This?" is in a minor key (Aeolian mode) that uses each of the three forms. Example 8.65a illustrates a section of the melody and the triads used to harmonize it. The functions of each triad are placed below the staff and are indicated with the roman numerals. Notice that four of the first six pitches of the melody clearly express the tonic triad A–C–E:

8.65a   *What Child Is This?*

The arrows indicate the triads used to harmonize every two measures of the melody.

Example 8.65a illustrates that in measures 3 and 4, the subtonic triad, G major (VII), is outlined by four of the five pitches of the melody. Measures 5 and 6 suggest that either the tonic A minor (i) or the submediant F major (VI) could be used to harmonize the melody at this point; the example illustrates the submediant. *Prior to measure 6, only the pure minor form has been used to create and harmonize the melody.*

Observe in example 8.65b that the G♯ in measure 6 is the first indication of the presence of the harmonic minor form. Scale degree 7 (G) of the pure minor is raised to G♯, which provides a leading tone to the tonic. In measures 7 and 8, the leading tone, G♯, is part of a three-note pattern (**arpeggio**) outlining the dominant triad which eventually will resolve to the tonic. When combined as one musical thought, measures 1 through 8 comprise the **antecedent phrase** of this tune.

8.65b   *What Child Is This?*

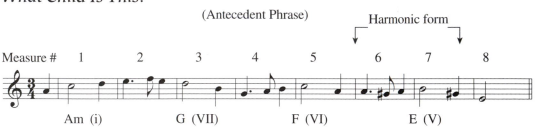

Example 8.65c illustrates the **consequent phrase** (the second part of the main melody) of "What Child Is This?":

8.65c   *What Child Is This?*

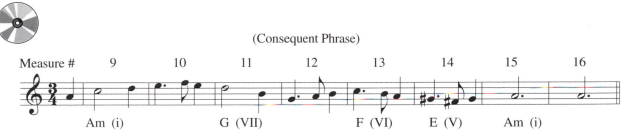

Measures 9 through 13 employ the pure form of the minor and are harmonized in the same fashion as measures 1 through 5 in example 8.65b.

Observe in example 8.65d that at measure 14 the melodic form of the minor mode has been used, and F (scale degree 6) which has been raised to F♯, ascends in the melodic minor scale to A. (The pitch immediately following F♯ is G♯ because the sharp on the first G is retained throughout the measure.)

8.65d   *What Child Is This?*

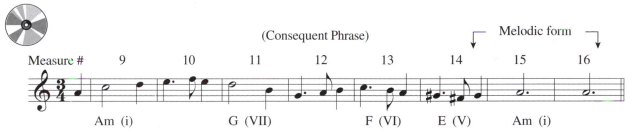

Although the antecedent and consequent phrases of this melody have employed the three forms of the minor mode, the melody is described as being in the key of A minor.

It is important to realize that in measures six and seven in example 8.65b, the harmonic form of the minor creates the leading tone (G♯), which defines the tonic. In measure 14 of example 8.65d, the melodic form of the scale, which raised F to F♯ from the pure form, was used to avoid the awkward interval of the augmented 2nd, which would have occurred between F and G♯. The resulting melody is smoother and more graceful, and may be sung without difficulty. Try singing the melody in example 8.65d using the F♮ (pure form) instead of F♯ and you will quickly observe the inelegance avoided by using the melodic form of the scale.

Now let's address the second question: How will I know which form of the minor to use when writing music? The answer is: Use all of the forms you need to achieve your musical goals.

When writing music in the pure form of the minor, the music will sound very "modal," with the key center not as clearly defined as it would be if you were employing the leading tone, provided by using the harmonic minor form. If possible, play the diatonic triads that exist in the pure form of A minor on a piano or guitar, and notice that the lack of a leading tone results in a rather weak tonicization of A minor.

8.66a

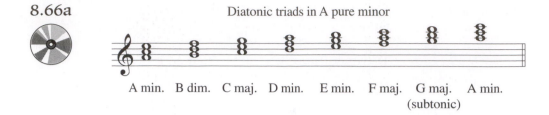

Diatonic triads in A pure minor

A min. B dim. C maj. D min. E min. F maj. G maj. A min.
(subtonic)

While the overall sound is quite beautiful and exotic, the pure minor form will not be as effective at clearly establishing the tonic triad. If you prefer the sound of this minor form then there is no need to use the other forms unless you find it desirable or helpful. If possible, play the tonic and dominant triads using the pure and harmonic forms of A minor, and you will easily perceive the power of the leading tone (G♯) in the harmonic form!

8.66b

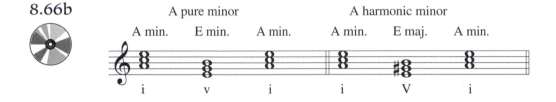

A pure minor

A min.   E min.   A min.

i   v   i

A harmonic minor

A min.   E maj.   A min.

i   V   i

The most necessary form of the minor is the harmonic minor, because it provides a leading tone. Composers use any form of the minor as needed, and choose triads because of the way they sound. Let your musical ear be the judge when deciding whether or not to use any particular form of the minor.

If you were to compose a song in minor and not change key anywhere in the piece, you could simply use the pure form and the listener would have no problem identifying the tonal center. The musical result would be a true expression of the Aeolian mode, which is the pure form of the minor scale. However, what usually happens is that compositions that are longer than two or three minutes tend to require more harmonic complexity to maintain the interest of the listener, and in these instances the harmonic minor assists in helping to establish shifting minor key tonal centers.

A SUMMARY OF THE DIATONIC TRIADS IN THE HARMONIC AND MELODIC MINOR FORMS

The **harmonic minor form** establishes three permutations of the pure form and results in *a diminished triad* on scale degree 7, *a dominant triad* on scale degree 5, and *an augmented triad* on scale degree 3. These triads, especially the dominant (V), add important harmonic functions to the music and increase the palette of tonal colors a songwriter may use to harmonize a melody. In addition, the melodic form of the scale smoothes out the awkward interval of the augmented 2nd between scale degrees 6 and 7 of the harmonic minor form and produces three additional triads with different tonal colors.

By using the triads of the various forms of the minor and other triads not strongly associated to the key, songwriters may inject many interesting approaches to harmonizing a melody.

The tunes of the songwriters who have written **standards** (tunes that have lasted many decades) are worth studying. Generally, within two and one half minutes of music, the melodies change keys at least once, the basic sound of a triad is enhanced by the use of extended harmonies, **nondiatonic triads** are used to harmonize a melody, and harmonic dissonance (tension) is carefully woven into the melodic and harmonic fabric of the tune.

All serious songwriters should carefully study the harmonic approaches of some of America's best songwriters of the twentieth century, such as George Gershwin, Irving Berlin, Cole Porter, Hoagy Carmichael, Vernon Duke, Duke Ellington, Harold Arlen, Jerome Kern, Johnny Mercer, Frank Loesser, Rodgers and Hart, and Lerner and Loewe. You may think their songs are out of date, but their harmonic approaches to writing and harmonizing melodies are inspirational!

REVIEW OF PRINCIPLES

Principle 1
To identify the keys in which a diatonic triad will occur, ascertain the quality of the triad, then compare it to the diatonic triad qualities of the scale degrees in both major and minor keys.

Principle 2
What is true for the key of C major and its relative minor is true for all keys.

ANSWER SHEETS TO CHAPTER 8

Exercise 1

8.10a

I	ii	iii	IV	V	vi	vii°
E♭ maj.	F min.	G min.	A♭ maj.	B♭ maj.	C min.	D dim.

8.10b

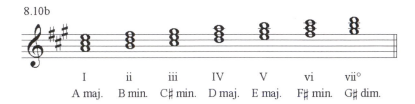

I	ii	iii	IV	V	vi	vii°
A maj.	B min.	C♯ min.	D maj.	E maj.	F♯ min.	G♯ dim.

8.10c

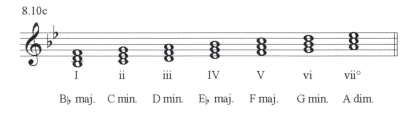

I	ii	iii	IV	V	vi	vii°
B♭ maj.	C min.	D min.	E♭ maj.	F maj.	G min.	A dim.

8.10d

I	ii	iii	IV	V	vi	vii°
E maj.	F♯ min.	G♯ min.	A maj.	B maj.	C♯ min.	D♯ dim.

Exercise 2

8.18

Pure form

Diatonic triads for B minor

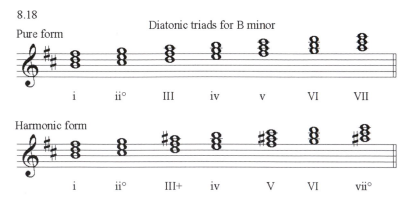

i	ii°	III	iv	v	VI	VII

Harmonic form

i	ii°	III+	iv	V	VI	vii°

Melodic form

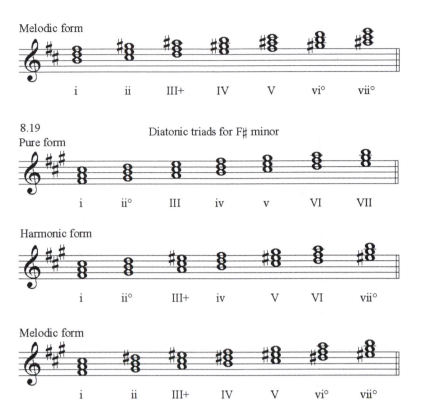

8.19   Diatonic triads for F♯ minor

Pure form

Harmonic form

Melodic form

Exercise 3

8.30a

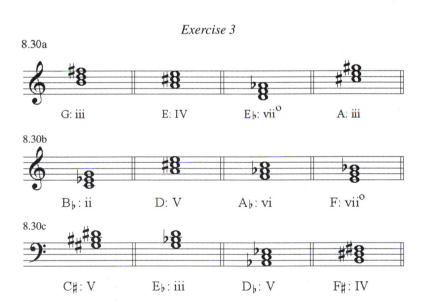

8.30b

8.30c

Exercise 4

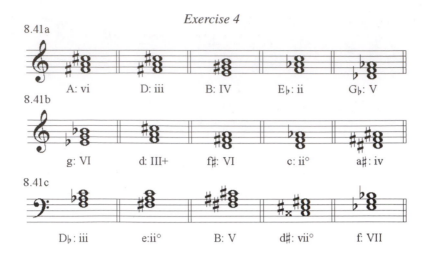

8.41a
A: vi   D: iii   B: IV   E♭: ii   G♭: V

8.41b
g: VI   d: III+   f♯: VI   c: ii°   a♯: iv

8.41c
D♭: iii   e:ii°   B: V   d♯: vii°   f: VII

Exercise 5

8.53a

A Major

Major Keys:	A:	I
	E:	IV
	D:	V

Minor Keys:	f♯:	III
	e:	IV
	d:	V
	c♯:	VI
	b:	VII

8.53b

E Minor

Major Keys:	D:	ii
	C:	iii
	G:	vi

Minor Keys:	e:	i
	d:	ii
	b:	iv
	a:	v

Exercise 6

8.63

D Minor

Major Keys:	C:	ii
	B♭:	iii
	F:	vi

Minor Keys:	d:	i
	c:	ii
	a:	iv
	g:	v

8.64

E Major

Major Keys:	E:	I
	B:	IV
	A:	V

Minor Keys:	c♯:	III
	b:	IV
	a:	V
	g♯:	VI
	f♯:	VII

WORKSHEETS FOR CHAPTER 8

Name

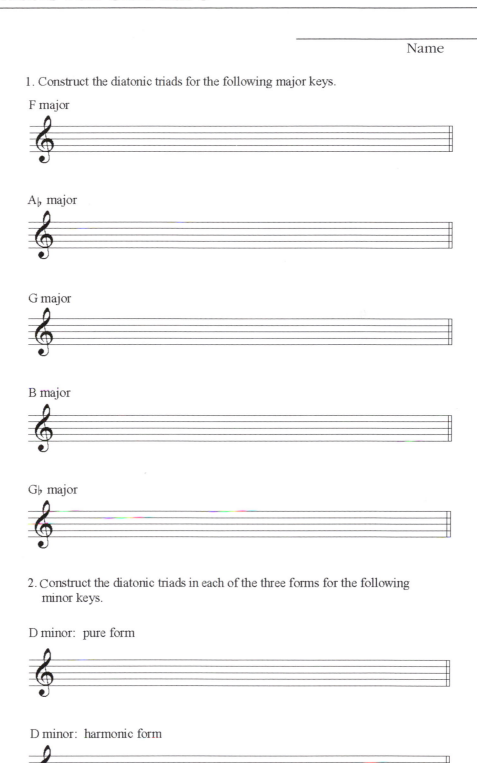

1. Construct the diatonic triads for the following major keys.

F major

A♭ major

G major

B major

G♭ major

2. Construct the diatonic triads in each of the three forms for the following minor keys.

D minor: pure form

D minor: harmonic form

_____
Name

D minor: melodic form

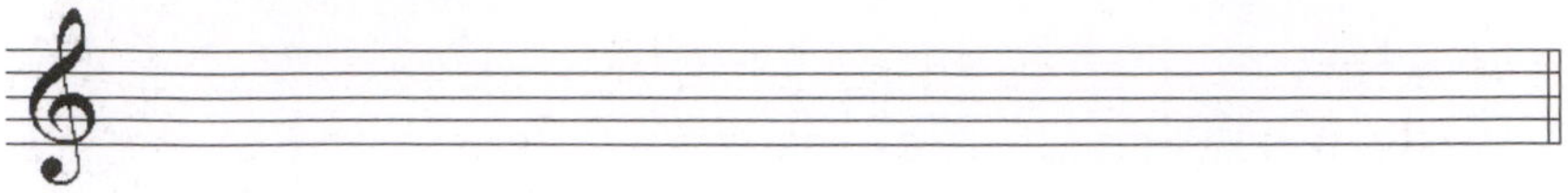

C♯ minor: pure form

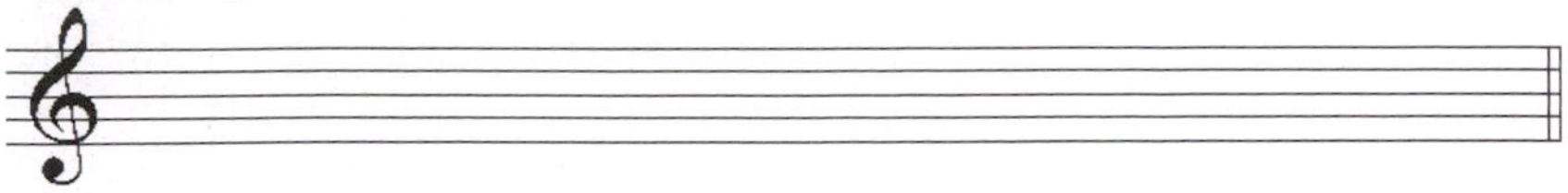

C♯ minor: harmonic form

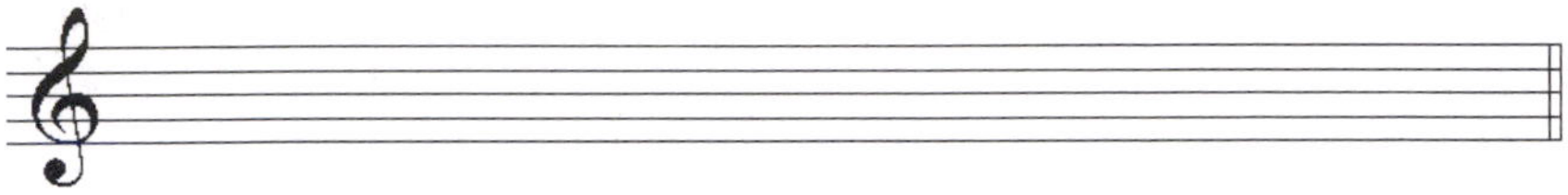

C♯ minor: melodic form

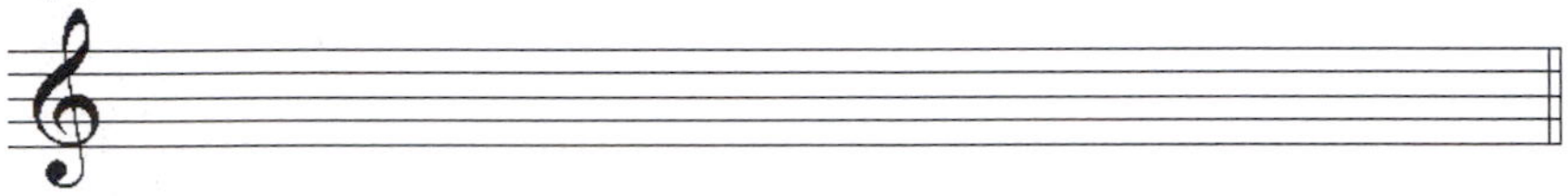

B♭ minor: pure form

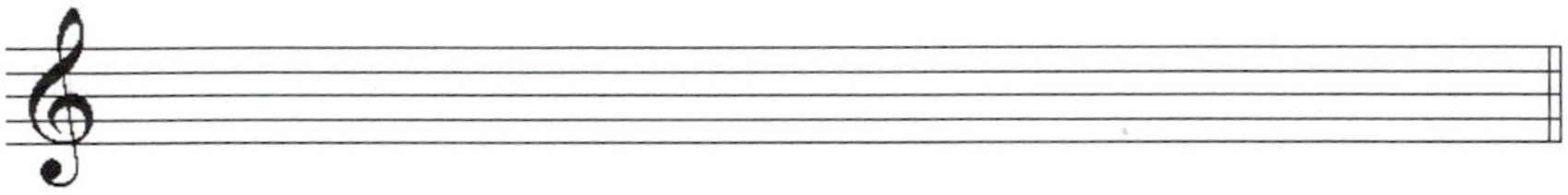

B♭ minor: harmonic form

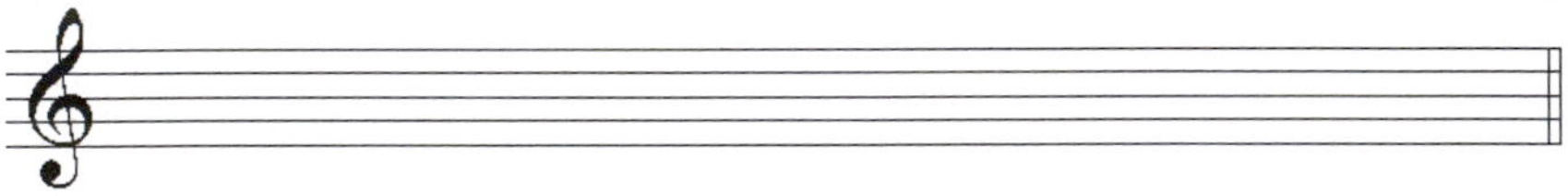

B♭ minor: melodic form

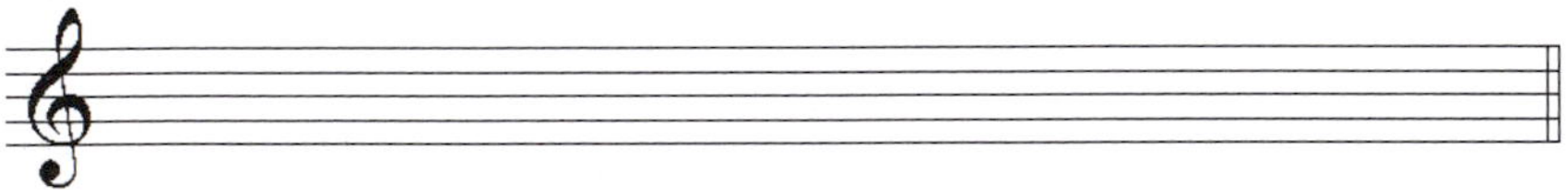

Name _____

3. Construct the triads indicated.

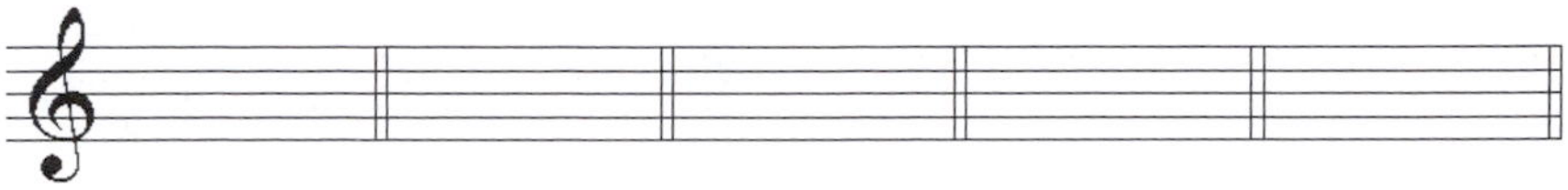

Ab: IV   G: vi   D: vii°   Eb: iii   F#: ii

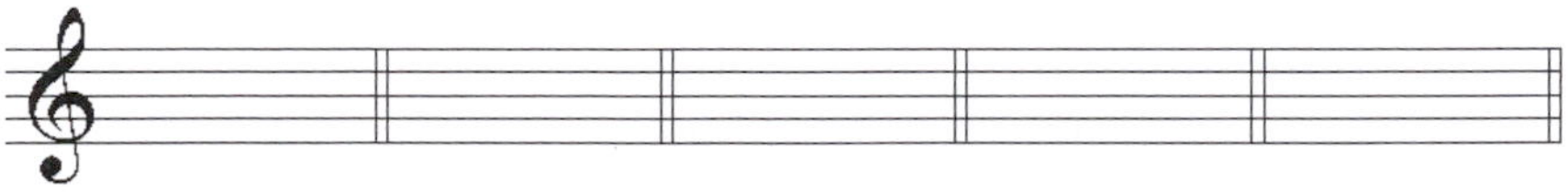

e: V   d: ii°   ab: vii°   b: III+   g#: VI

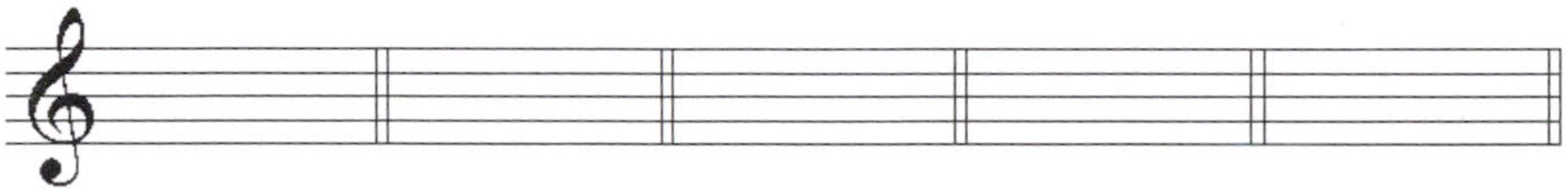

G: iii   E: vi   F#: vi   Bb: IV   Db: vii°

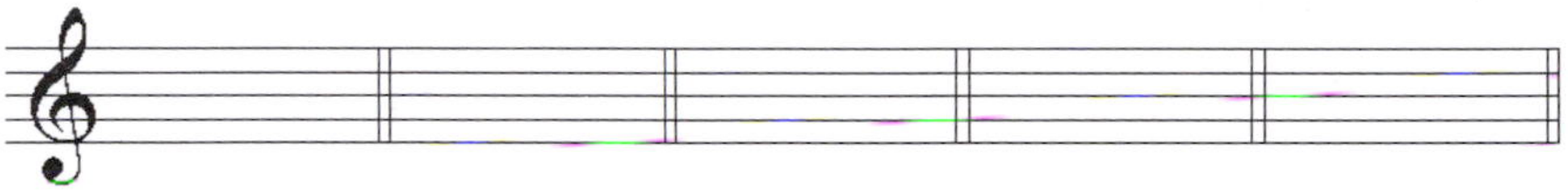

a: vi°   f: IV   b: ii°   g#: vii°   eb: iv

4a. Determine the possible diatonic functions of the Bb major triad in both major and minor (all forms) keys.

MAJOR KEYS AND FUNCTIONS   MINOR KEYS AND FUNCTIONS

_____   _____

_____   _____

_____   _____

                        _____

                        _____

4b. Determine the possible diatonic functions of the G major triad in both major and minor (all forms) keys.

MAJOR KEYS AND FUNCTIONS   MINOR KEYS AND FUNCTIONS

_____   _____

_____   _____

_____   _____

                        _____

                        _____

4c. Determine the possible diatonic functions of the F# minor triad in both major and minor (all forms) keys.

MAJOR KEYS AND FUNCTIONS   MINOR KEYS AND FUNCTIONS

_____   _____

_____   _____

_____   _____

                                            _____

4d. Determine the possible diatonic functions of the C minor triad in both major and minor (all forms) keys.

MAJOR KEYS AND FUNCTIONS   MINOR KEYS AND FUNCTIONS

_____   _____

_____   _____

_____   _____

                                            _____

Find additional Skill Development Drills on the accompanying CD-ROM and on the book companion Web site: http://music.wadsworth.com/kinney1e.

9
❦

Transposition

It is the melody which is the charm of music, and it is that which is most difficult to produce.

—Joseph Haydn

Transposition is the process of rewriting or performing an existing piece of music at a higher or lower pitch level. This process is often necessary to accommodate the pitch ranges of singers and instruments, and make it possible for instruments that are not manufactured at **concert pitch** (the pitch at which nontransposing instruments play, such as a flute or piano) to sound concordant with those that are manufactured at concert pitch. For example, each note played on an alto saxophone sounds a major 6th lower than written. If the written pitch G were to be played on an alto saxophone, it would sound like a piano's B♭ (a major 6th below G)!

If you ever have tried to sing a favorite song out of your comfortable singing range, and then changed the starting note up or down to make singing easier, you have performed a transposition. Also, if you play a piece of music on a transposing instrument such as the clarinet, trumpet, or saxophone, you need to rewrite it (or mentally transpose each note) in order to play along with a guitar or a piano (or the guitarist or pianist needs to transpose his or her music).

During the developmental stages of some instruments in the nineteenth century, the physical designs made it difficult to play chromatically altered pitches in tune. Before the mechanical systems were fully perfected, instruments were constructed in different keys in order to avoid having to play numerous accidentals. The mechanical problems have been solved and instruments are now able to play in any key desired, but the notation for these instruments has not changed.

When a transposing instrument's **fundamental** (written C) is sounded, it produces a concert pitch that designates how the instrument is identified. Two examples of this are the trumpet in B♭ and the horn in F. When a written C is performed on these instruments, the actual pitch one perceives is different for each.

9.1

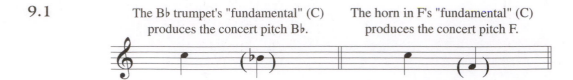

The Bb trumpet's "fundamental" (C) produces the concert pitch Bb.   The horn in F's "fundamental" (C) produces the concert pitch F.

Let's begin the study of transposition by learning how to rewrite an existing piece of music at a higher or lower pitch in order to accommodate the particular requirements of a voice or an instrument.

THE TECHNIQUE OF TRANSPOSITION

Imagine that you and your friends are preparing to sing "Happy Birthday" at a celebration, and you wish to play along with the melody on a nontransposing instrument such as the flute, violin, or keyboard. If you needed to read the music, the first part of the melody, in the key of F major, would appear as follows:

9.2   *Happy Birthday*

Hap - py birth - day to   you! Hap - py birth - day to   you! Hap - py...

Now, let's suppose that after practicing the melody a few times in this key, you decide that it sounds too low and wish to raise each pitch one diatonic whole step. You will need to *transpose* the key signature and the pitches from the key of F major to G major. Your first step will be to change the key signature from one flat to one sharp. (Key signatures were discussed in Chapter 4.)

9.3

F Major   G Major

Now write each pitch of the melody one diatonic whole step higher.

9.4   *Happy Birthday*

Hap - py birth - day - to   you! Hap - py birth - day to   you! Hap - py...

If you think the original key of F major is too high, you may wish to transpose it down one whole step to Eb. In this instance, you would need to change the key signature as follows.

9.5

Now write each pitch that was written in the key of F major down one diatonic whole step.

9.6   *Happy Birthday*

Hap - py birth - day to you! Hap - py birth - day to you! Hap - py...

If the melody you are going to transpose has a chromatically altered note (sharp, flat, or natural), you will have to be careful because the chromatic alteration will not always transpose using the same accidental.

Let's transpose the first phrase of "The Star-Spangled Banner" both higher and lower by one diatonic whole step. In the key of C major, the first few measures of "The Star-Spangled Banner" appear as follows.

9.7   *The Star-Spangled Banner*

O say can you see, by the dawn's ear - ly light...

When this melody is transposed one diatonic whole step higher to the key of D major, please notice that the F♯ in measure 3 of example 9.7 will transpose to a G♯, as illustrated in the following example.

9.8   *The Star-Spangled Banner*

O say can you see, by the dawn's ear - ly light...

When this section of the melody is transposed down one diatonic whole step from the key of C major to the key of B♭ major, the F♯ in the third measure of example 9.7 will transpose to an E♮.

9.9   *The Star-Spangled Banner*

O say can you see, by the dawn's ear - ly light...

Let's suppose you wanted to transpose the "The Star-Spangled Banner" up a major sixth from the key of C major to the key of A major. You may be thinking that it will take a great deal of time to transpose each note up this distance. Not true! Once you have determined the new key signature located a major 6th above C (key of A), all of the pitches will transpose accordingly without the need to compute a major 6th above each pitch.

9.10   *The Star-Spangled Banner*   Be careful!

The only note that will require your attention is the F♯.

9.11   *The Star-Spangled Banner*   F♯ transposed up a
                                                        major 6th to D♯.

Exercise 1

Transpose the following musical phrase as indicated.

9.12

Transpose one whole step higher.

9.13a   (original phrase)

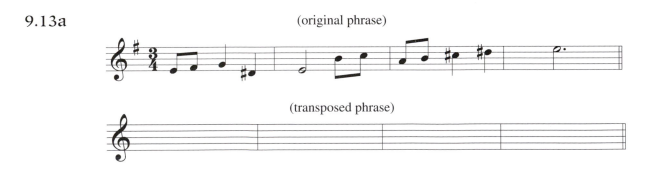

Transpose one whole step lower.

9.13b

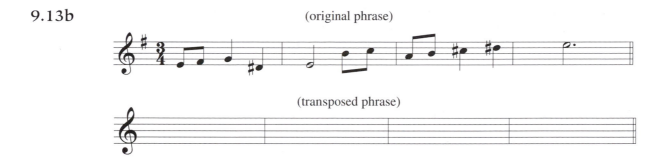

Transpose a perfect 5th higher.

9.13c

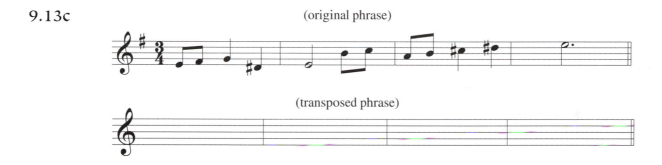

Transpose a minor 3rd lower.

9.13d

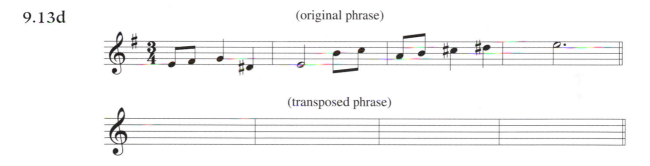

Transpose the phrase down one octave and write in the *bass clef*.

9.13e

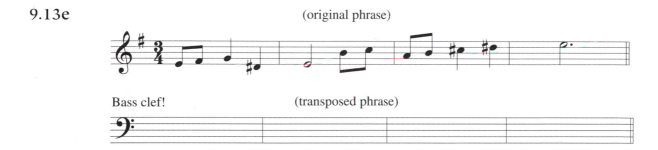

THE PROCESS OF TRANSPOSING FOR INSTRUMENTS

There are many woodwind and brass instruments requiring transposition that are used primarily within an orchestral setting, such as the trumpet in E♭, English horn in F, clarinet in D, and the oboe d'amore in A. Rather than investigate the process of transposition for each of these instruments, we will explore the transposition requirements of some of the more commonly used instruments, such as the B♭ clarinet; B♭ trumpet; horn in F; the various saxophones; and those instruments that transpose by the octave. Once you have learned how to transpose for these instruments, you may apply this knowledge to any instrument requiring transposition.

When writing music for a transposing instrument, the primary issue is to realize that when a pitch is played, the sound produced (the concert pitch) is different from that of the written note. Before attempting to transpose for an instrument, it is necessary to *determine exactly where a written pitch will sound when it is played!* Once you know this information, you will be able to easily determine how to write for any instrument requiring transposition. Please memorize the following principle.

Principle 1

Before attempting to transpose for an instrument, it is necessary to determine exactly where a written pitch will sound when it is played.

Let's apply **Principle 1** and learn how to transpose music for the B♭ trumpet and the B♭ clarinet.

Both instruments produce pitches sounding one full step (a major 2nd) lower than written. This means that when playing a written G, the concert pitch produced (the pitch you would hear on the piano) is F.

9.14　　　　　　　B♭ Trumpet and B♭ Clarinet

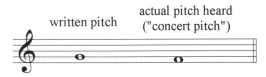

Because every pitch played on either instrument sounds a major 2nd lower than written, music for these instruments must be transposed up a major second. The tune of "Happy Birthday," when performed in the concert key of F major, will have to be written up a major 2nd in the key of G for the B♭ trumpet and the B♭ clarinet.

9.15　　　　　　　"Happy Birthday," written in the concert key of F major.

Hap - py birth - day to you! Hap - py birth - day to you! Hap - py...

9.16   "Happy Birthday," transposed for B♭ Trumpet and B♭ Clarinet.

Now let's suppose that a guitarist or pianist has decided to play "Happy Birthday" in the key of F major and wishes to have an alto saxophonist play along. The alto saxophone is a transposing instrument that sounds a major 6th lower than written. This means that every note played on the instrument will produce a concert pitch a major 6th lower, as illustrated in the following example.

9.17   Alto Saxophone

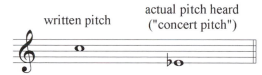

In order for the alto saxophone to perform "Happy Birthday" with the piano or the guitar, every note must be transposed a major 6th higher from the concert key of F major to the key of D major. Why? Because, every note played on the instrument will sound a major 6th lower than the written note!

9.18a   "Happy Birthday," written in the concert key of F major.

9.18b   "Happy Birthday," transposed for the alto saxophone (from the key of F major to D major).

Let's transpose "Happy Birthday" for the horn in F. This instrument sounds a perfect 5th lower than written, as illustrated in the following example.

9.19   Horn in F

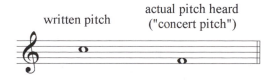

In order for the horn in F to perform "Happy Birthday" in the key of F major along with a concert pitched instrument such as the piano or guitar (or flute and violin, for example), the music and the key signature must be transposed up a perfect 5th from the key of F major to the key of C major. Why? Because, every note played on the instrument will sound a perfect 5th lower than the written note!

9.20a   "Happy Birthday," written in the concert key of F major.

Hap - py birth - day to you! Hap - py birth - day to you! Hap - py...

9.20b   "Happy Birthday," transposed up a perfect 5th to the key of C major.

Hap - py birth - day to you! Hap - py birth - day to you! Hap - py...

READING A TRANSPOSED INSTRUMENTAL PART FROM A SCORE

You have been learning the process of transposition for vocalists and for various transposing instruments. Now let's reverse the process and convert a transposed piece of instrumental music into the concert key in which the piece sounds. This skill is necessary when, for example, two transposing instruments, such as the trumpet and the horn in F, are both reading a piece of music written for the horn. How will the trumpet need to transpose the music in order to play along with the horn? Or, suppose the reverse situation occurred and the horn player had to transpose the trumpet part.

The following example illustrates "Mary Had a Little Lamb" written for the horn in F.

9.21   *"Mary Had a Little Lamb," for Horn in F*

Ma - ry had a lit - tle lamb, lit - tle lamb, lit - tle lamb.

Ma - ry had a lit - tle lamb, its fleece was white as snow.

When the music in example 9.21 is performed on the horn in F, the concert key the listener perceives will be C major, because the horn sounds a perfect 5th lower than written.

9.22

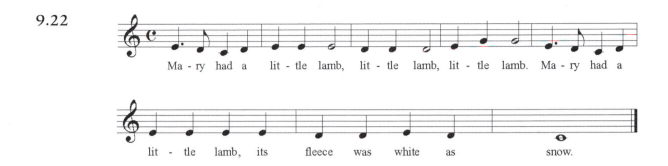

In order for the trumpet to play along with the horn, the music in the key of C would need to be transposed up one step to the key of D, because the B♭ trumpet sounds one step lower than written.

9.23   *"Mary Had a Little Lamb," written in the key of D major*
        for the B♭ trumpet

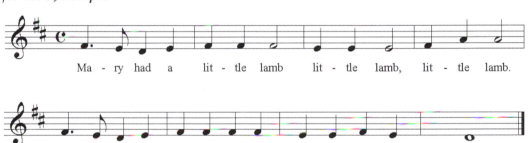

Therefore, if a trumpet player were playing the horn part (example 9.21), the music would need to be transposed down a perfect 4th in order for the players to sound in **unison** (playing at the same pitch). If the horn player were to read a trumpet part, the reverse would be true; the music would have to transposed up a perfect 4th to sound in unison with the trumpet.

Skill Development

Let's suppose that a clarinetist wanted to play along with an alto saxophonist and needed to read the saxophone music. The music for the clarinet would have to be transposed.

How would the clarinetist transpose the music for "Mary Had a Little Lamb" when it is written for the alto saxophone? For our purposes, the tune is written in the key of D major, as illustrated in the following example.

9.24   *"Mary Had a Little Lamb," written in the key of D major
            for alto saxophone*

Ma - ry had a   lit - tle lamb, lit - tle lamb, lit - tle lamb.

Ma - ry had a   lit - tle lamb, its   fleece was white as   snow.

Process

Step 1. Determine how the music will sound at concert pitch (**Principle 1**). The alto saxophone sounds a major 6th lower than written. This means that the concert key signature and every note of the melody will be a major 6th below what is written in example 9.24.

Step 2. Now transpose each pitch down a major 6th and change the key signature. Because the music for the alto saxophone is written in the key of D major, descending a major 6th will place the music in the concert key of F major. (Remember that the "concert key" is the key that you are actually hearing as it would sound on the piano or any other concert-tuned instrument.)

9.25   *Alto saxophone part transposed to concert sounding pitches*

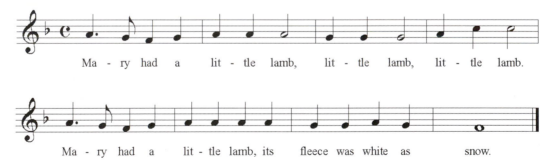

Ma - ry had   a   lit - tle   lamb, lit - tle   lamb, lit - tle   lamb.

Ma - ry had a   lit - tle lamb, its   fleece was white as   snow.

Step 3. In order for the B♭ clarinet to sound at concert pitch, it needs to transpose every note (and the key signature) in example 9.25 up one step. Why? Because every note the clarinet produces sounds a major 2nd lower than written! This will place the clarinet in the key of G major, and the transposed music will look as follows.

9.26 *"Mary Had a Little Lamb," transposed up a major second for the B♭ clarinet.*

Ma - ry had a lit - tle lamb, lit - tle lamb, lit - tle lamb.

Ma - ry had a lit - tle lamb, its fleece was white as snow.

Now let's see how well you understand the process of transposition! Below is a section of the famous tune "Lazy River," which was composed during the early part of the twentieth century by the great American songwriter Hoagy Carmichael. The melody is extremely chromatic and challenging to transpose. The first part of the melody looks as follows.

9.27 *A section of "Lazy River"*

Exercise 2

Transpose the excerpt from "Lazy River" in example 9.27 for the B♭ trumpet. (Be sure to transpose the key signature!)

9.28

Transpose the same excerpt for the alto saxophone.

9.28b

9.29a

When transposing a piece of music for an instrument, remember to keep the instrument's playing range and characteristic sound in mind. For example, if "Lazy River," as it is written in example 9.27, were to be transposed for the tenor saxophone, the upper pitches would be in the extreme high register of the instrument. The tenor saxophone sounds a major 9th lower than written, so its music must be transposed up a major 9th to sound at concert pitch. Not only would some of the pitches of "Lazy River" *nearly* be out of the playing range of the instrument at this transposition, but the higher pitches would sound odd because the sound of the tenor sax is strongest in the range written below one ledger line above the staff. An appropriate solution to this problem is to transpose the entire concert key of the melody down a few steps. The following example illustrates how example 9.27 has been transposed for the tenor saxophone, resulting in upper pitches close to the top of its range. The resulting notes in the second and third measures are not written in the best range for the tenor saxophone.

9.29b   9.29c   *Lazy River*

The normal playing range
for the tenor saxophone.

TRICKS OF THE TRADE

When transposing a piece of music written in a concert key for the alto saxophone, you learned that you must write each note up a major 6th because the instrument sounds a 6th lower than written. In examples 9.18a and 9.18b, "Happy Birthday," which was written in the key of F major, needed to be transposed to the key of D major so that the alto saxophone could play along with a concert pitched instrument. Once again, this is illustrated in the following examples.

9.30a   "Happy Birthday," written in the concert key of F major.

9.30b   "Happy Birthday," transposed for the alto saxophone (from the key of F major to D major).

It is not uncommon for an alto saxophonist to be asked to transpose music written for concert pitched instruments. For example, let's say you are in a band and have a piece of music from which a pianist or guitarist is playing, and then ask an alto saxophonist to play along. It is expected that an accomplished saxophonist will transpose each note up a major 6th at first sight! Transposing up a major 6th is not a simple task, and the likelihood of making an error is great.

You have learned one method of transposing up a 6th; here is another. The alto saxophonist can (1) add three sharps to the key signature (this will adjust the key signature up a major 6th); (2) read the music a third below each pitch; and (3) play these pitches up one octave.

If an alto saxophonist were to apply this mental process to the tune of "Happy Birthday," it would appear as follows.

9.31a   "Happy Birthday," written in the concert key of F major.

9.31b   Key signature   "Happy Birthday," with
             has been adjusted   transposed notes and key signature.

Original notes
are on the top.

When the notes in parentheses are played up one octave, the resulting pitches will sound a major 6th higher than the original tune in the concert key of F major (see example 9.30b)! This method of transposition is an extremely valuable musical tool for alto saxophone players and is relatively easy to learn.

The technique of adding three sharps to a key signature, in order to transpose a key up a major 6th from the original key, *does have its limitations*. It works exceedingly well when adding three sharps to a key signature written in flats because sharps negate flats; this is explained in the section on parallel minor keys in Chapter 4. But, when adding three sharps to a key signature written in sharps, you must be careful not to exceed writing seven sharps. Why? There are only seven different sharp keys. This means that if the concert key is written in five or more sharps, you will not be able to add three sharps to it.

Let's look at this issue more closely by placing the excerpt of the tune to "Happy Birthday" in the concert key of B major.

9.32   "Happy Birthday," written in the concert key of B major.

If an alto saxophonist were asked to perform this music with a concert-sounding instrument, the music would have to be transposed up a major 6th from the key of B major to G♯ major. The key of G♯ major does not exist! What is the solution in this instance? The music for the alto saxophone would have to be transposed up an enharmonic 6th to the key of A♭ major. This process would need to be applied whenever the concert key signature has five or more sharps. Because most music is not written in these keys, this issue is not a major concern, but certainly it has the potential to occur.

Now let's explore another way to utilize transposition when the instrument is the baritone saxophone.

The baritone saxophone, which is the largest saxophone commonly used in today's music, is a popular instrument in jazz, rock and roll, funk, and in concert bands. Its main purpose is to reinforce music written for the trombone or a bass instrument, such as the tuba or string bass. It may also be featured playing the melody, and was the main instrument for jazz greats Gerry Mulligan and Nick Brignola.

The baritone saxophone's fundamental (written C) produces the pitch E♭, like the alto saxophone, but sounding one octave lower. The instrument therefore sounds a major 13th lower than written! (Recall from Chapter 6 that a major 13th is a compound interval equal to an octave and a major 6th.)

9.33

Alto Saxophone
Plays C—Sounds E♭

Baritone Saxophone
Plays C—Sounds E♭, one
octave lower than the alto

The baritone saxophone produces pitches that sound in the bass clef. However, music for all of the saxophones is written in the treble clef, so that players are able to play any of the various saxophones.

Because the baritone saxophone is primarily responsible for supporting the bass, it is not uncommon for composers to write music for it that duplicates, or "doubles," the string bass or trombone part note for note.

The first few measures of the tune "Happy Birthday" could have a bass part, as illustrated in the following example.

9.34

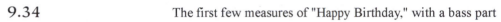

The first few measures of "Happy Birthday," with a bass part

Piano

If a baritone sax player were asked to read the bass part (the music in the bass clef), and play along with a concert pitched instrument (such as a piano, guitar, flute, or violin), each note would need to be transposed up a major 13th. This is not an easy task, and the likelihood for making errors is extremely high!

The solution to this problem is quite simple. The baritone sax player would simply need to (1) change the clef sign from the bass to the treble, and (2) add three sharps to the key signature to produce the key of D, which is a 6th above F. (Remember, the first sharp will negate the flat and leave two remaining sharps.)

9.35a

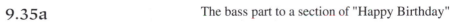

The bass part to a section of "Happy Birthday"

Example 9.60b illustrates the same music transposed for the baritone saxophone.

9.35b   Baritone Saxophone part to a section of "Happy Birthday"

1. The treble clef sign has replaced the bass clef
2. The original bass clef notes remain unchanged
3. The key signature has been adjusted

Although this transposition method may be applied to numerous musical situations, it has the same limitations that pertain to the method for alto saxophone, because it will not function when the concert key signature of a piece of music is written in five or more sharps. (Most songs avoid these keys.)

TRANSPOSING CHROMATICALLY ALTERED PITCHES AS ALTERED SCALE DEGREES

When a musician is required to transpose a piece of music in which there are numerous chromatically altered pitches (naturals, sharps, and flats), it is sometimes helpful to determine how a pitch's *associated scale degree* has been altered.

Principle 2

When transposing chromatically altered pitches, it is occasionally easier to think of them as altered scale degrees.

You will recall from Chapter 3 that each degree of a scale may be identified with a number. For example, the C major scale has pitches located on scale degrees 1 through 8.

9.36   C Major Scale

Let's suppose that a piece of music is written in C♯ minor and employs the harmonic minor form. (For a review of minor scales, see Chapter 3.) This form would include the pitch B♯. If a musician needed to transpose this note up a perfect 5th (such as for the horn in F), B♯ would transpose to F𝑥!

9.37   Original pitch   Transposed up a 5th

When transposing from the key of C♯ minor up a perfect 5th to G♯ minor, it is much simpler to think of B♯ as scale degree 7 raised one half step rather than to compute a perfect 5th above B♯.

Let's apply this process and transpose the first part of "The Star-Spangled Banner" from the key of C major to the key of F major.

9.38   *"The Star-Spangled Banner"*

This entire melodic fragment must be transposed up a perfect 4th. To accomplish this, first the key signature must be changed from the key of C to the key of F by adding B♭, and then each pitch must be transposed a perfect 4th higher. The only pitch requiring a chromatic alteration when it is transposed will be the F♯ in the fourth measure. In this instance, if you are adept at quickly constructing any interval above a pitch, you will determine that a perfect 4th above F♯ is B♮. However, another way to think about this chromatically altered note is to realize that it is *scale degree 4 raised one half step*.

9.39   *"The Star-Spangled Banner"*

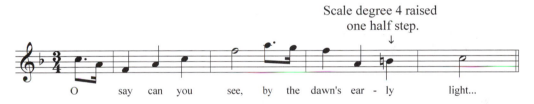

Complete the following transpositions. Try to think of the chromatic pitches as altered scale degrees.

Exercise 3

9.40a   Transpose up a major third. Do not forget to adjust the key signature! ☺

9.40b   Transpose up a perfect 4th.

9.40c   Transpose down one octave. Write the melody in the bass clef.

Exercise 4

Refer to the Transposition Chart in the Appendix (pages 427–431) and transpose the melodic fragment for the following instruments.

9.41a   Transpose for B♭ trumpet.

9.41b   Transpose for alto saxophone.

9.41c   Transpose for bass clarinet.

9.41d   Transpose for guitar.

9.41e   Transpose for horn in F.

READING PITCHES IN THE MOVABLE C CLEFS USING THE PROCESS OF TRANSPOSITION

In Chapter 1 you were introduced to four movable C clefs: soprano clef, mezzo soprano clef, alto clef, and tenor clef. In each of these clefs, middle C was located on the line at which the center of the clef was placed on the staff.

9.42

Because the majority of musicians read either the treble or bass clef, it is somewhat difficult for most to fluently identify pitches written in the movable clefs. It is possible, however, to apply your knowledge of transposition to assist in this process.

Please observe that middle C, which is located on the bottom line of the soprano clef, would look like an E if it were written on the same line in the treble clef.

9.43

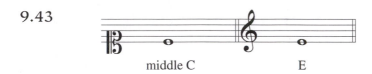

middle C   E

When the written E, in example 9.43, appears on the bottom line in the soprano clef, it may be thought of as having been renamed (transposed down one line) to be called middle C. Therefore, it is possible to identify the *letter name* of any note written in the soprano clef by imagining that it is written in the treble clef and identifying it by the letter name of the pitch a 3rd below it, regardless of the accidental used. Example 9.44a illustrates this concept.

9.44a

The name of this pitch?

Read the note in the treble clef down a 3rd. Db becomes Bb.

944b

Bb

Skill Development

Identify the following two pitches written in the soprano clef.

9.45

?   ?

Process

Step 1. Imagine that the two pitches are written in the treble clef and then transpose them down a 3rd.

9.46

The pitches in example 9.47 now may be easily identified as F♯ and G♭.

9.47

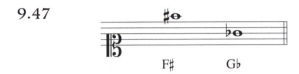

Exercise 5

Identify the following pitches using the same method.

9.48

TIP. It is important to realize that while this method will provide you with an efficient means of *identifying* the names of pitches written in the soprano clef, it does not necessarily place pitches at their correct octaves. This will be true for the remaining movable C clefs as well.

READING PITCHES IN THE MEZZO SOPRANO CLEF

Reading pitches in the mezzo soprano clef requires using the bass clef and applying the same process you learned in the previous section. Observe that middle C in this clef is placed on the second line of the staff and is identified as B in the bass clef.

9.49

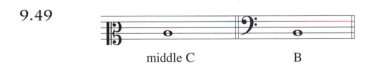

It is now possible to determine the letter name of any note written in the mezzo soprano clef, by imagining that all pitches will be identified by the letter name of the nearest note above it in the bass clef. This is illustrated in the following example.

9.50a

The name of this pitch?

Read the note in the bass clef
one letter name above.
A♯ becomes B♯.

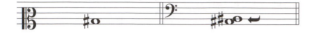

9.50b

B♯

Skill Development

Identify the following pitches in the mezzo soprano clef.

9.51

?   ?

Process

Step 1. Imagine that the two pitches are written in the bass clef and then transpose them to the nearest pitches directly above them.

9.52

?   ?

The pitches in example 9.52 now may be identified as C♭ and E♯.

9.53

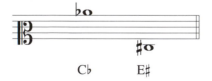

C♭   E♯

Exercise 6

Identify the following pitches.

9.54

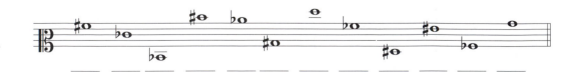

READING PITCHES IN THE ALTO CLEF

Reading pitches in the alto clef will once again require using the treble clef. Observe that middle C in this clef is placed on the third line of the staff and is identified as B in the treble clef.

9.55

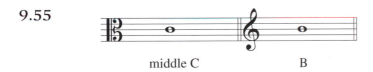

middle C   B

The letter name of any note written in the alto clef may be identified by the letter name of the note that is directly above it in the treble clef, as illustrated in the following example.

9.56

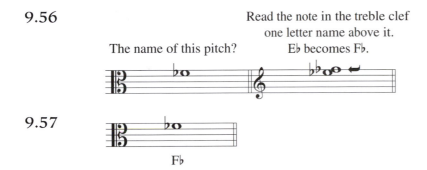

The pitches in example 9.59 may now be identified as D and G.

9.57

F♭

Skill Development

Identify the following pitches in the alto clef.

9.58

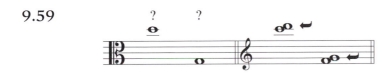

Process

Step 1. Imagine that the two notes are written in the treble clef and then transpose them to the nearest note above.

9.59

The pitches in example 9.59 may now be identified as D and G.

9.60

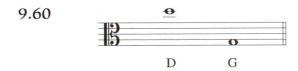

D   G

Exercise 7

Identify the following pitches.

9.61

READING PITCHES IN THE TENOR CLEF

Reading pitches in the tenor clef will require using the treble clef. Observe that middle C in this clef is placed on the fourth line of the staff and is identified as D in the treble clef.

9.62

middle C   D

The letter name of any note written in the tenor clef may be identified by the letter name of the note directly below it in the treble clef. This is illustrated in the following example.

9.63a

Read the note in the treble clef
one letter name below it.
The name of this pitch?   B♭ becomes A♭.

9.63b

A♭

Skill Development

Identify the following pitches in the tenor clef.

9.64

?   ?

Process

Step 1. Imagine that the two notes are written in the treble clef and then transpose them to the note directly below.

9.65

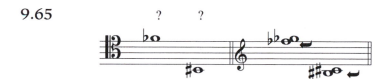

The pitches in example 9.65 now may be identified as F♭ and B♯.

9.66

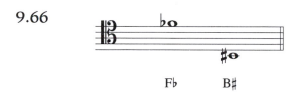

Exercise 8

Identify the following pitches.

9.67

REVIEW OF PRINCIPLES

Principle 1
Before attempting to transpose for an instrument, it is necessary to determine exactly where a written pitch will sound when it is played.

Principle 2
When transposing chromatically altered pitches, it is occasionally easier to think of them as altered scale degrees.

ANSWER SHEETS TO CHAPTER 9

Exercise 1

Exercise 2

Exercise 3

Exercise 4

Exercise 5

9.48

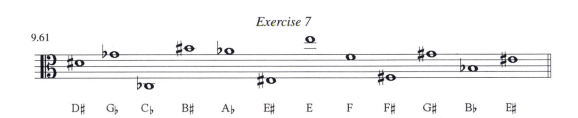

B   D♭   G   E♯   A♭   E   A   D♭   A♯   G   C♭   F

Exercise 6

9.54

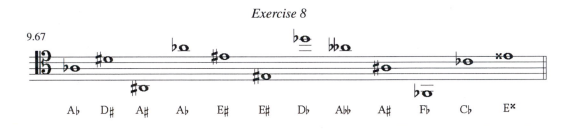

A♯   E♭   D♭   D♯   C♭   B♯   F   A♭   F♯   G♯   A♭   B

Exercise 7

9.61

D♯   G♭   C♭   B♯   A♭   E♯   E   F   F♯   G♯   B♭   E♯

Exercise 8

9.67

A♭   D♯   A♯   A♭   E♯   E♯   D♭   A♭♭   A♯   F♭   C♭   E𝄪

WORKSHEETS FOR CHAPTER 9

Name

1. Transpose the following melody for the instruments indicated.

a) Alto Saxophone:

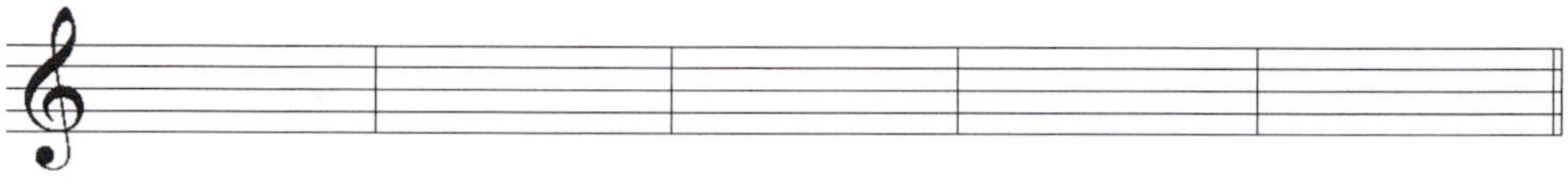

b) Horn in F

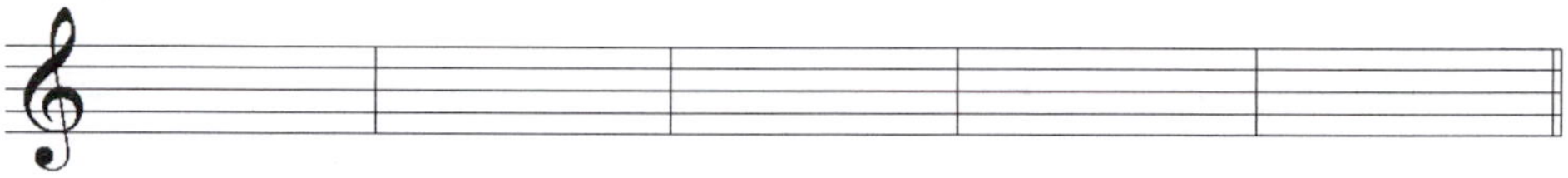

c) Guitar

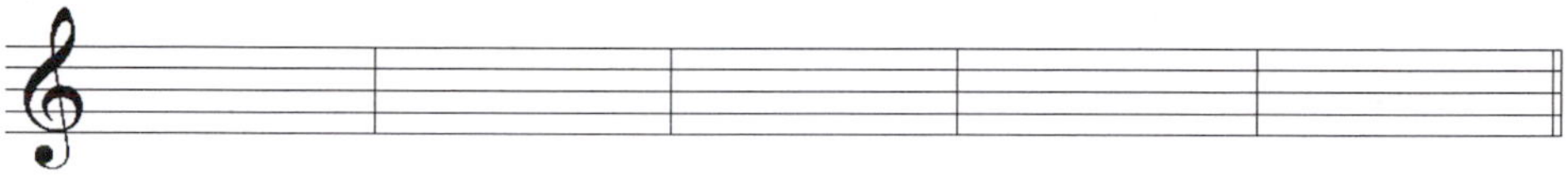

d) Tenor Saxophone

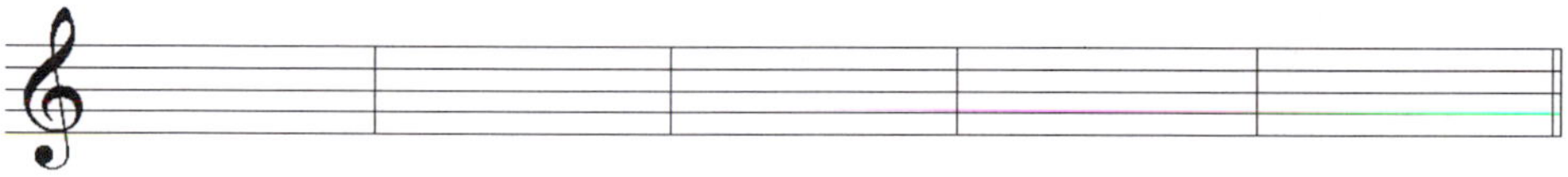

e) Transpose down one octave into the bass clef for the trombone.

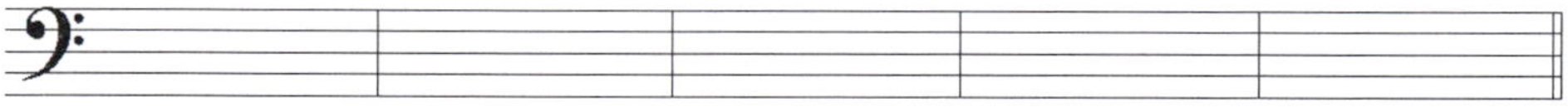

Name

2. Transpose the following melody into the treble clef for the baritone saxophone.

3. Transpose the folowing melody for the piccolo.

4. Identify the following pitches.

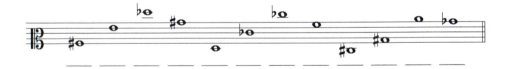

Name

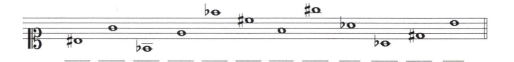

5a. Transpose the following notes, written for the trumpet, to their concert sounding pitches.

5b. Transpose the following notes, written for the alto saxophone, to their concert sounding pitches.

5c. Transpose the following notes, written for the horn in F, to their concert sounding pitches.

5d. Transpose the following notes, written for the guitar, to their concert sounding pitches.

5e. Transpose the following notes, written for the double bass, to their concert sounding pitches.

Find additional Skill Development Drills on the accompanying CD-ROM and on the book companion Web site: http://music.wadsworth.com/kinney1e.

Appendix

A SECTION OF THE PIANO KEYBOARD

THE MAJOR KEY SIGNATURES

Minor keys are indicated in the parentheses.

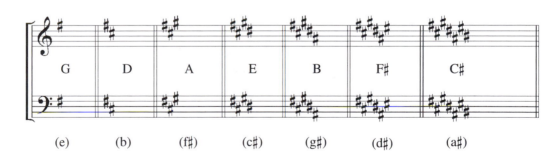

G	D	A	E	B	F♯	C♯
(e)	(b)	(f♯)	(c♯)	(g♯)	(d♯)	(a♯)

F	B♭	E♭	A♭	D♭	G♭	C♭
(d)	(g)	(c)	(f)	(b♭)	(e♭)	(a♭)

The Circle of Fifths

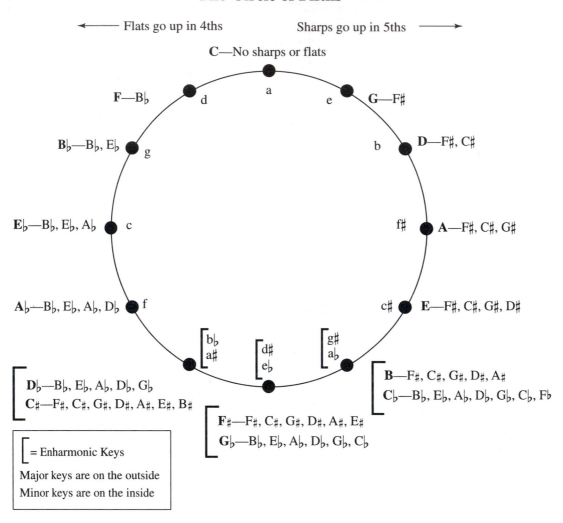

← Flats go up in 4ths   Sharps go up in 5ths →

C—No sharps or flats

F—B♭

G—F♯

B♭—B♭, E♭

D—F♯, C♯

E♭—B♭, E♭, A♭

A—F♯, C♯, G♯

A♭—B♭, E♭, A♭, D♭

E—F♯, C♯, G♯, D♯

⎡ b♭
⎣ a♯

⎡ d♯
⎣ e♭

⎡ g♯
⎣ a♭

B—F♯, C♯, G♯, D♯, A♯
C♭—B♭, E♭, A♭, D♭, G♭, C♭, F♭

D♭—B♭, E♭, A♭, D♭, G♭
C♯—F♯, C♯, G♯, D♯, A♯, E♯, B♯

F♯—F♯, C♯, G♯, D♯, A♯, E♯
G♭—B♭, E♭, A♭, D♭, G♭, C♭

⎡ = Enharmonic Keys

Major keys are on the outside
Minor keys are on the inside

TRANSPOSITION CHART

The Playing Ranges and Transposition Requirements of Some Commonly Used Instruments

INSTRUMENT	WRITTEN RANGE	ACTUAL SOUND	TRANSPOSITION

Strings *(A small quarter note indicates the possible range.)*

Instrument		Actual Sound	Transposition
Violin		as written	none
Viola		as written	none
Cello		as written	none
Double Bass		one octave lower	up one octave
Mandolin		as written	none
Guitar		one octave lower	one octave higher

INSTRUMENT	WRITTEN RANGE	ACTUAL SOUND	TRANSPOSITION
Woodwinds			
Piccolo		one octave higher	down one octave
Flute		as written	none
B♭ Clarinet		major 2nd lower	up a major 2nd
Bass Clarinet		major 9th lower	up a major 9th
Bassoon		as written	none
B♭ Soprano Saxophone		major 2nd lower	up a major 2nd
Alto Saxophone		major 6th lower	up a major 6th

INSTRUMENT	WRITTEN RANGE	ACTUAL SOUND	TRANSPOSITION
Tenor Saxophone		major 9th lower	up a major 9th
Baritone Saxophone		major 13th lower	up a major 13th

Brass

INSTRUMENT	WRITTEN RANGE	ACTUAL SOUND	TRANSPOSITION
Trumpet in C		as written	none
Trumpet in B♭		major 2nd lower	up a major 2nd
Horn in F		perfect 5th lower	up a perfect 5th
Tenor Trombone		as written	none

INSTRUMENT	WRITTEN RANGE	ACTUAL SOUND	TRANSPOSITION
Baritione or Euphonium		as written	none
	or		
		major 9th lower	up a major 9th
Bass Trombone		as written	none
Tuba		as written	none

Percussion

Xylophone		octave higher	octave lower
Marimba		as written	none

Instrument	Written Range	Actual Sound	Transposition
Timpani		as written	none

Glossary

accidental A symbol such as a sharp, flat, or natural sign used to chromatically alter a pitch.

accolade A type of bracket used to connect two or more staffs (staves) (also known as **brace**).

alla breve A simple meter time signature indicating that there are two beats per measure, with the half note receiving the beat (also known as **cut time**).

anacrusis The "pickup" note (or notes) at the beginning of a musical melody or phrase that precedes the accented first beat of the designated meter of the music.

antecedent phrase The first half of a proportional melody that, by itself, is an incomplete statement of a musical idea. It is complemented by a consequent phrase.

arpeggio The pitches of a chord played successively rather than simultaneously.

arranger An individual who reworks the main elements of an already composed piece of music to suit his or her needs.

art song Solo vocal music accompanied by piano, popular in the nineteenth century.

atonality Music in which there is no key center.

augmented interval Any major or perfect interval made larger by one half step.

augmented triad A major triad with the 5th raised one half step.

bar line The line used to separate measures on the staff.

bass clef The clef generally used to write those pitches that occur below middle C on the piano keyboard; also known as the **F clef**.

beam The line used to connect those pitches that comprise the division and subdivision of one beat.

beat The regularly occurring pulse within a piece of music.

blue notes The lowered 3rd, 5th, and 7th chord tones of a 7th chord that are freely used to add expression to the performance of the "blues" style.

brace A type of bracket used to connect two or more staffs (staves) (also known as **accolade**).

chord A combination of three or more tones sounded simultaneously.

chord cluster A combination of tones that produce dissonance.

chromatic half step The distance of a pitch located one semitone above or below a given pitch with the same basic letter name; G to G♯.

chromatic scale A twelve-note scale in which all pitches are one half step apart.

church modes The ancient scales that serve as the basis for the music of the Roman Catholic Church.

circle of fifths The ordering of the major and minor key signatures in a circular pattern in which all keys are separated by the interval of the perfect 5th.

close position When the root, 3rd, and 5th of a triad (chord) are voiced so closely that no chord tone may be inserted between any two adjacent chord tones.

commercial music Popular music such as show tunes and songs, as opposed to the music performed in concert halls by symphony orchestras, opera companies, and concert soloists.

common time A meter in which there are four beats per measure, with the quarter note receiving one beat.

composer A person who creates original musical compositions.

compound interval The basic distance between two pitches that are more than an octave apart.

compound meter When a pulse or beat is divided by thirds.

concerto A musical composition for soloist and orchestra, usually in three sections called "movements."

concert pitch The pitch at which nontransposing instruments play.

consequent phrase The second half of a proportional melody that brings the initial phrase (antecedent phrase) to a conclusion.

consonance The lack of musical tension within a musical composition.

crescendo The gradual increasing of the volume of the music over a period of time.

cut time A simple meter time signature indicating that there are two beats per measure, with the half note receiving the beat (also known as **_alla breve_**).

D.C. al Coda A musical term that directs the musician to repeat from the beginning of a composition, play to the coda sign (⊕), and then skip to the final coda section.

D.C. al Fine A musical term that directs the musician to repeat from the beginning of a composition and stop at the _Fine_.

decrescendo The gradual decreasing of the volume of the music over a period of time.

diatonic Refers to pitches occurring on adjacent scale degrees.

diatonic half step A pitch one semitone above or below a given pitch with a different letter name; G to A♭ or G to F♯.

diatonic triads Those triads that occur on each scale degree within a given key.

diminished interval Any minor or perfect interval brought closer together by one half step.

diminished third The intervallic distance of two half steps written as a 3rd.

diminished triad A major triad with the 3rd and 5th lowered one half step.

dissonance Musical tension among the harmonies within a composition.

double flat An accidental (♭♭) that lowers a pitch two half steps.

double sharp An accidental (𝄪) that raises a pitch two half steps.

doubly augmented interval An augmented interval made larger by one half step.

doubly diminished interval A diminished interval that is brought closer together by one half step.

downbeat The recurring accented first beat within any given meter.

duplet A rhythmic pattern occurring in a compound meter in which two notes are to be performed in the time it takes to play three notes of the same rhythmic value.

D.S. al Coda A musical term that directs the musician to repeat to the sign (𝄋), play up to the coda sign (⊕), and then skip to the final coda section.

D.S. al Fine A musical term that directs the musician to repeat to the sign (𝄋)) and play to the *Fine*.

dynamics The volume levels at which sounds are played.

enharmonic Two pitches that sound the same but are written differently.

enharmonic equivalent A pitch that sounds exactly the same as another pitch but is written differently.

extended chord A chord that includes pitches added to it beyond the 7th.

F clef The clef generally used to write those pitches that occur below middle C on the piano keyboard (**also known as the bass clef**).

first ending The section of a composition that will not be repeated when, after repeating the beginning (or a previously played section) of the piece, it is encountered for the second time.

first inversion When the 3rd of a chord is placed in the bass.

flag The curved line attached to the stem of the note.

flat An accidental (♭) that lowers a pitch one half step.

fundamental The concert pitch produced when a transposing instrument plays its written C.

G clef The clef generally used to write those pitches that occur above middle C on the piano keyboard (also known as the **treble clef**).

Grand Staff (Great Staff) The combination of the bass and treble clefs on which musical pitches are written.

half step The smallest distance between adjacent pitches on the piano keyboard (also known as the **semitone**).

harmonic interval The perceived distance between two simultaneously sounded pitches.

harmonic minor form The altered form of the pure minor scale in which scale degree 7 is raised one half step to create a leading tone.

harmonic minor scale The form of the pure minor scale when the pitch located on the 7th scale degree is raised one half step.

harmonic progression The aural perception of the forward motion of the root movements associated with chords as they occur over time.

harmonize To add pitches above and/or below a melodic line.

harmony The relationship between and among simultaneously played pitches.

hook A rhythmic or melodic fragment of a song established in the listener's memory by continual repetition.

imperfect consonance The intervals of the major and minor 3rd and 6th.

improvising The extemporaneous creating of music without any pre-established musical plan.

interval The distance between pitches.

inversion (chord) When the root of a chord is not placed in the bass.

inversion (interval) When the pitches of an interval exchange their positions so that the originally written lower pitch is placed above the upper pitch or the originally written upper pitch is placed below the lower pitch.

jazz An American style of instrumental and vocal music that had its beginnings in the early twentieth century and emphasizes improvisation, blues, and swing.

key (key center) The established tonal center toward which the pitches of a composition gravitate.

key signature The necessary sharps or flats that indicate those pitches of a scale or composition needing to be adjusted in order to establish a specific tonal center.

leading tone The pitch that is located one half step below the tonic in major and minor keys.

ledger lines The lines placed above and below the staff that enable the writing of pitches outside the range of those pitches written between the first space above and below the staff.

major interval The distance between the lower and upper pitches of an interval in which the upper note is in the key of the lower note, except for the intervals of the prime, 4th, 5th, and octave.

major scale A seven-note scale comprising a specific pattern of whole steps and half steps, in which half steps occur between scale degrees 3 and 4, and 7 and 8.

major triad A three-note chord comprising pitches placed at the intervals of a major 3rd and a perfect 5th above the root.

measure A section of written music placed between two bar lines.

melodic interval The distance between two consecutively played pitches.

melodic minor scale A variation of the pure minor scale in which scale degrees 6 and 7 are raised while ascending and lowered while descending.

meter A regularly reoccurring pattern of strong and weak beats over time.

meter signature Indicates the number of beats per measure and the rhythmic value of the note receiving one beat (also known as the **time signature**).

metronome An adjustable mechanical device used to indicate the speed of the beat.

metronome marking The indication of the appropriate tempo of a piece of music, printed above the first measure of a composition.

microtonal music Music constructed using quarter-tone pitches.

microtone An interval smaller than the semitone.

middle C The pitch located on the one ledger line that separates the treble and bass clefs of the Grand Staff.

minor interval A major interval brought closer together by one half step.

minor scale A scale consisting of eight pitches in which half steps occur between scale degrees 2 and 3, and 5 and 6. All other adjacent scale degrees are separated by one whole step.

minor triad A major triad with the 3rd lowered one half step.

mode A scale comprised of an organized pattern of whole and half steps.

modulation A change of key within a composition.

montuno A section within a composition designated for solo improvisation, performed over a repeated chord progression.

movable C clef The clef that may be moved to each of the five lines on the staff to indicate the relocation of middle C.

musical alphabet The alphabet letters A through G that are used to identify all of the basic pitches used in music.

natural minor scale A scale consisting of eight pitches at which half steps occur between scale degrees 2 and 3, and 5 and 6. All other adjacent scale degrees are separated by one whole step (also known as the **pure minor scale**).

natural sign An accidental (♮) that cancels a sharp or flat.

nondiatonic triads Chromatically altered triads that occur in a piece of music and do not function as diatonic triads.

nonfunctioning dominant The minor dominant triad located on scale degree 5 in the pure minor scale.

nonharmonic tone A dissonant tone that embellishes the consonant harmonies within a composition.

note head The oval-shaped part of a written note, with or without an attached stem.

octave Any two pitches separated by twelve half steps, such as C to C.

open position When the root, 3rd, and 5th of a triad (chord) are voiced so that it is possible to insert a chord tone between one or more pairs of adjacent chord tones.

parallel major The major key associated with a minor key with the same tonic; C major is the parallel major to C minor.

parallel minor The minor key associated with a major key with the same tonic; C minor is the parallel minor to C major.

pentatonic scale A five-note scale without half steps.

perfect consonance The intervals that have no musical tension (dissonance): the perfect octave, perfect prime, perfect 4th, and perfect 5th.

perfect 5th The distance of seven half steps between two pitches.

perfect 4th The distance of five half steps between two pitches.

perfect interval The intervals of the octave (twelve half steps), prime (no half steps), 4th (five half steps), and 5th (seven half steps).

pitch The highness or lowness of a sound as it relates to the frequency of sound waves.

polytonality Music in which one tonal center is not clearly established because of the simultaneous use of two or more keys.

pulse The beat in music that reflects the speed of the tempo.

pure minor scale A scale consisting of eight pitches at which half steps occur between scale degrees 2 and 3, and 5 and 6. All other adjacent scale degrees are separated by one whole step (also known as the **natural minor scale**).

quartal harmony Chords and melodies which are based on using the basic interval of the fourth.

quarter tone A pitch located within half the distance of a semitone.

relative minor The minor key that shares its key signature with a major key.

relative pitch The ability to identify or produce a pitch using a reference pitch.

repeat sign A musical symbol used to indicate that a section of music is to be replayed.

rhythm The perceived relationship among sequential sound duration patterns occurring over time.

rhythmic mode mixture Rhythms occurring in compound meters that are used in simple meters and vice versa.

rhythmic value The designated length of a sound.

root The fundamental pitch that generates the 3rd and 5th of a triad.

root position When the root of a triad (chord) is in the bass.

scale An organized set of pitches arranged from low to high or high to low.

scale degrees The numerically identified steps of a scale.

second ending The portion of a composition that is played after repeating the beginning (or a previously played section) of the piece, and then skipping the first ending.

second inversion When the 5th of a chord is in the bass.

semitone The smallest distance between adjacent pitches on the piano keyboard (also known as the **half step**).

sharp An accidental (♯) used to raise a pitch one half step.

simple interval The distance between two pitches within the span of one octave.

simple meter When a pulse, or beat, is divided by halves.

solfège (solfeggio) The singing of pitches using established Italian nouns (in some cases French) to designate each scale degree: *do, re, mi, fa, sol, la,* and *ti.*

solmization Assigning syllables, rather than letter names, to identify pitches.

sonata An instrumental composition, usually in three movements, that features a soloist accompanied by an instrument such as the piano (or the soloist accompanying himself or herself on an instrument).

standards Commercial music written throughout the twentieth century that is still being performed today.

stem The line attached to the note head of a pitch written on the staff.

subdivision The dividing of the beat into smaller rhythmic units.

subtonic The scale degree one full step below the tonic.

symmetrical Scales are called symmetrical when the distances between all consecutive pitches are the same.

symphony A composition for an orchestra, usually in three or four movements.

tempo The speed at which a musical composition is to be performed.

tempi The plural of tempo (in Italian).

tertian harmony Harmony based on the basic interval of the 3rd.

tetrachord Four pitches that span the interval of the 4th.

tie A musical symbol that is used to connect two pitches in order to increase the rhythmic value of the first pitch.

time signature The numbers placed at the beginning of a musical composition indicating the number of beats per measure and the type of note value that will receive one beat (also known as the **meter signature**).

tonal music Music in which there is a clearly established key center.

tonic The first scale degree of a major or minor scale and the pitch toward which all other pitches of a tonal composition gravitate.

tonicize The process of musically establishing the tonal center of a piece of music.

transposition The process of rewriting or performing an existing piece of music at a higher or lower pitch level.

treble clef The clef used to write those pitches that occur above middle C on the piano keyboard (also known as the **G clef**).

triad A three-note chord constructed using the basic interval of the 3rd.

triplet A rhythmic pattern occurring in a simple meter in which three notes of equal rhythmic value are played in the time in which it takes to play two of the notes.

tritone The distance of three whole steps (augmented 4th or diminished 5th) between two pitches.

unison The interval in which there are no semitones; pitches are performed simultaneously (or in octaves) without harmony.

upbeat The unaccented part of the beat which is counted as "and."

voicing The way in which the pitches of a triad are written in open or close position.

whole note The rhythmic value of a pitch that receives four beats in simple quadruple meter.

whole step The distance of two half steps between two adjacent pitches.

whole-tone scale A six-note scale in which all pitches are separated by one whole step.

Index

Name

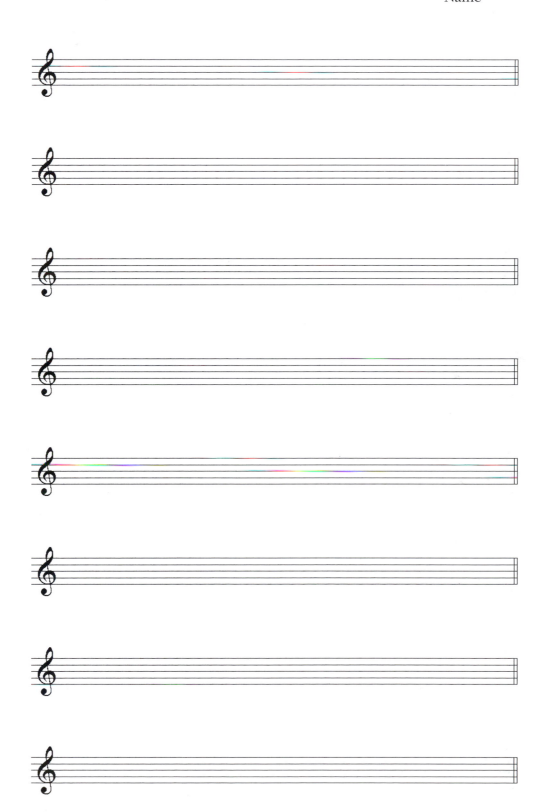

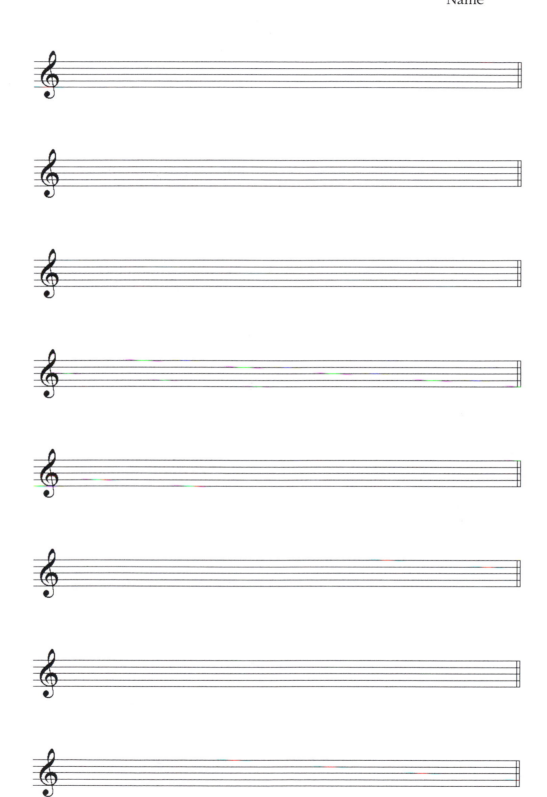

Name

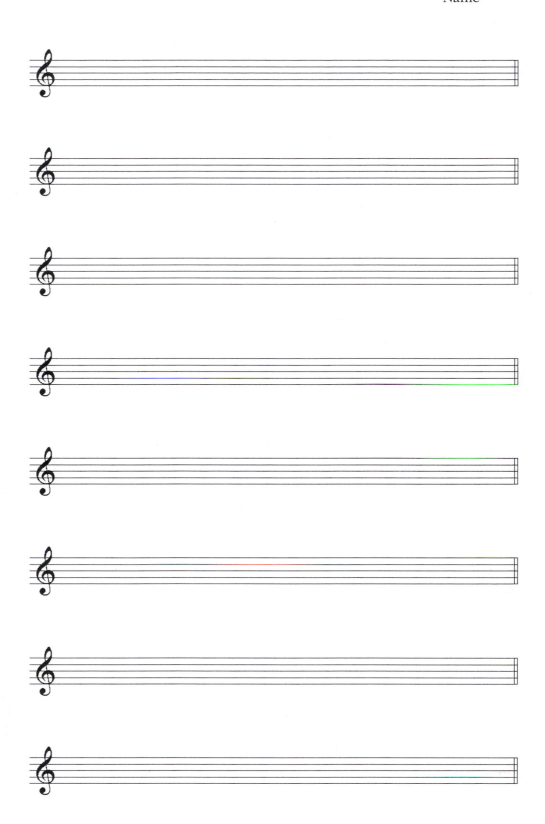